Engineering-Grade OT Security

Acknowledgements

The best practices and insights I relate in this book are drawn from a decade of working with cybersecurity leaders and practitioners at Waterfall Security Solutions, Waterfall's customers, as well as a wide variety of other security experts. My heartfelt thanks to all these people who contributed to my understanding of the practices and principles that I document here. In particular, a big thank you to Mark Fabro at Lofty Perch, who introduced me to modern approaches to modeling cyber risk and cyber Design-Basis Threat concepts, and Rees Machtemes, who explained in some detail the obligations of engineers to their profession.

I also thank my dedicated reviewers for their very valuable feedback: Dr. Jesus Molina, Dr. Wm. Arthur (Art) Conklin, Terry Ingoldsby, Andrea Ginter, Courtney Schneider, Alan Dewar, Rachel Ginter, Betty Wong, Chris Aziz, Rees Machtemes, Bryan Owen, Amir Ashuri, Daniel Ehrenreich, Elisha Olivestone, Simon Llewellyn and the Security Architects team at the Canadian Centre for Cyber Security.

For the record, while I am grateful to everyone who has contributed to this book and to my understanding of these issues, no reader should assume that any of these good people agree with anything I have written. In fact, most of them have expressed disagreement with at least some of the points I make. This book expresses my own best judgement, not necessarily that of anyone else.

Andrew Ginter

Prologue – How Much Is Enough?

"How much is enough" is a key question. How much engineering? How much cybersecurity? For which kinds of industrial operations and automation systems? And more importantly, *why?* Corporate directors are asking these questions, as are executives, managers, and individual practitioners. How can we determine how much is enough? How can we communicate these decisions to our businesses and project teams? And how can we justify and defend our decisions in this space?

To start to answer these questions, let's dig a little deeper. This is my third attempt at a book to answer important questions in OT security and cyber risk management. My first attempt to "solve" the industrial cybersecurity problem, *SCADA Security – What's broken and how to fix it* (the "red book"), had mixed reviews. Feedback from experts ranged from:

> *"Andrew, I disagree so fundamentally with your premise that I could not finish reading the book."*

To:

> *"Andrew, it must have taken weeks of your life to write all this down, but everything you've written here is obvious. What would possess you to spend so much effort documenting the self-evident?"*

From disagreeing fundamentally, to so obviously true it was not worth writing down, and everything in between. That feedback taught me two things:

1) Experts disagree. There is no consensus in this industry as to what is the right way to "do" industrial cybersecurity.
2) Nobody likes a critic.

To elaborate a moment on the second point – the title of the book says it all: *What's broken.* I criticized an approach to industrial cybersecurity that was and is still widely used, an approach that I saw as inadequate to the needs of important industrial and critical infrastructure sites. I naively expected that I could "show people the error of their ways" and that they would "follow me to the light." Instead, proponents of the approach I criticized got their shovels out and started digging deeper. In hindsight, criticism is easy. Producing something new that others can criticize is much harder and much more valuable. My apologies to everyone whom I offended.

In my second effort, *Secure Operations Technology* (the SEC-OT "black book"), I went to the other extreme and took a deliberately journalistic approach. Do you want to know what the world's most secure industrial sites do differently? Well first they inventory their information flows. Then they put engineering-grade measures in place to control the most dangerous information flows, and so on. No value judgements. If you see value in any of the techniques, then cherry pick them as you will.

Feedback on the black book was positive but confused. The approach I described clearly had value, was clearly being used successfully at very important industrial sites, but one practitioner after another struggled with the question *"how much is enough?"* I heard the question applied to the IEC 62443 standard – the world's most detailed industrial security standard. I heard it applied to the SEC-OT methodology in my black book. I heard it applied to all the variations of standards and frameworks in between. "What kind of systems deserve which kind of protection?" "Are nation-states *really* coming after me?" And "It's great that the most secure systems do that stuff, but what should I do, to which of my systems, and *why*?"

After years of reflecting on the feedback, I conclude that the *"experts disagree"* and *"how much is enough?"* issues are two symptoms of the same problem. One way to look at protecting industrial processes from cyber attacks is to see the solution as a coin with two sides – one side is engineering for cyber risk, and the other is information cybersecurity. A bit more sophisticated way to understand things is to say that the solution space is a continuum, with engineering at one extreme and cybersecurity at the other, and every site winds up using a mix of engineering and information cybersecurity techniques.

In this perspective, experts disagree because nobody is or can be an expert on the entire space – there is too much to know. Instead, each of us is an expert at some part of the space, the part which of course, we are utterly convinced is the most important part of the space, because that's what we do. Every expert I asked about these issues over these last many years admits that each end of the spectrum and each approach to the problem has a role to play. Engineering-grade mitigations *must* feature heavily when securing nuclear generators and passenger rail switching systems. These are physical environments where the worst-case consequences of cyber attacks can be horrific. Information-centric cybersecurity clearly has a role to play in arenas where industrial automation systems look and act a lot like IT systems. And there is a lot of space between these data points.

More recently, I have concluded that neither of these ways of seeing the problem are accurate. In my experience, almost all the time, *almost everyone uses everything*, to similar degrees. Engineering-grade protections for public safety and worker safety are designed into everything from cell phone batteries to automobiles and rail switching systems. IT cybersecurity is pretty much everywhere as well or should be. More fundamentally, the most sophisticated IT cybersecurity systems that I have ever seen are the ones deployed at nuclear generators and passenger rail systems – *the very same industries* where engineering-grade solutions are also deployed the most intensely.

This is not a coin with two sides where you must pick one. This is not a spectrum, where you can go "all engineering" at one extreme or "all cybersecurity" at the other. *In practice, everyone uses everything* – the question we urgently need answered is not *"which one?"* but *"how much of each?"*

In this book, in hopes of answering the question *"how much is enough?"* I adopt not a critical voice, and not a documentary voice, but a prescriptive one. "Do this, to that, for this reason." How can I prescribe a solution, or a path to selecting a solution? The answer is that industrial cybersecurity is all about risk. This does *not* mean that we can do whatever we feel like and pretend that we are "risk based." The engineering profession has an obligation to protect public safety, worker safety and national security in their physical, automation and cybersecurity designs. The profession has an obligation to put reasonable protection in place for all threats, including hurricanes, earthquakes, explosions, *and cyber attacks*. For that matter, the cybersecurity profession has many of the same responsibilities when practitioners are active in the OT / industrial space.

Each of these professions has only just started taking steps towards defining professional standards for reasonable protection from cyber sabotage of physical operations that puts public safety and national security at risk. This book is in part a primer to help a wider group of practitioners contribute to these discussions.

Back to the question – if engineering and OT security practitioners have an obligation to put reasonable protections in place for threats to public safety and to other stakeholders, what exactly is "reasonable" in this decision space? That is the question for the ages, for the courts, for the ethics committees, and for each of us in the space to wrestle down. Much of my advice is based on my understanding of established decision processes in the engineering space with respect to other kinds of threats and risks. In my experience, the engineering perspective on risk and how to address it in the design of systems and protections is very relevant to cyber threats, at least for the most consequential of systems.

And as the threat environment continues to deteriorate, the answer to *"what is reasonable?"* is evolving and will continue to evolve. What I have written here is my understanding of today's perspective of "reasonable."

Thank you for taking on the task of reading what I've written – I did spend a very long time writing it, throwing it out, and then starting again from scratch. Twice. I really do hope that *somebody* reads this material and hope even more that you / they derive some benefit from it.

Is this my last book? Maybe, maybe not. I see my retirement coming some time in the next half decade, because I suffer increasingly from the boring complaints of the aged. If I do not write another book, then this is my last opportunity to scrape together what bits of wisdom I possess in hopes that the next generation of practitioner can benefit from them somehow.

I hope you find this material persuasive, and if not persuasive, then at least useful.

Andrew Ginter

Chapter 1 - Introduction

If we want to answer the question *"how much is enough?"* in the industrial / OT security space, we must look at consequences. Worst-case consequences of compromise drive the decision process.

What does this mean? Well, much has been written about the differences between conventional IT networks and Operational Technology (OT) or industrial control system (ICS) networks: patching is harder in OT networks, anti-virus is harder, OT networks use very old protocols and computers, and there is enormous resistance to change from the people who manage these networks. These differences are, however, all superficial. The fundamental difference between these two kinds of networks is consequences: most often, the worst-case consequences of cyber attacks are sharply, qualitatively different on IT vs OT networks.

What is the difference? Ransomware hits our IT network and what do we do? We detect, respond, and recover. We identify the affected computers and isolate them. We take forensic images for the security analysts, and we erase the equipment. We restore from backups. We repeat. This costs time and effort. The attack may have stolen intellectual property and/or personally identifiable information (PII), and we suffer lawsuits as a result. These are all business consequences. Said another way, on IT networks, the goal for managing cyber risk is to prevent business consequences by protecting the information – protecting the confidentiality, integrity, and availability of business information.

On OT networks, however, the worst-case consequences of compromise are very often physical. Explosions kill people, industrial malfunctions cause environmental disasters, the lights go out, aircraft drop out of the sky, or our drinking water is contaminated. The cyber risk management goal for OT networks is generally to assure correct, continuous, and efficient operation *of the physical process*. The goal is not to "protect the information" but rather to protect physical operations from information, more specifically from cyber attacks that may be embedded in information. This is the fundamental difference between IT and OT networks: neither human lives, nor damaged turbines, nor environmental disasters can be "restored from backups."

This means that even if we could somehow wave a magic wand and render all industrial networks fully patched, fully anti-virus-ed, fully encrypted, and otherwise completely up to date with modern IT cybersecurity mechanisms, this fundamental difference would remain. The difference in consequence, today and always in the days ahead, demands a different approach to risk management in safety-critical and reliability-critical networks versus business networks. In this book, Chapters 2-3 are introductory material. We come back to consequence in much more detail in Chapter 4, and consequence plays a role in all the chapters that follow.

Government Intervention?

But before we dig into the question of how to protect industrial systems from the most consequential threats, we should address the question *"why?"* Why ask the question about cybersecurity at all? Are governments not supposed to be the ones to save us from the most powerful attacks from other nations and from organized crime? Well, it turns out that governments cannot protect us from powerful cyber attacks in the same way as they do from physical attacks.

For example, some governments have declared that significant cyber attacks on critical infrastructures shall constitute acts of war. Significant attacks on critical infrastructures have occurred however, with neither physical retaliation nor declarations of war by those same governments. In part this is because reliable attribution of cyber attacks can be made arbitrarily difficult by attackers – after the attack, we do not know who to declare war against. In part the problem is that the consequences of launching an all-out physical war are truly monstrous and are widely seen as a disproportionate response to a cyber attack, even an attack on critical infrastructures.

Many governments have invested heavily in protective measures for their infrastructures: establishing threat information sharing systems, providing classified threat briefings, establishing national cyber emergency response teams, imposing cybersecurity regulations and sometimes even mandating central government security and incident monitoring systems. Most governments also have powerful systems in place to ferret out spies, terrorist conspiracies, sleeper cells and even systems to identify trustworthy employees who are becoming susceptible to compromise or blackmail because of gambling debts, extra-marital relationships, and other aspects of their personal lives.

While these measures have enormous value, governments are neither omniscient nor omnipotent. Many kinds of cyber attacks take place much faster than any of these government initiatives can respond. None of these government programs can defeat fast-moving cyber attacks, only individual industrial/OT sites can provide credible protection against such attacks. Hence this book – to look at what individual industrial sites and enterprises must do to protect themselves.

Threat

OT cyber risks are of course part of deciding *"how much is enough?"* and these risks are increasing for most industries. Current indications are that the risks will become much worse before they get any better. Why? Well, consider mega-trends. For forty years now, we have automated physical operations with computers in the name of increased operating efficiencies. The problem is that computers run software, and almost all software can be manipulated by cyber attacks, by exploiting defects in the software, by stealing credentials for the software, or by many other means. Thus, for forty years we have, in the name of increased efficiencies and automation, steadily deployed more and more *targets* for cyber sabotage attacks. For just as long, we have connected our computers, because data in motion is the lifeblood of modern automation. But - all cyber sabotage attacks are information, and every flow of information can encode cyber attacks. Thus, for forty years we have steadily increased the number opportunities to attack our ever-increasing pool of targets. Neither of these trends will reverse any time soon. The OT cybersecurity problem will get much worse before it gets better.

Another big problem with OT cyber risk is that our enemies are automating as well and increasing the sophistication of their attacks and attack tools. A recent report[1] showed that before 2019, it was very rare to have more than one or two cyber attacks per year that caused physical consequences in manufacturing or critical industrial infrastructures. Since then, ransomware attacks with physical consequences in these industries have more than doubled every year. It will take only another few doublings for cyber attacks to become a serious, widespread impediment to correct, continuous and efficient industrial operations. Today, no expert believes that we will ever return to a state where we suffer only one or two cyber attacks per year with physical consequences.

As for attack automation, at this writing, the tools and techniques used by ransomware groups trail nation-state attack tools and techniques by less than half a decade. What we see nation states doing to each other today, we must expect criminal groups to be doing to all of us who have money within a handful of years.

The same is true in IT networks. In those networks, cybersecurity attacks, monitoring and other defenses are in constant change, as the defenders seek to invest optimally and minimally to stay one step ahead of their attackers. This constant change, however, is a poor fit for many industrial environments where engineers must strictly manage change to control risks to safe and reliable operations. An extreme example – in many jurisdictions, such as Germany, it is effectively illegal to apply patches and security updates to automation systems in passenger trains without approval by the government regulator[2]. More fundamentally, in some systems and some industries, staying one step ahead of

---

[1] *2023 Threat Report,* https://waterfall-security.com/2023-threat-report, by Waterfall Security Solutions and ICSStrive

[2] In many jurisdictions, a supplier must submit a safety case to a rail system operator. That case must be approved by an independent Safety Assessor hired by the operator. The safety case is then submitted by the operator to the regulator, who issues a Permission to Operate for the specific line or fleet. The safety case includes software versions and checksums of critical systems and any modification to these checksums must repeat the entire process.

our attackers is a poor fit for our need to assure correct and reliable operations over the entire decades-long expected lifetime of our investments in physical infrastructures.

All this means that today, board members and executives may have a very hard time discharging their obligations to manage exposures to cyber risks. When a CISO reports to the board that they invest steadily in reducing OT cyber risk, how is the board to know if that executive is talking about investments in slow-moving government initiatives, in "constant change" initiatives that may be difficult to apply to some industrial operations, or in engineering-centric mechanisms some, but never all, cyber risk completely off the table. Board members need to stop asking *"have we got this covered?"* and start asking more specific questions.

Security Engineering

There is good news as well in this space – in many cases, the engineering profession has powerful tools at their disposal to address physical risk, tools that can be applied to OT cyber risks much more widely than they are applied today. For example, mechanical over-pressure valves prevent pressure vessels from exploding. These valves contain no CPUs and are therefore un-hackable. Torque-limiting clutches prevent turbines from disintegrating, contain no CPUs, and are thus un-hackable. Unidirectional gateways are physically able to send information in only one direction and are physically unable to send attack information in the other direction. Today, these powerful tools are too often neglected because they have no analogue in the IT security space, and so are not mentioned in most cybersecurity standards, regulations and advice that have been published over the last two decades.

Digging a bit deeper, the engineering profession has managed risks to public safety for over a century. It is because poor engineering poses risks to public safety that the engineering profession is a legislated, self-regulating profession in many jurisdictions, similar to the medical and legal professions. The engineering profession has an enormous contribution to make to managing OT cyber risks, but this is poorly understood both inside and outside of the profession.

Why? In part, it is because are perhaps fifty times as many IT security practitioners in the world as OT security practitioners, and so IT experts are often the first people consulted when we need industrial cybersecurity solutions. Most IT security experts, however, are not engineers and so are not aware of the responsibilities of, nor the contributions that can be made by, the engineering profession.

The engineering profession is not much better off. If cyber attacks with physical consequences continue more than doubling annually, then the OT cyber problem will reach crisis proportions before the end of the decade, but in most jurisdictions, the engineering profession has not yet come to grips with these risks to public safety and to physical operations. At this writing, it is unclear whether there has ever been a case of an engineer being disciplined or losing their license for failing to apply robust cyber risk management to industrial designs. While some jurisdictions, such as the United Kingdom, have added "cybersecurity and data protection" to their code of ethics, most engineers are still not aware of rapidly changing expectations for industrial cybersecurity in their practices.

There is progress though. In the last half decade, several approaches to robust security engineering have crystalized:

- **Process engineering:** The *Security PHA Review*[3] textbook documents an approach for using routine Process Hazard Analysis engineering reviews to put in place unhackable physical mitigations for cyber threats to worker, environmental and public safety,
- **Automation engineering:** The *Countering Cyber Sabotage – Introducing Consequence-driven Cyber-informed Engineering* (CCE) textbook[4] is primarily about risk assessment, but includes several chapters on unhackable mitigations for cyber threats, including unhackable digital mitigations for cyber threats to equipment protection, and
- **Network engineering:** This author's *Secure Operations Technology* (SEC-OT) text[5] describes the engineering perspective of protecting correct physical operations from attacks that might be embedded in incoming information flows, rather than trying to "protect the information."

In this theme, the US Department of Energy (DOE) also released a *National Cyber-Informed Engineering Strategy* in 2022. The strategy seeks to develop an engineering body of knowledge to, among other things, "use design decisions and engineering controls to mitigate or even eliminate avenues for cyber-enabled attack or reduce the consequences when an attack occurs." We look at the strategy in more detail in Chapter 4.

Network Engineering

Network engineering lives at the boundary between engineering-centric mitigations for cyber risk and information-centric mitigations. Connectivity between OT / industrial automation systems, between OT systems and IT systems, and between all of this and Internet-based cloud services continues to increase. On the surface, this trend demands that we encrypt everything, thus protecting the information. And, because no operating system nor cryptosystem is perfect, we must also deploy at least the "detect," "respond" and "recover"

---

[3] Security PHA Review for Consequence-Based Cybersecurity, *Edward Marszal, and Jim McGlone,* 2019, International Society for Automation

[4] *Countering Cyber Sabotage – Introducing Consequence-driven Cyber-informed Engineering,* Andrew A. Bochman and Sarah Freeman, 2021, CRC Press

[5] *Secure Operations Technology,* Andrew Ginter, 2018, Abterra Technologies Inc.

pillars of the US *National Institute for Standards and Technology Cybersecurity Framework*[6] (NIST CSF). Since connectivity leads sooner or later to intrusions, then we must use sophisticated intrusion detection techniques, in hopes that when we are compromised, we can detect the attacks, respond to them, and recover normal functionality again before we suffer downtime, equipment damage, casualties, or other unacceptable consequences.

Industrial network engineers, however, have always been uneasy with protecting information. Consider a six-story catalytic cracking tower full of high-pressure, high-temperature hydrocarbon liquids and gasses. Imagine we are standing in front of the cracker watching a technician carrying out routine maintenance. In front of us are two analog gauges reporting temperature and pressure, and a dial controlling the flow of fuel to the cracker's furnace.

We look over our shoulder and notice that, outside the fence, someone is sitting with a telescope pointed at the gauges, taking notes. We tap the technician on the shoulder. "That person over there seems to be writing down our settings," we say. They are stealing information. What does the technician do? They might call corporate security. Depending on policy, they might shrug their shoulders and go back to work. The consequence of stealing that information is a business consequence – it is somebody else's problem.

Now imagine that the person behind the telescope cuts a hole in the fence, runs up to us, cranks the furnace fuel feed dial hard to the right, and runs away. What does the technician do? They scream for security. They run to the dial and returns it immediately to the correct position. Over-heating the cracker risks damage to the catalyst and possibly an explosion and fire.

The point here is that monitoring information that leaves the site is just information – with value comparable to the value of any other information in an IT network. All control information that enters the industrial site, however, is a potential threat. Calling both examples simply "attacks on information" and saying "encrypt everything to protect the information" ignores this fundamental difference.

In many, but not all, industries, the goal for most network engineers is not to "protect the information" but rather to prevent unacceptable physical consequences of cyber attacks. Universal connectivity lets monitoring information leave the plant, yes, but it also lets potentially dangerous control information enter the plant. Encryption provides no protection against a compromised cloud that sends attack information into the plant *inside* of an encrypted, authenticated connection.

Putting cryptographic and other protections in place for monitoring information that leaves the site makes sense. The business and societal consequences of an attacker stealing monitoring information are similar to the consequences of an attacker stealing other kinds of business information. Putting

---

[6] *Framework for Improving Critical Infrastructure Cybersecurity, Version 1.1,* 2018, National Institute of Standards and Technology

information-protecting mechanisms in place for control information is often woefully inadequate, because at many industrial sites, the consequences of compromised controls are completely unacceptable.

Engineers are also uneasy with the focus on detect, respond, and recover activities. Hoping that we can detect attacks in progress and respond in time to prevent unacceptable physical consequences is not good engineering. Engineers do not "hope" their bridges will not collapse, nor "hope" that their 300-ton steam turbines will not shake themselves to pieces. Engineers design systems that simply *do not* fail in the face of a defined set of threats. That said, yes engineers often do monitor or periodically inspect their finished products to ensure that they are holding up as designed, but any engineer caught "crossing their fingers" in a design, risks being drummed out of the profession.

We look at this topic in much more detail in Chapter 5.

This Book

In this book, we introduce OT cybersecurity, security engineering and *Secure Operations Technology* concepts and techniques to a non-technical audience. The goal of these introductions is to provide a grounding in cybersecurity and cyber risk concepts sufficient to enable both technical and non-technical readers to engage in useful and informed dialog when addressing the question *"how much is enough?"* With the grounding in place, the book walks through decision criteria and a decision process to decide what is reasonable – how much is enough?

As a result, this book is written mostly at a high level, to be universally understood. After all, almost no cybersecurity experts are also engineering experts, almost no engineering experts are also cybersecurity experts, and few business decision makers or board members are either of the above. Thus – if from time to time the discussion here slips into a bit of the technical, never fear. We will return quickly to the high-level kind of discussion essential to our broad audience. And if you are already a technical reader grounded in ICS and cybersecurity concepts, you may wish to skip Chapters 2 & 3.

Summary

Worst-case consequences of compromise define the difference between most IT and OT networks. Consequences on IT networks are generally business consequences, while OT consequences are very often physical. The goal of IT security teams is most often to manage business risk by protecting information. The goal of OT security teams is often to manage physical risk, not by protecting information, but by protecting physical operations *from information*, more specifically from cyber-sabotage attacks that may be embedded in information.

Cyber risk to both IT and OT networks continues to increase. Continued business and physical automation each deploy more and more targets for cyber attacks, while increased connectivity creates steadily more opportunities to communicate those attacks to the ever-increasing number of targets. Governments are generally expected to protect us from the worst kinds of physical attacks but cannot protect OT sites from fast-moving cyber attacks – OT sites must protect themselves from such attacks. None of this will change any time soon – the OT cyber problem will get much worse in the years ahead.

The good news is that the engineering profession has powerful, though mostly neglected, safety, equipment protection, and other tools that can be applied to the task of protecting public safety and physical operations from cyber risk. Network engineering is emerging as an important engineering-grade protection. Network engineering is focused on controlling the flow of potentially dangerous information – any information that enters control-critical networks is almost always much more dangerous than information leaving such networks for use by cloud systems and other business automation.

The new Cyber Informed Engineering Strategy (CIE) is an important effort intended to, in part, increase awareness of engineering approaches to reducing or eliminating many cyber risks. Safety engineering, protection engineering and network engineering are approaches that belong in the emerging CIE body of knowledge.

Network engineering lives at the boundary between engineering and cybersecurity approaches to addressing cyber risk to physical operations and in part is focused on the difference between monitoring and control information. Monitoring information sent to IT networks is most often able to cause only business consequences. Control information sent from external IT, Internet and other networks *into* important control networks is very often able to cause dangerous malfunctions of physical operations.

Deciding when, where, why, and how much we need to apply the tools, is the topic of this text.

Chapter 2 – OT / Industrial Control Systems

To understand how to deal with OT cyber risks, we need some understanding of what a control system is and how it works. In this chapter we introduce OT systems for a non-technical audience.

Where to begin? The field of automation engineering has been around for almost as long as the engineering profession has existed. More recently, in 2005, the Gartner Group coined the term "operational technology" (OT). In the beginning, the term was used by IT teams to mean more or less, "all that industrial and engineering stuff that we IT people do not understand." Engineers have only much more recently started to use the "OT" term, primarily when interacting with enterprise security teams. Engineers use the term to refer to the computers and networks that control important, complex, and often dangerous physical processes. Many of these physical processes constitute critical industrial infrastructures: water treatment systems, passenger rail systems, and the electric grid. These physical processes are powerful tools, and their misoperation generally has unacceptable physical consequences. Preventing such misoperation is the goal of OT cyber risk management.

Thus, while the term "OT risk" is new, people were monitoring, controlling and to some extent automating physical processes with dials, gauges, and analog control loops before there were computers, and have been using computers to assist with such control almost since the first computers were invented. As with any old field, the terminology is arcane. The first computers used in operations were so woefully under-powered that each computer could do only one kind of thing, and so every little thing that a computer did was given a different name.

For example, control systems are sometimes called SCADA systems, where SCADA stands for "Supervisory Control and Data Acquisition." A SCADA system is an industrial control system that uses a wide-area network (WAN) to communicate over long distances. Electric grids, pipelines and water distribution systems use SCADA systems. In contrast, "DCS" stands for "Distributed Control System." A DCS is an industrial control system where no WAN is involved, and the entire physical process is contained in one site. Power plants, refineries and chemical plants use DCSs. Historically, SCADA systems and DCSs were different – one kind of software could not control the other kind of process. Nowadays, general-purpose control system software has all the features of both SCADA systems and DCSs, making the difference between the two terms more usage than technology.

The modern term encompassing DCSs, SCADA systems and all other kinds of control systems is "industrial control system" (ICS). That said, every industry tends to use variations of the term. Many refineries call their control systems Process Control Networks (PCNs). Railway operators call some of their control systems switching systems, and yet others signalling systems. Building owners and operators call them Building Automation Systems.

Industrial processes can be classified as well. Critical industrial infrastructures are generally examples of "process industries." In process industries, the material being manipulated is more or less "goo" at some point in the physical process: water purification systems manipulate water, refineries manipulate oil, and pipelines move fluids. Electric grids are considered process industries as well, because electricity is produced in a continuous stream that can be modelled as more or less a fluid. Even transportation and traffic control systems are considered by many to be process systems, though this pushes the concept a bit.

Within process industries, there are batch industries and continuous industries. Batch industries, such as refining and pharmaceuticals, are industries where the production line does not run continuously. Instead, the physical process produces identifiable batches of outputs. Continuous industries, such as water treatment plants, power plants and offshore oil production platforms, consume inputs and produce outputs more or less constantly. Worst case consequences of cyber sabotage in process industries can be spectacular. These industries are sometimes called "boomable" industries – with one of the main jobs of the control system being to stay "left of boom".

Discrete manufacturing is the opposite of process manufacturing. While process industries work with continuous inputs to produce continuous or discrete outputs, discrete manufacturing assembles small, discrete inputs into larger discrete outputs, such as automobiles, aircraft, and home appliances. There are many similarities between process and discrete manufacturing, but there are significant differences as well. Discrete manufacturing often consists of individual machines or "production cells," each with a technician responsible for operating and/or repairing machines in the cell. Each machine tends to have its own small, local "human-machine interface" (HMI).

Whereas process industries are often "boomable," worst case consequences of cyber attacks on discrete manufacturing tend to be threats to product quality – which can be very important in fields such as aircraft manufacturing – and threats to individual technicians operating the equipment. A machine that turns on while a technician has their hand or body inside the machine can injure or kill the person, but generally poses no threat to other technicians in the plant, nor to public safety.

An important aspect common to all SCADA systems is the human operator. Control systems for important industrial facilities almost always have human oversight. System operators are charged with ensuring the safe and reliable operation of the physical process. These operators use tools known as human-machine interface (HMI) software. This software almost always includes a graphical visualization of the state of the physical process, and often includes other elements such as alarm managers and historical trending tools called process historians.

In many industries, by policy and sometimes by law, process operators are required to permit the physical process to operate only if they have a high degree of confidence that the process is operating safely. If the operator ever loses such confidence, for example because their displays freeze, or a message pops up saying, "you have been hacked," they must act. An affected operator may transfer control of the process to a secondary or redundant HMI or control system. However, if after some seconds or minutes the operator is still not sufficiently confident of the correct and safe operation of the physical process, then that operator must return the process to a known-safe state – most soften by triggering an emergency shutdown of the physical process.

This means that most often, the simplest way that cyber attacks can cause physical consequences is for the attack to impair the operation of some part of an operator's HMI or the systems supporting the HMI. The simplest physical consequences of such attacks are shutdowns of the physical process. Many industrial processes can be shut down much faster than they start up and can take days to recover full production again after an emergency shutdown. In some cases, regulatory approvals must be obtained before restarting physical processes, delaying plant restarts by as much as months. Worse, emergency shutdowns often put physical stress on industrial equipment, stress that can lead to either immediate equipment failures or to premature equipment aging.

While safe and reliable operations are the top priority in almost all industrial networks, confidentiality can be a priority as well. For example, pharmaceutical firms often regard the detailed processes used to manufacture their outputs as closely held trade secrets. Discrete manufacturers sometimes regard the programs and settings for industrial robots and other manufacturing equipment the same way. Enterprise security teams have an important role to play in protecting this information.

Field Devices

HMIs and other high-level monitoring and control software tend to run on conventional computers. In contrast, field devices are the specialized computers that are physically and electrically connected to the sensors and actuators in the physical process. The most common such devices are known as:

- Programmable Logic Controllers (PLCs) – which often can be programmed with a visual "ladder logic" programming language that mimics electric circuit diagrams, and which typically support up to several hundred physical sensors and actuators,
- Remote Terminal Units (RTUs) – which generally have more permanent firmware, and are most often located in distant locations such as electric substations,

- Flow computers – which tend to encode specialized logic to calculate fluid volumes from temperature, pressure, velocity, and other measurements,
- Intelligent Electronic Devices (IEDs) – which represent an attempt to give a single standard name (with an unfortunate acronym) that applies to all the above devices, and
- Many other devices with specific names in specific industries such as pump-off controllers for oil wells, Computer Numerical Controllers (CNC) for lathes and drills, and Proportional Integral Derivative (PID) controllers for "smooth" control of complex processes such as automobile cruise control.

All the above controllers and control systems tend to simultaneously support multiple engineering objectives: to operate a physical process in pursuit of an organization's mandate to produce electricity or gasoline or whatnot and to do so safely, reliably and without undue risk of costly equipment damage.

In contrast, Safety Instrumented Systems (SIS) and protection equipment are specialized field devices. Safety Instrumented Systems have only one job – to sample their inputs every few milliseconds, carry out a deterministic set of calculations, and use those inputs and calculations to determine whether the physical process is still in a safe state. If the process ever deviates from a safe state, the SIS triggers an emergency return to a safe state – most commonly an emergency shutdown. In a real sense, SIS do not care what the mission of the organization is – the job of the SIS is to prevent disaster, nothing more.

Protection systems, most commonly known as protective relays, similarly have only one job: to detect conditions such as excessive vibration, over-heating and electrical faults that might damage long-lead-time physical equipment. When protective relays detect a dangerous condition, just like safety systems, the relays trigger an emergency return to a safe state.

In recent years, the term "edge computer" has been added to the terminology mix. An edge computer is any computer that, like a field device, is close to the physical process *and* communicates directly or indirectly with a cloud system. The term was initially coined in the context of the Industrial Internet. Today, most vendors have rebranded most of their field devices as "edge" devices, and so the term has been rendered nearly meaningless.

Field devices historically used specialized real-time operating systems. Today, most new devices use either a hardened version of Microsoft Windows, or a Linux derivative. This means that IT-style attack tools increasingly work against field level devices. This also means that increasingly, standard IT-style defensive tools have at least some chance of working for these devices as well. One complexity in applying conventional cybersecurity defenses to field devices is support by device vendors. For many reasons, some very reasonable and some less so, vendors tend to honor support agreements and warranties for their devices only if the devices are running vendor-approved software exclusively, and not any third-party cybersecurity add-ons.

Device Communications

The market for field or edge devices is extremely fragmented. Historically, a great many of these providers, large and small, chose to implement their own proprietary communications protocol to communicate with their devices. Almost none of these protocols originally supported encryption or cryptographic authentication. Modern versions of many protocols do support these functions, but few engineering teams enable these features.

This means that once an attacker or their malware can connect to a device, they can most often gain complete control of the device. They can tell PLCs to turn on equipment that is supposed to be turned off. They can tell protective relays and safety systems to ignore unsafe conditions. They can very often persuade field devices to report that "all is well" to the human operator throughout these malicious manipulations. They can often load new firmware into the device that shuts the device down so thoroughly that correct firmware can no longer be loaded into the device – *"bricking"* the device – putting into a state where the device must be physically replaced with a new one. Many practitioners call devices designed or deployed without authentication as "insecure by design."

This reluctance to use cryptographic tools and role-based access controls can be distressing to "protect the information" people, but the reluctance has at least two sources:

1) Account management, encryption and cryptographic key management adds a degree of complexity and thus risk to reliable physical operations. Couple this with the fact that cyber threat and risk awareness among many engineers is still poor, and we have a situation where encryption/security vs. complexity/risk decisions may be misinformed.
2) Engineers in many industries have the means to make small changes to physical processes and automation networks that entirely eliminate important classes of cyber risks, thereby legitimately reducing the need to implement universal cryptosystems.

We revisit the topic of encryption many times throughout this text. That said, it is pretty much universally understood that when edge devices communicate with the cloud, those communications *must* be encrypted and authenticated.

One communications protocol worth mentioning specifically is the Open Platform Communications (OPC) protocol[7]. OPC is widely used to simplify communications with the very diverse world of field devices. The original OPC Data Access (OPC-DA) protocol is Windows DCOM-based and is in widespread use. The protocol provides a standard for communication with industrial devices. An OPC server is a piece of software that exposes the standard application programming interface (API) to control system components and translates that

[7] Technically, OPC is a COM/DCOM API, not a communications protocol, but common usage is that that OPC+DCOM together constitute a protocol.

API directly or indirectly into device communications for a specific set of field devices. If there are many vendors' devices and protocols in an industrial network, there tend to be many OPC servers, one per field device protocol. Less commonly used variants of standard OPC programming interfaces include OPC for Alarms and Events (OPC A&E) and OPC Historical Data Access (OPC-HDA).

OPC Unified Access (OPC-UA) is a modern re-write of the above OPC variants. OPC-UA drops support for DCOM and adds support for a variety of more modern transports. The most widely used transport for OPC-UA is an XML-based SOAP, HTTP and HTTPS transport that is very compatible with Internet-based web services and cloud services. OPC-UA communications are therefore encrypted much more often than other device protocols, but managing encryption keys and certificates on industrial networks is still difficult.

Purdue Model

The term "Purdue Model" is used widely in industrial cybersecurity circles as a reference model for industrial network segmentation. The term refers to what was originally a naming convention for industrial devices developed by Purdue University. The original purpose was to take the huge space of industrial "things," each with a different name, and classify them as to their function. This provided engineers a simpler and more general terminology to refer to entire classes of devices and systems.

Later, cybersecurity practitioners started encouraging automation engineers to use firewalls to segment industrial networks, grouping devices and systems with similar functions and communications needs into sub-networks. As it turned out, the Purdue Model provided a nearly ideal categorization for these "similar function" groupings, and so became, not just the de-facto naming convention, but the de-facto way to segment industrial networks as well. The model itself is very detailed, but the most-often cited categorizations include:

- Level 0 (L0) – the physical process, such as furnaces, boilers, distillation towers high-voltage transformers and associated sensors and actuators, such as physical switches and temperature and pressure transmitters,
- Level 1 (L1) – field devices or specialized computers directly connected to sensors and actuators in the physical process such as PLCs, RTUs and flow computers,
- Level 2 (L2) – DCS systems and other control systems for an individual site or sub-process,
- Level 3 (L3) – SCADA systems and other system-wide or plant-wide infrastructure,
- Level 4 (L4) – Business networks, and
- Level 5 (L5) – the Internet and cloud-based systems.

Safety Instrumented Systems (SIS) and protective relays are all lumped with field devices in Level 1. As we move up the hierarchy of levels, we almost always see many-to-one relationships. An L2 DCS network may monitor and control many L1 device networks. An L3 SCADA or plant network most often monitors and controls many L2 production units. The L4 corporate IT network of course is connected to many L3 networks, one in each plant the corporation operates. Very often there are firewalls and demilitarized zones (DMZs) – networks between networks – between these levels as well. In fact, DMZs between L3 and L4 systems are so common that many practitioners refer to such DMZs as Level 3.5 networks.

Note that product vendors can be very fussy about the firewalls deployed within what those vendors see as their sphere of influence. In the lower-numbered networks, it tends to be harder to deploy arbitrary third-party firewalls than in the higher-numbered networks.

Engineering Change Control

Patching and applying security updates to some industrial networks is very hard. Why? Consider a typical refinery. The entire site goes down once every three years for a retrofit where every piece of physical equipment, large and small is inspected. What is worn out is replaced, and what is old may be upgraded. Necessary new systems and upgrades are installed. Control system computers and devices are similarly examined and replaced or upgraded. The entire process incurs enormous change. Engineering teams plan for, study, prototype, analyze and test every change for safety and reliability, sometimes for up to six years prior to the three-year outages. There are frequently two engineering upgrade teams working in parallel, staggering their results into three-year production outages, because there is that much work and analysis involved in these outages.

But when everything is re-assembled, do we simply turn everything back on? Well no. Despite up to six years of analysis, we may have missed something. Every change is a risk, and we've changed everything. So, what do we do? Typically, all vacations are cancelled. All vendor representatives and services contractors are summoned to the site. Everyone starts putting in 12-hour days, and the plant is started and is brought up to 5% of capacity. Every technician, vendor and engineer is walking around the site, looking at things, listening to them, feeling them if it's safe to touch them, and sometimes even sniffing at them. The plant operators, their supervisors and the engineers are clicking through the HMI screens, looking at every bit of each screen to see if both the plant and the screens are working as expected. The cyber people are looking at memory usage, network communications, and logs.

Nobody and nothing is perfect. We find problems, and we fix them. We bring the plant up to 25% of capacity. To 50%. And eventually to 100% of capacity. It's been two weeks. Everyone is exhausted. Most of us haven't seen our families in all that time, and still, we look for problems. We find fewer and fewer new problems. Each problem is triaged. Low-priority problems are documented and handed off to the team preparing for the next outage, three years from now. We start to stand down. At three weeks, the plant is at full capacity, the vendors have all gone home and we are back to a normal staff. Success!

But wait – on the Tuesday following, Microsoft issues a Windows security update with 17 fixes in it. Do we apply that update? If we do, will we introduce new problems that impact safe operations? Will we introduce a problem that trips the plant? How can we know? We do not have the source code for the changes, and even if we did, we most likely cannot find people who can analyze that much code with the degree of engineering confidence that we need. If we cannot analyze the code, must we shut down again, apply the patches, bring everyone back and start the commissioning process all over again?

Many industrial sites delay security updates. They delay installing updates until they are confident that the update will not impair operations unacceptably. Sometimes it takes months of testing on a test bed to prove that the update is safe. Sometimes the patch is simply delayed until the next outage in three years.

Every change is a risk and engineering change control (ECC) is the discipline that engineering teams use to control that risk. Equipment that a vendor has certified for safety at a cost of up to a half million dollars cannot be used with security updates until the vendor re-certifies the equipment using the changed operating system. Other equipment is not updated until the engineering team is satisfied with the risk, and even then, the teams tend to apply the update to the least vital equipment first to see if the patch causes problems. Then they apply it to the machines that serve as backups for vital redundant equipment. Then they switch over to the updated backups. If there are any problems, they switch back to the unpatched primaries, and so on.

This is in sharp contrast with some aspects of enterprise cybersecurity programs that in some domains apply constant, aggressive change to stay ahead of the adversary: the latest security updates, as quickly as practical, the latest anti-virus signatures, and the latest software versions and keys and cryptosystems. These "constant change" practices fly in the face of the ECC discipline. There is simply no way to keep industrial equipment patched as aggressively as we patch enterprise networks. One consequence of this limitation is that most industrial equipment is vulnerable to known exploits for much longer periods of time than is typical of enterprise equipment.

All this said, however, while ECC is misunderstood by many IT practitioners, ECC is *misapplied* by many engineers. When short production outages are acceptable – outages that are due to either malfunctioning patches or cyber compromise, then it is a mistake to use the ECC discipline as an excuse to delay patches. That we *must* use ECC in safety-critical applications is no excuse delaying patching in *all* industrial networks. Yes, patching can cause downtime, but so can cyber attacks. Chapters 7-8 focus on determining what is *reasonable* in different circumstances. ECC is critical in some industrial networks, but not in all.

IT/OT Integration

An important trend in SCADA systems since roughly the mid-1990's is what the Gartner Group has coined "IT/OT integration". The group observed that since both SCADA/OT and IT networks increasingly use the same computing hardware, operating systems, platform applications and networking components, there are cost savings and other benefits to merging these technology teams, application platforms, networks, and business practices. Why, for example, would it make any sense to use one relational database vendor's product in a SCADA network when the business had already purchased an enterprise-wide license to deploy a different vendor's databases?

The "IT/OT integration" term has since expanded in scope to encompass interconnected IT and OT networks that enable the business automation that relies on access to OT data. Predictive maintenance systems, for example, monitor how long and how intensely every bit of industrial equipment has been used, automatically order parts, and schedule repairs and crews to minimize maintenance and outage costs. Today, most IT and engineering practitioners have forgotten the original meaning of the term and equate "IT/OT integration" with "increased IT/OT connectivity." Again, this is proving to be a problem because increased connectivity increases cyber risks to physical operations, often to unacceptable levels.

Summary

Industrial control system (ICS) terminology is old and varied – DCS, PCN, SCADA and many other specific kinds of systems are today called ICS by engineering teams and are increasingly called Operational Technology (OT) by both IT and engineering teams. The Purdue Model classifies systems by role and by communications patterns and has emerged as a natural ICS network segmentation model.

Field devices connect to the physical process – sensors and actuators on boilers, conveyors and much more. Safety Instrumented Systems are special field devices tasked with protecting human life. Protection systems / relays are special devices tasked with preventing damage to costly equipment. OPC is a widely used standard interface to the huge diversity of field devices, protocols and vendors. Today, many field devices are deployed with plain text communications protocols, because there are significant technical and cultural challenges to deploying encrypted field device communications.

All changes to the most sensitive physical and cyber industrial systems pose a potential threat to safe and reliable operations. Engineering change control (ECC) is the discipline by which engineering teams manage this risk by managing change. ECC is necessary, expensive and conflicts with many aspects of IT-inspired cybersecurity, for example encryption systems and security update programs.

Today, IT/OT integration means, among other things, connecting IT and OT networks to enable business efficiencies. Of course all such connections introduce new attack opportunities, which is a very large part of today's OT cyber risk management challenge.

Chapter 3 – Cyber Attacks

An essential step in understanding cyber risk, and understanding how to manage that risk, lies in gaining some understanding of how cyber attacks work. In this chapter we introduce cyber attacks on OT targets for a non-technical audience.

Today's pervasive sophisticated threat is targeted ransomware. A typical attack proceeds as follows in what is known as the "cyber kill chain" for industrial control systems:

1) The attackers do some homework and choose a target organization. They find a potential victim or twenty within that organization on social media and learn about their current projects, colleagues, suppliers, and other contacts. Or attackers scan for public-facing servers, such as remote access servers, that provide access to the organization.
2) The attack then establishes a foothold by crafting and sending very convincing emails to victims, either persuading them to provide the attackers with credentials, or persuading them to click on a malicious attachment. Credentials to the victim's email account are particularly useful, since the attacker can use those credentials to reset the victim's passwords in many other systems. Or attackers exploit a vulnerability / defect in the remote access servers to gain access to the target network. In the worst case, if the servers are fully patched, attackers wait until a new vulnerability is announced and exploit it in the brief window between the announcement and when the servers are patched.
3) The foothold is established, most often by malware called a Remote Access Trojan (RAT). The RAT connects across the Internet to the attacker's command and control center (C2), a server that is usually disguised as a website. The easiest disguise is to copy a similarly named legitimate website. The attacker connects to the RAT via the C2 and starts giving it commands.
4) The attackers escalate privilege (optional). Usually, the RAT is running as part of a compromised user account, and so has permission to do anything that user can do. Attackers will often look around the compromised system and network for password files or misconfigurations that let the RAT assume powerful "system" privileges or something close to that. For example, the attacker could persuade the user that to view an apparently attractive video, they must first download and install new video decoder driver. The user clicks "install," and Windows asks if they want to run the installer with system privileges. The user says "yes," and the attack software is installed with system privileges.

5) Acquire domain privileges (optional). Often attackers can use local system privileges to find passwords, password hashes, Kerberos tickets or other technical means to make a Windows Domain Controller do their bidding. With these credentials, the attackers can create new accounts, change passwords, make all machines in the domain install an "emergency security update" that is actually ransomware, or more.
6) Use the compromised machines and compromised credentials to attack other machines. This is known as "pivoting" an attack through compromised systems.
7) Hide extra RATs (optional). Often attackers will hide copies of their RAT on machines they do not obviously compromise. They may even hide a different RAT on these machines. This way, if the victim organization does not pay the ransom and instead, restores obviously compromised machines from backups, the attackers can easily come back into the organization and try again later.
8) Look around to find and steal information (optional). Many ransomware groups steal customer or other sensitive information as well as use their malware to encrypt important servers. The double threat – pay me to decrypt your network and pay me to keep me from releasing your data into the Internet – is generally more effective than either single threat at persuading the victim to pay the ransom.
9) Sabotage operations and demand a ransom to restore them.

Details of this last step vary, depending on the ransomware group and the target they have selected. The simplest sabotage is simply to encrypt large parts of the IT network. A more sophisticated attack group might want to shut down a factory, and so might use stolen credentials to log into OT servers in the factory through the IT/OT firewall and plant a copy of the RAT into the factory. The process above repeats inside the factory until critical systems are encrypted and the factory shuts down. There are no easy fixes for these attacks. For example:

- Two-factor authentication (2FA) makes it harder for attackers to use stolen passwords to log in but does nothing to prevent RATs coming in as downloads or attachments, nor does 2FA prevent RATs from propagating from IT to OT networks via server-to-server communications, which cannot use 2FA.
- Anti-virus can detect known RATs, but ransomware groups routinely re-compile and rebuild their RATS to evade anti-virus systems. Worse, "living off the land" attacks have no RATs – instead, attackers use operating system components and other tools that are already installed on compromised machines to enable remote control.
- Intrusion detection systems may raise alerts when suspicious activity on a machine is detected, but such alerts are routinely missed. Worse, more clever attack groups often launch noisy attacks against irrelevant targets in the

victim organization while they are carrying out their more subtle, targeted RAT manipulations. The noisy attacks generate a lot of alerts and distract human security analysts in the organization's Security Operations Center (SOC) from the real attack.

This is the modern style of ransomware attacks. Sometimes the process above takes months. Sometimes it moves from "get a foothold" to "demand a ransom" in as little as 45 minutes. This class of attack nets ransomware criminals billions of dollars per year world-wide. As with any industry of that size, an entire economy has emerged to exploit the opportunity:

- Powerful RATs are available for purchase, complete with support contracts,
- Other elements of these attacks are available as a service – criminal organizations providing expert RAT operators for example, or professional ransomware call centers staffed with negotiators, and
- Professional money laundering operations turn bitcoin ransoms into "clean" cash, for a fee.

The tools and techniques used by today's ransomware groups trail those used by nation states by less than five years. There was a day when many owners and operators thought "I'm not important enough for a nation state to come after me." Today that line of reasoning is clearly mistaken – what we saw nation states doing to each other five years ago, we see ransomware doing to everyone with money today.

Three Ways Ransomware Impacts Operations

Ransomware attacks can impact operations in one of three ways:

1) The attacks may reach all the way into OT networks and encrypt critical servers, thus shutting down industrial sites. For example, the EKANS or "Snake" ransomware includes code to specifically target OT networks and routinely shuts down discrete manufacturing sites.
2) The attacks may impair only IT assets, but a victim organization may not be confident of the strength of their OT protections, and so decides to shut down physical operations out of "an abundance of caution."
3) The attacks may impair only IT assets, but physical operations may depend on those assets for minute-by-minute operations. For example, recent passenger rail attacks crippled signage so that passengers did not know on which platform their train was waiting.

Note that there are OT cyber experts who split hairs, arguing that cyber attacks that impair only IT networks should not be counted as "OT cyber incidents" because it is IT security teams who should be responsible for dealing with these incidents. These experts argue that calling such incidents "OT cyber incidents" puts the onus for addressing these incidents into the hands of OT security teams, when really the responsibility for protecting IT networks should lie with IT teams.

Try to ignore this finger-pointing. Cyber attacks that cause an organization to shut down physical operations constitute cyber risks to physical operations, no matter whose computers were impaired by the attacks. Addressing these risks most often requires a cross-functional effort, an effort that is not alien at all to most industrial organizations, since the trend for 20 years has been closer integration of IT and engineering teams.

While there are many examples of ransomware impacting physical operations, a widely reported incident was the Colonial Pipeline outage. Ransomware hit the Colonial IT network and America's largest gasoline pipeline went down for 6 days. The pipeline normally delivers 40% of the gasoline used in the country's Northeast region. That the pipeline was down, and that the outage was highly publicized, led to gasoline shortages and line-ups at gas stations. In addition, there were reports of members of the public trying to stockpile gasoline in garbage bags and other containers not designed to store the substance – a very dangerous practice.

In the investigation that followed, Colonial Pipeline's CEO testified under oath[8] as to the sequence of events:

- Ransomware infected the IT network,
- The IT team notified the pipeline operations team,
- Within 50 minutes of being notified, the Operations Supervisor entered a stop work order to halt operations throughout the pipeline, out of concern that the malware might spread to operations.

The CEO testified that at the time of the shutdown, there was no evidence that the ransomware had penetrated to the OT network, but that the supervisor had the authority to stop the pipeline if they felt that safety was at risk.

In what sense might safety be at risk? The CEO did not say, but it is common knowledge that all pipelines come with risks. One of the most significant risks is a "pressure hammer" or "hydraulic hammer." This is a pressure wave that moves through the pipeline at the speed of sound in the fluid the pipeline carries. The wave is triggered by conditions that include suddenly closing valves on the pipeline while fluid is moving through the pipeline at speed. The commonplace manifestation of this phenomenon in household plumbing is the "knocking" noise some plumbing makes when taps are turned off. In very large pipelines, this phenomenon is much more dangerous and can cause pipeline ruptures. The worst-case possibility would be something like a rupture of the gasoline pipeline under pressure in a population center, with a subsequent ignition, explosion, and fire. It is therefore completely understandable that Colonial Pipeline halted operations.

Unconfirmed reports subsequently claimed that the shut-down was not

[8] https://www.congress.gov/117/meeting/house/112689/witnesses/HHRG-117-HM00-Wstate-BlountJ-20210609.pdf

because of the danger, but because the custody transfer system hosted on the IT network and was crippled by the ransomware attack. A custody transfer system tracks the movement of product through the pipeline. As a rule, pipeline owners or operators do not own the material passing through their pipelines. In the Colonial Pipeline case, presumably the refineries own the gasoline, jet fuel and other materials until those materials are delivered to consumers at points along the pipeline. The custody transfer system is vital in tracking what is in the pipeline and who owns every barrel of that product as it passes through.

The Colonial CEO said nothing about this in his testimony, and so we should take him at his word – the pipeline operator made the call to shut down operations, following standard operating procedures. However, it seems plausible, whether it was a factor at Colonial or not, that at least some pipelines may not be able to restart in similar circumstances until the custody transfer system is working again. An inability to track product valued at hundreds of millions of dollars per day passing through a pipeline would lead to massive lawsuits if any pipeline were restarted in such circumstances.

The public reports of the attack on Colonial Pipeline thus illustrate two of the three ways that ransomware can impair physical operations. The pipeline was shut down according to standard operating procedures because the IT network was impaired, and because the operator could not be confident of safe operation of the pipeline in this state. And unconfirmed reports suggested that physical operations depended on the IT-based custody transfer system. If those reports were accurate, then it would mean that, even if safety were not an issue, the pipeline could not have restarted until at least some of the IT-based systems the pipeline depended on were restored to normal functionality.

Safety and Protection System Attacks

The Triton attack used the above targeted attack techniques to remotely reprogram SIS equipment in two petrochemical facilities in the Middle East. The attack caused expensive shutdowns but was caught before the impaired safety systems could contribute to explosions or worker casualties. Russia's second attack on the power grid in Ukraine in 2016 used malware that appeared to be designed to cripple protective relays. The attack managed to shut off power to Kyiv for an hour in December but failed in the attempt to manipulate protective relays and electric power flows in such a way as to damage the substation's high voltage transformers.

Both attacks were attributed to Russian-backed cyber attack groups. Both attack groups seemed very good at the cyber attack end of things but seemed much less capable on the engineering side of things. Future attacks targeting safety and protection systems are not likely to suffer this deficiency – the engineering knowledge that is needed to sabotage safety and protection systems is widely available in industrial automation communities.

Supply Chain Attacks

In 2017, a Russian-backed attack group inserted the NotPetya malware into a security update for a Ukrainian tax package. The malware was promptly auto installed at hundreds of sites and erased thousands of hard drives. Noteworthy OT victims were Maersk, the world's largest container shipping company that suffered a 6-day outage, and Merck, a pharmaceutical company that won a $1.4 billion USD settlement from their insurer Zurich for damages suffered in the NotPetya attack. In 2021, only 4 years later, ransomware was distributed through a compromised cloud-based security update server at Kaseya to 800 victims within a 45-minute period. In this case, ransomware actors trailed nation-state tactics by only 4 years in using cloud-based security update servers to distribute their attacks.

These attacks are examples of supply chain attacks. The problem with the "supply chain" term is that it is too broad. The term encompasses any or all of the following:

- Back doors may be deliberately inserted into software by vendors under the influence of hostile governments. For example: many western governments have banned Huawei and ZTE as suppliers of products or components for 5G wireless service because of concerns over back doors.
- Software vulnerabilities may exist in components which are then assembled into solutions and re-sold. When vulnerabilities are announced in components, or components of components, how can the high-level system vendors know about these vulnerabilities and act to evaluate and/or remediate them? How can end users be aware of how vulnerable their software is? Software Bill of Materials (SBOM) technologies are emerging to fill this gap.
- Malware may be surreptitiously inserted into otherwise-legitimate software products and services. Examples here include NotPetya, Kaseya and the SolarWinds Orion attacks. SolarWinds was a particularly advanced attack – a Russian-backed group is accused of inserting a RAT into the build process of the SolarWinds Orion product's security updates. Those compromised updates were then installed at up to 18,000 customer sites. It took over 6 months before the malware was discovered.

Again, the "supply chain" term is deceiving because it covers all these very different scenarios. A board who is told that "the supply chain problem is under control" needs to dig deeper. Which part of it is under control? Are we doing supply security audits to ensure our suppliers are trustworthy? Do we demand that our suppliers use SBOMs to ensure that the products they supply us have been patched for important vulnerabilities? Or have we taken steps to ensure that malware that arrives in security updates, either that we download or that is automatically downloaded and installed from or via the cloud, is dealt with somehow?

Stuxnet

Stuxnet is a historical attack that still confuses many. The Stuxnet malware appears to have destroyed roughly 1000 gas centrifuges in Iran's uranium enrichment program. The malware spread between sites on USB keys but spread across networks very aggressively within sites – across and through firewalls once it had a foothold on an IT network. The malware was extremely sophisticated and appears to have embodied a deep knowledge of the structure of the site it targeted. The malware included mechanisms to disable or avoid specific anti-virus and other security products and included mechanisms to identify specific industrial equipment and configurations that were unique to the uranium enrichment site.

After the attack, firewall vendors made much of the fact that the malware spread between sites on USB keys, ignoring the fact that the malware spread through firewalls within sites. Whitelisting vendors made much of the fact that the malware defeated anti-virus systems but not whitelisting systems, ignoring the fact that whitelisting systems can be defeated as well. There is circumstantial evidence that the malware was designed without technology to defeat whitelisting only because there were no whitelisting systems deployed at its target. Some intrusion detection vendors proudly pointed out that, unlike their competitors, their own systems would have detected the Stuxnet worm, again ignoring the fact that with sufficient effort, all detection systems can be spoofed. Stuxnet *needed* to spoof only certain systems – those systems that were installed at the targeted facility and associated facilities. The result was widespread confusion among IT and OT security practitioners.

In the years that followed the Stuxnet attack, there was widespread speculation as to when we might see "the next Stuxnet." At the time, Stuxnet was unique in many ways, including:

- The worm succeeded in destroying over 1000 gas centrifuges,
- Stuxnet exploited four "zero day" vulnerabilities – security vulnerabilities that were previously unknown or little known, and for which no security updates existed,
- The worm was autonomous – it had RAT capabilities but once loose on a network, the malware spread automatically and carried out its sabotage without need for human supervision,
- Stuxnet was targeted – despite an apparent coding error let the worm spread world-wide, the worm brought about malicious outcomes in apparently only one site on the planet – Iran's uranium enrichment site, and
- The worm included code to mask its effects – the only thing that Iranian operators saw while their centrifuges were disintegrating was green lights on their HMIs.

Despite widespread speculation, nothing close to this attack has been seen since. This is in no small part because of the complexity and cost of creating and deploying such a worm. Finding or purchasing zero-days is expensive, designing very capable autonomous malware is much more expensive than designing remote-control malware, and designing highly targeted malware is extraordinarily expensive.

How Worried Should We Be?

So, given this litany of sophisticated attacks, how worried should we be? Are these attacks, however sophisticated, rarities or commonplace? The answer to these questions by different kinds of stakeholders can be very confusing. Some examples:

Vendors of cybersecurity solutions have an interest in exaggerating attack statistics. For example, to many vendors, it is fair to count every message that every IT/OT firewall drops as an attack that was defeated. Indeed, some vendors count every message that a power utility's Internet firewall drops as an attack prevented on critical infrastructure, while others count every instance of malware that an email system diagnoses and discards at a power or water utility as an attack on critical infrastructure. Few observers find these reports of millions of attacks per year to be persuasive.

Governments have expert advisors with a deep understanding of what is possible and of how well or poorly prepared are different manufacturers and critical infrastructures. These agencies continue to issue warnings and advice based on these expert opinions, but for every expert with one opinion we can very often find another with the opposite opinion. This debate confuses everyone from owners and operators to the public at large. And it helps little when agencies and experts give in to temptation and quote the questionable vendor statistics to support their positions.

Experts debate the definition of an OT cyber incident. Some experts maintain that every error by an operator and every software defect that results in physical consequences is an OT cyber incident, and so report that as many as hundreds of people are killed every year in such incidents. Other experts disagree, arguing that, while human errors and software flaws that result in physical consequences *could* be reproduced by attackers to bring about the same consequences, in fact it is much more difficult for outsiders to execute such attacks than it is for software vendors to make coding mistakes, or for insiders to make mistakes in operations.

Software vulnerability repositories each year document thousands of defects in IT and automation software, hardware, designs, and implementations. A fraction of these vulnerabilities are ranked as the most serious kinds of vulnerabilities. Some experts point to these numbers as evidence that urgent action is needed to address OT cyber risks. Other experts disagree, again pointing out that vulnerabilities are not attacks, and that while an individual vulnerability may be trivial to exploit by an attacker with direct access to the affected automation systems, gaining such access is generally not trivial.

Furthermore, even with access to exploit a vulnerability, directing that exploit in such a way as to cause an unacceptable physical consequence most often demands considerable engineering expertise.

Government agencies, academic researchers and others accumulate repositories of attacks and compromises of different kinds of targets, including critical industrial infrastructures, but almost no such repositories classify consequences in useful ways. Attacks that are easily defeated before they come anywhere close to an unacceptable consequence are not distinguished from near misses. Attacks that risk only business consequences are not distinguished from attacks that put physical operations at risk. Almost no agency tracks or makes it possible to search for and summarize cyber attacks that caused physical consequences. Numbers that government agencies and researchers quote from these repositories vary wildly, because of the differing criteria for counting attacks and consequences, which does not increase the confidence of observers trying to understand what action they need to take in response to today's pervasive threat environment.

Other repositories report both attacks in the public record and attacks that were somehow privately disclosed to the repository. All such repositories claim to investigate thoroughly all reports they receive before publishing those reports, but many researchers find these confidential reports less than credible, in part because the researchers are unable to access the confidential reports and verify the data.

How are we to deal with these many conflicting inputs? Well, there are nuggets of truth and insights to be drawn from all these inputs. For example:

- Automation errors, omissions, defects, and safety consequences do say something about physical consequences that are possible, physical consequences that we should be considering in our threat models. These possibilities are important to determining network criticality in Chapter 7.
- Vulnerability reports do give us an idea of how much trouble we are in. This is especially true in automation systems where the systems exhibiting these vulnerabilities are easily reachable from the Internet, and especially when these reports describe vulnerabilities in the very security systems that we deploy to defend our automation systems to prevent attacks from the Internet and other sources from reaching those automation systems.
- Since the threat environment has become steadily more threatening over the course of the last thirty years, it should come as no surprise that forward-looking statements by government and academic experts are more alarming than backwards-looking statements based on statistics. We need to base our security planning on forward-looking research.

But – given the on-going controversy about the role of each of the above kinds of reports, consider a view of past OT cyber incidents that is incontrovertible.

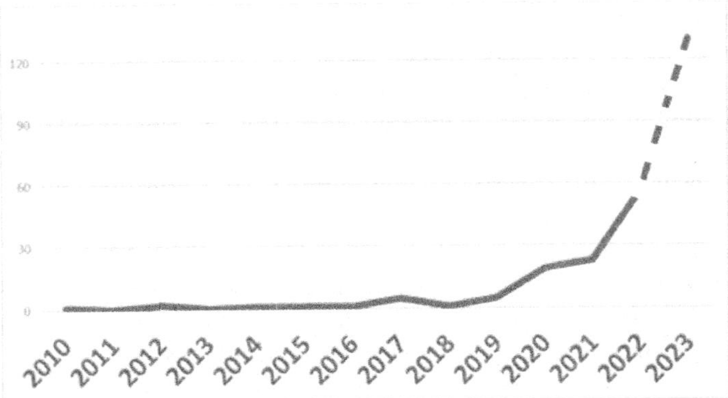

Figure (1): Consequential Cyber Attacks

The figure is a chart of cyber attacks in the public record that had physical consequences in discrete and process manufacturing industries[9]. The figure does not include hospitals, banks, nor governments. It is focused on power plants, rail systems, automobile, cell phone manufacturers, and the like. The figure does not include errors and omissions, nor does it include private disclosures that cannot be verified in records accessible to the public. A quick tour of the numbers includes:

- 2010 – Only one cyber attack in these industries had physical consequences – the Stuxnet worm destroyed over 1000 uranium gas centrifuges. Stuxnet infected over 100,000 other machines world-wide, but there was no public report of any physical consequence from any of those other infections, however much they might have cost to clean up.
- 2011 – No cyber attacks with physical consequences were reported.
- 2012 – Israeli hacktivists take credit for shutting down passenger rails in Iran, and the US DHS reports that malware delayed the scheduled restart of a large power plant by 3 weeks.
- 2013 – No cyber attacks with physical consequences were reported.
- 2014 – The German BSI reports a steel mill suffering massive damages because of a cyber attack. The mill was never named, but the attack was widely reported.
- 2015 – A group suspected to be Russian-backed turned off the power to 225,000 Ukrainians for up to 6 hours.
- 2016 – A group suspected to be Russian-backed turned off the power to citizens of Kyiv for one hour.
- 2017 – Five attacks with physical consequences, with the NotPetya attack being by far the most serious. NotPetya affected hundreds of enterprises and

[9] *2023 Threat Report*, Waterfall Security and ICS Strive, https://waterfall-security.com/2023-threat-report

impaired physical operations at Merck Pharmaceutical, Maersk Shipping, and others – but it was a single attack that embedded malware in a Ukrainian tax package.

- 2018 – A ransomware attack shut down semiconductor fabrication at TSMC for several days.
- 2019 – Five attacks, the most prominent being the ransomware attack on Norsk Hydro that shut down several sheet aluminum plants for up to a week.
- 2020 – 18 attacks, all ransomware, each shutting down between one and 14 plants for up to two weeks.
- 2021 – 23 attacks, all but one ransomware, most shutting down multiple manufacturing sites, with the most prominent attack being on Colonial Pipeline, producing widespread gasoline shortages in the Northeast United States.
- 2022 – 57 attacks, most were ransomware but including 5 hacktivist attacks, together shutting down oil terminals, rail systems, copper mines, Bridgestone tire factories, and many more.

What is clear from the numbers above is that cyber attacks with physical consequences were a largely theoretical risk in the 20-teens. In the 2020's, ransomware attacks with physical consequences have increased dramatically and are, at this writing (2023), more than doubling every year. This represents a state change in the threat environment. At present, there is no reason to believe that attacks with physical consequences in these industries will ever return to the zero-or-one attacks per year state of the 20-teens.

The numbers above are arguably the most conservative possible interpretation of the threat environment. In many of the world's jurisdictions, attacks such as these are considered state secrets and are not reported publicly. This makes it certain that the numbers above are an under-estimate of cyber attacks with physical consequences in the tracked industries.

Despite this conservatism, it is clear that the OT security threat environment is worsening, and even the most cautious and conservative of experts are predicting continued worsening in the future. In the 2020's, OT cyber risk changed fundamentally, from a largely theoretical risk well understood by only experts, to a clear and growing threat to safe, reliable, and efficient physical operations.

Summary

Modern ransomware and other sophisticated attacks operate by remote control – an attacker issues commands to a compromised machine from across the world, sees the results of those commands and repeats. Using a compromised machine to attack other machines accessible to the compromised machine is called "pivoting" an attack from one machine to another. Ransomware groups, nation-state intelligence agencies and military organizations and other sophisticated threats all make heavy use of this approach – the approach is very effective.

Ransomware is the most widespread perpetrator of targeted, pivoting attacks, and is responsible for most OT shutdowns since 2020. There are three ways ransomware can impact operations:

- Ransomware can target OT systems directly,
- Ransomware can target only IT systems, but fear of propagation into OT networks causes OT shutdowns in "abundance of caution," scenarios and
- Ransomware can target only IT systems, but physical operations rely on services provided by crippled IT systems and so must shut down.

A handful of "famous" attacks are worth studying, because everyone in the industry talks about them. These include:

- **Colonial Pipeline** – a remote-controlled ransomware attack triggered a shutdown "in an abundance of caution," with unconfirmed reports of OT dependencies on IT systems,
- **Triton** – a remote-control attack that targeted Safety Instrumented Systems (SIS), putting human lives at risk,
- **Ukraine Power Grid** – the first attack shut off power to 225,000 residents for up to 6 hours, while the second turned off power for only an hour, but appears to have been designed to damage high-voltage transformers and so impair power to the region for much longer,
- **NotPetya** – malware hidden in a security update spread indiscriminately, erased hard drives, and crippled over one hundred victim organizations, some of them with very large, very expensive physical operations, and
- **Stuxnet** – tightly-targeted malware that destroyed 1000 uranium gas centrifuges in Iran's nuclear weapons program.

While there are only a handful of cyber attacks with physical consequences that most practitioners are aware of, there are reports of thousands and even millions of attacks on OT systems. These reports tend to be very confusing, because the criteria for inclusion in these summaries and reports are inconsistent and often opaque to the readers of the reports. The most cautious threat report counts only public reports of deliberate cyber attacks that caused physical consequences in process and manufacturing industries. Even by this ultra-conservative measure, the number of attacks resulting in physical consequences is growing rapidly. At the current rate of increase, this class of attack is expected to reach crisis proportions by 2027-2028.

Chapter 4 – Security Engineering Approaches

Having defined the problem, what is the solution? The comparatively new discipline of security engineering should provide much of an answer. Security engineering is not just cybersecurity, consisting instead of a collection of approaches including cybersecurity, safety engineering and others.

Security engineering is about addressing cyber risk to physical operations with both cybersecurity and engineering techniques, as appropriate to the systems and to the risks. How to do this is a little complicated, because much of security engineering is unique to specific industries, and even within industries, varies between large and small operations. A small shoe factory for example, almost certainly has a very different risk profile and set of cyber and physical due-care expectations than does a business producing aircraft parts, or a passenger rail system moving tens of thousands of passengers per day.

This said, the available cyber risk management solutions range from "IT centric" to "engineering centric" and everything in between. The IT-centric end of the spectrum is well documented and widely understood. The engineering-centric end of the spectrum is much less well understood. In this chapter we introduce security engineering, contrast it with IT-style cybersecurity, and survey the body of security engineering knowledge.

IT-Centric Security

There is widespread consensus among experts that IT-centric solutions are the right way to protect business-critical networks and systems, and many of these tools and approaches are important in safety-critical and reliability-critical networks as well. Essential elements of the IT-centric approach include:

- A recognition that Internet connectivity for all business and consumer computing systems has increased dramatically in the last 25 years, and that this trend shows no sign of slowing down.
- Sending ever-increasing amounts of important information across the Internet demands strong encryption. To a very real extent in IT-centric systems, "Encryption is the answer, what was the question?"
- IT systems pull gigabytes or terabytes of information from the Internet every day, most of it *inside* of encrypted connections. A measurable fraction of that information – researchers report a bit less than 1% – is attack information. Given this volume of attacks, it seems inevitable that every IT network will sooner or later be breached. As a result, it is vitally important that we develop sophisticated abilities to understand our systems, anticipate

attacks, and in the terminology of the *NIST Cybersecurity Framework*, to detect, respond, and recover from cyber attacks.

None of these elements is controversial on business or consumer networks. Of course, encryption is vital – none of us can afford to have our bank accounts or credit card credentials stolen, and few of us care to have "big brother" in the form of governments, businesses or others looking over our shoulders to see what we are reading, what we are posting, and who we are communicating with.

And yes, it seems pretty much inevitable that all IT systems will eventually be breached. It is therefore vital that we have sophisticated security and intrusion monitoring systems, staffed by experts who assume we have been compromised and who actively, deliberately, and systematically set out to find what has been compromised. We need additional experts poised to respond promptly and decisively when we are compromised. Routine IT security operations systematically search for and detect compromised equipment, isolate that equipment, take forensic images for later analysis, erase the equipment, and restore it from backups. And then do it again. And again.

NIST Framework

This IT-centric security (IT-SEC) approach has been practiced and studied for decades, and as a result is reasonably mature. The NIST Framework for Improving Critical Infrastructure Cybersecurity (NIST CSF) for example, is seen by most practitioners as a comprehensive list of security measures that should be considered for every IT cybersecurity program. The pillars of the NIST CSF are:

- **Identify** – determine who is responsible for security, what assets need protection, policies needed to protect those assets, and so on,
- **Protect** – prevent cyber attacks from reaching or impairing the assets,
- **Detect** – recognize that no protective regime is perfect and so actively monitor and search for attacks in progress,
- **Respond** – develop a robust capacity to respond to and shut down attacks in progress, when they are detected, and
- **Recover** – develop the capacity to recover computer systems promptly and reliably to normal operations when operations have been impaired by a cyber attack.

A sixth pillar *Govern* is part of the *NIST CSF 2.0* draft, focused on processes and risk. Dozens of measures or controls are associated with each of these pillars, controls which may be accomplished by people, process, technology, or a combination thereof.

The framework, however, has limitations. For starters, no framework is a prescription for how to secure a system, and the NIST framework is no exception. Frameworks are more like checklists of things to *consider* for inclusion in a specific program. It is up to the practitioner to look through the list and decide which of these measures may be appropriate to their organization's needs, and to what degree they may be appropriate.

Second, while the framework reflects inputs from a wide variety of IT, OT, military and other practitioners and academics, the language of the framework is very abstract. "Critical infrastructure" is defined by NIST to include everything from power plants and nuclear weapons systems to banks and large retailers. The problem with this generality and abstraction is that it is easy for each of these kinds of practitioners to see their own preconceptions reflected in the framework, with no real understanding of each others' perspectives. Enterprise security personnel looking at the framework see "detect, respond and recover," with no understanding that these elements of the framework have a different role in power plants than they do in banks.

Third, the framework is very abstract. For example, search an online version of the framework – the word "firewall" does not appear in the framework. Protecting networks is a measure in the *protect* branch of the framework, but how to do that is left to standards such as NIST 800-53, which are cross-referenced to measures in the framework. Interpreting the framework and applying it to any given organization or installation takes a lot of knowledge.

Finally, the NIST CSF is all about cybersecurity. The framework says nothing about engineering approaches to managing physical risk due to cybersecurity, a topic we now explore.

Engineering-Centric Security

Engineers responsible for power plants and refineries look at the IT approach to cybersecurity and see assumptions and approaches that simply do not seem to fit the needs of many industrial sites:

- No OT engineering team on the planet has "increase connectivity with the Internet" as a strategic goal. Instead, increased manufacturing and business efficiencies are the most common engineering goals, and those goals must always be pursued in a way that incurs acceptable levels of physical risks. Yes, IT connectivity and even Internet connectivity has efficiency and other benefits, and so the key question that engineers must ask routinely is *"How many of those benefits can we enjoy, without incurring unacceptable physical risk?"* Engineers seek the benefits of connectivity, not connectivity itself.
- Encryption, and especially the very technical topic of encryption key management, while straightforward on IT networks and in the upper levels of industrial networks, is very difficult to do deep inside heavily protected industrial networks.
- Intrusion detection, response and recovery are important capabilities to have in the engineering-centric approach, but in critical networks, engineers must give a higher priority to *preventing* attacks than is possible in IT networks.

This last assertion is particularly difficult for many practitioners to accept, so consider an analogy. Imagine that we are guests on a tour of a large power plant. We are in the control room. There are four operator workstations, one for each half-gigawatt generating unit in the plant. Each operator station has an operator sitting 24x7 at a large, curved desk, using a bank of screens as an HMI. Two supervisors are in the room as well, each responsible for two of the operators.

While we are standing there in the tour group, a stranger wearing no name badge runs into the room and pushes one of the operators out of their chair. The intruder sits down and starts moving the mouse and typing on the keyboard. What happens? Chaos ensues. Everyone starts screaming for security. All the able-bodied people in the room jump on the intruder and drag them out of the chair. Security shows up and drags the intruder, kicking and screaming, out of the room.

The operator is restored to their chair and every expert in the room – including both supervisors and our tour guide, look anxiously over their shoulder as they to determine what just happened. Did the intruder change anything? Is the generating unit at risk? Do we need to shut the unit down? Do we need to trip the entire plant? Minutes go by, then tens of minutes. The experts determine that no harm was done. The lights stay on.

Our tour guide returns to our group and says "I'm – I'm very sorry that you had to see that. The tour is over, sorry – I will take you back to security."

We put our hand up and ask, "A question while we walk back – a question about what we just saw. That intruder who took over the HMI – how long is an acceptable amount of time to have that intruder operating the physical process? How long is an acceptable risk?"

The room goes silent. Every head in the room turns to us. Our tour guide stares at us in shock, long enough for us to start to become uncomfortable. Eventually our guide coughs and says, "I'm sorry, but that's entirely the wrong question. The right question is 'How did that person get in here, and what are we going to do to make sure this *never* happens again?'"

Detecting intrusions takes time. Deciding that the alerts and other evidence we have in front of us really does constitute a situation worthy of investigation takes time. Scrambling an incident response team takes time. That team determining that this really is an intrusion and not some sort of false alarm takes time. And once the team determines that they do have an intrusion, dealing with the intrusion takes time. For all that time, our adversary has control of some or all computers on our industrial network. In many industrial systems, this is unacceptable.

Engineering teams must never confuse preventing intrusions into control-critical networks with detecting, responding, and recovering from intrusions. The latter is important, yes – our power plant story did have a physical security team that responded to the physical intrusion after all. But in many cases, there is no acceptable amount of time for an intruder to maliciously operate powerful, dangerous physical processes.

More to the point – with intrusion detection, response and recovery on IT networks, enterprise security teams *hope* to discover attacks before we incur material business damages. In many engineering contexts, *hope* is unacceptable. Engineers use physics, mathematics, and experience to design bridges that will withstand a defined load for a defined period of time to a very high, mathematically determinable degree of confidence. Yes, there is an inspection regime to ensure that the bridges have been constructed according to engineering specifications, and to ensure that the bridges are not wearing out or corroding faster than projected. However, no engineer designs a bridge *hoping* that it will hold up to its specified load for a specified number of decades. *Hope* is not good engineering.

Similarly, in the world of OT cyber risk, our automation for powerful, dangerous physical processes often should be designed to withstand a specified cyber threat load, at least until the next opportunity to redesign, update and redeploy the automation and its security system. This means that:

- Since we cannot update important automation systems constantly, we must *anticipate* the worsening threat environment for at least the next 3-5 years, possibly for the next 15 years,
- We must *define* the capabilities of the threat actors that our security engineering designs are going to defeat reliably over the course of that time,
- We must of course deploy those security systems, and
- We must monitor our defenses and the threat environment to ensure that our defenses have been deployed correctly, and that the threat environment has not evolved in unanticipated ways that put our physical operations at unexpected risk.

Intrusion detection, response and recovery capabilities are still important to industrial security programs. Nobody operates the power plant in the above example without a physical security team ready to respond to intrusions, but in most kinds of industrial sites, the priority for these three pillars of the NIST CSF is rather different from the priority on IT networks.

Security Engineering

In many jurisdictions, engineering is a regulated profession because of the risks to worker safety, public safety and to the public welfare posed by poor engineering practice. Civil engineers who design bridges and skyscrapers are regulated, power engineers who design the power grid are regulated, and chemical engineers who design refineries are regulated. If a professional engineer in any of these jurisdictions ignores engineering best practices, produces a flawed design, and that design then fails in such a way as to cost billions of dollars or kill dozens of people, that engineer is thrown out of the profession. They never practice again. The time has come for security engineering to become a recognized part of the engineering profession, at least for designs where public safety is at risk.

To create this specialization, we must develop a body of knowledge and of practice that moves from today's most common cybersecurity positions of "unacceptable outcomes *seem* unlikely" to a position where critical sites are reliably protected from unacceptable outcomes of cyber attacks across a specified range of attack capabilities. The range of attack capabilities from which we are reliably protected must include all capabilities that are easily available to our adversaries, whoever those adversaries might be. At the very minimum, the ruled-out capabilities must include those widely available to today's ransomware criminal groups. Engineering-grade techniques must stand the test of time as well. Engineering-grade security must reliably defeat not just yesterday's and today's attacks, but tomorrow's as well, at least until our next scheduled opportunity to redesign our security systems, with a generous margin for error.

For example, consider the design of a pedestrian bridge across a busy thoroughfare next to a football stadium. What load must such a bridge be designed to carry? The maximum load occurs when the stadium is emptying after a game and people are crossing the bridge en masse, shoulder-to-shoulder. Engineers model that load as the entire bridge covered in two meters / 6.5 feet of water. People are mostly water, and the average person's height is less than two meters. That weight and weight distribution is the specified maximum load for the bridge. And then, the engineer designs the bridge to carry ten times that specified load, "just in case." These are people using the bridge after all – failure under load is unacceptable.

This is deterministic, engineering-grade design. This is our goal for security engineering when the worst-case physical consequences of compromise are unacceptable. In this book, we define engineering-grade designs as any design that:

- Reduces the risk of unacceptable consequences of defined classes of cyber attacks to acceptable values,
- Carries out this reduction in a way that is predictable and mathematically modellable,
- Brings about this reduction for a predictable period of time, no matter how the threat environment might evolve in the interim.

A couple of words of caution about this definition:

- Not all unacceptable consequences have engineering-grade solutions. For example, this author is not currently aware of any engineering-grade design able to prevent ransomware attacks from regularly compromising Internet-exposed IT networks, no matter how unacceptable the consequences of a compromised IT network may be.
- Not even engineering-grade solutions can eliminate all risk, hence the use of the word "defined" in the definition above.

For example, an over-pressure valve can still be physically sabotaged by a malicious person at the industrial site carrying a hammer or other tools. When we evaluate engineering-grade solutions, we need to be aware of residual risks, and we must consider what measures may be appropriate to address those risks, or not. This kind of risk management is the subject of Chapters 6-8.

Security PHA Review

There are several engineering approaches than can be used to eliminate entire classes of consequences from risk equations. The first and perhaps simplest is *Security PHA Review*[10] (SPR), a powerful methodology for eliminating safety consequences of cyber attacks. In the title of the book, PHA stands for "Process Hazard Analysis" – a safety review methodology that is widely practiced and is required by law in some jurisdictions, for all industrial facilities with material risks to the safety of workers, the environment, or the public. The output of a PHA is most often a spreadsheet with columns including:

- **Consequence** – the explosion or fire or other hazardous outcome of a potential safety incident,
- **Causes** – any event, such as an equipment failure or error in carrying out an operating procedure, that might cause or lead to the consequence,
- **Cause likelihood** – the probability of each cause arising,
- **Safeguards** – equipment, automation, operating procedures, or other measures that reduce the likelihood of, or eliminate entirely the consequence, and
- **Unmitigated impact** – the severity of the consequence, often expressed as a qualitative impact rating between one and five for each of safety, the environment or equipment damage.

The Security PHA Review methodology reviews these outputs of a PHA and for each consequence, asks the question, "Can any of the causes of this consequence be brought about by cyber sabotage?" If the answer is "yes," then the methodology asks, "Are all the countermeasures that serve to prevent this consequence 'hackable' – capable of being brought about through compromise?

Exactly what constitutes "hackable" is a question of risk tolerance. Some practitioners decide that any computer that controls a safety function is hackable – all software has "bugs" or defects after all, and some of those defects are security vulnerabilities, either discovered or undiscovered. Other practitioners and sites will argue that only computers that are connected directly or indirectly to an Internet Protocol (IP) network are hackable.

Whatever the definition, if there is a reliable mechanical safety mitigation in place, then the consequence cannot in fact be brought about by a cyber attack.

---

[10] *Security PHA Review for Consequence-Based Cybersecurity*, Edward Marszal, and Jim McGlone, 2019, International Society for Automation

On the other hand, if an unsafe condition can be brought about by a cyber attack, and if all safety mitigations are hackable, then we have an OT cyber safety risk. A worst-case cyber attack will be able to bring about unacceptable consequences.

SPR advocates that, wherever practical, we eliminate the opportunity to bring about these unsafe conditions by deploying unhackable mitigations. Examples of unhackable mitigations include:

- Mechanical pressure-relief valves,
- Centrifugal over-speed switches,
- Excess-flow check valves, and
- One-way check valves.

All these examples are physical and mechanical. Computers may monitor the status of these mechanical protections, but no computer intervention is needed to trigger these devices to engage to shut down unsafe operations before they injure anybody. In addition, to qualify as unhackable, there must be no way for any computer or compromised computer to impede the mechanical operation of the device. With unhackable mitigations in place, the opportunity to cause safety consequences with a cyber attack, in a sense "vanishes."

We say "in a sense" because there is physically no way to make all risk vanish. Mechanical mitigations wear out and fail in mathematically predictable fashions. This is why the safety engineering discipline exists. That discipline considers factors such as the quality of the mitigations, the expected rates of failure, inspection disciplines able to detect failures, the time it takes to repair mitigations that have failed, and so on. The discipline uses these factors to calculate an acceptable level of safety, not just for this physical process, but for an entire plant, and indeed sometimes for an entire industry. Physical mitigations do not make risk vanish, they make cyber risks to safety vanish.

Furthermore, these mechanical mitigations are in a real sense "future proof." It does not matter how many passwords our enemies steal in the future, nor does it matter how sophisticated their malware becomes – if no computer can impair the operation of these safety measures, then no cyber attack can impair them, no matter how sophisticated that attack is today, or becomes tomorrow.

The SPR methodology is an engineering-centric methodology. Where are the over-pressure valves in the NIST CSF? There is no such thing – the NIST CSF is focused on cyber mitigations, not physical mitigations. There is no hint in the NIST framework of any of these engineering-grade approaches to dealing with cyber risk. Where are over-pressure relief valves in the very widely used IEC 62443 series of industrial cybersecurity standards? There is no hint of the valves in the 62443 standards either – like the NIST CSF, the 62443 family of standards is focused on cybersecurity, not engineering mitigations.

SPR-style physical mitigations for safety threats are well understood by safety engineering teams. Safety teams deploy this class of protection routinely. Better yet, the cost of such measures is modest. Augmenting computerized safety systems with mechanical and electrical safeties is generally accomplished at only a tiny fraction of the cost of a full-fledged cybersecurity program that provides anywhere near engineering-grade protections for safety computers. With physical risk-avoidance mechanisms in place, it is no longer necessary to accept the risk of cyber attacks causing these safety consequences.

Note that when unhackable safety mitigations are not possible, SPR recommends deploying software-based safety measures, protected to the greatest extent practical by conventional IT-centric security measures, in the hopes of bringing cyber risks somewhat closer to acceptable levels, and notes how expensive such cybersecurity programs are.

Consequence-Driven, Cyber Informed Engineering

A second approach to eliminating cyber consequences is Consequence-driven, Cyber-informed Engineering[11] (CCE), as documented in the text *Countering Cyber Sabotage*. The name of the methodology defines its approach: this is cyber-informed *engineering*, not cybersecurity.

While CCE is focused primarily on OT cyber risk assessment, the methodology also encourages organizations to focus cybersecurity programs initially on the most consequential threats and touches on powerful engineering-grade consequence-elimination techniques. CCE echoes some of the SPR advice and goes on to point out that some types of digital mitigations are also unhackable. Digital circuits and circuit boards can encode complex algorithms for avoiding safety threats as well as avoiding the risk of damage to very costly or difficult-to-replace equipment, provided that these electronics do not include a CPU or any other form of computer.

Digital circuit boards may use electrical relays, transistors, capacitors, gate arrays, custom ASICs, and other components to carry out complex calculations without involving computers. No cyber attack can impair the operation of these hard-wired circuits. Such digital circuits can, for example:

- Introduce unhackable delays between the time a motor is turned off and turned back on again, so that the motor can come to a complete stop to prevent being re-activated out of phase with the grid,
- Detect vibration or noise when a pump is spinning too quickly and cavitating, and thus causing serious damage to the pump, or
- Detect unusual current or voltage conditions, such as may occur naturally in a power grid or industrial installation during a lightning strike or may occur deliberately because of some kinds of cyber attacks.

Digital, unhackable mitigations for threats to worker safety and threats to costly equipment are well understood by engineering teams. Better yet, the cost of such

---

[11] *Countering Cyber Sabotage – Introducing Consequence-driven Cyber-informed Engineering (CCE),* Andrew A. Bochman and Sarah Freeman, 2021, CRC Press

measures is modest. Very often, the very "ladder logic" designs that engineers use to program safety automation can be directly converted into digital circuits. With unhackable digital protections in place, the opportunity to bring about unacceptable safety, equipment damage or other consequences vanishes. Even if an industrial network is compromised and every computer on the network issues every unsafe instruction the computer is physically and electrically able to issue, unhackable digital protections still do their job, most commonly bringing about an emergency shutdown when dangerous conditions are detected.

A word of caution here – while it is possible to design "unhackable" digital mitigations, not all CPU-less mitigations are unhackable. To be truly "unhackable" it must not be possible to physically damage the mitigation by manipulating its inputs. For example, many years ago, CPU-less CRT monitors could be set to a refresh speed of zero Hz. This led to enormous current being shunted through transformers, which subsequently over-heated and caught fire. Engineers designing these mitigations must design the circuit boards to withstand any possible combination of inputs (controls) to the boards, even those that "should" not occur in normal use of the circuits.

A more fundamental limitation of CCE, at least as the methodology is documented in the text Countering Cyber Sabotage, is that the methodology ignores network and information flow engineering as tools to prevent attack propagation, recommending only cybersecurity mitigations for that purpose.

That said, the methodology is useful as far as it goes, and we look closer at network engineering for reliability-critical infrastructures in the sections and chapters ahead.

Manual Operations and Resilience

Resilience is defined as the ability of a system to continue operating under stress – usefully, but in a potentially degraded mode. Resilience also refers to the ability of that system to return to something closer to normal operations when the stressor is removed. The widespread analogy is that resilience is like a spring: the spring deforms when force is applied but returns to its original form when the force is removed. The spring in the analogy is our physical industrial operations, and the force is a cyber attack.

Manual operations are the most widely described and most practical example of industrial resilience. Consider the 2017 ransomware attack on Norsk Hydro for example. When the attack was discovered, decision-makers evaluated very quickly what impact the attack might have on physical operations and decided that:

- Norsk's power plants were protected by OT security programs so robust that the malware had no real chance of propagating to those plants, and so the power plants were left running normally.

- The computers operating the company's aluminum smelters were at risk, and so the company shut down all those computers and continued operating the smelters manually, though presumably somewhat less efficiently, and
- The computers operating the company's sheet aluminum plants were at risk, the enterprise was not confident of the strength of the plants' OT security programs, and the facilities were so heavily automated that they could no longer be operated manually. The sheet aluminum plants were therefore shut down, out of an abundance of caution.

When physical infrastructure, such as the Norsk aluminum smelters, can be operated manually, without computers, that is a powerful fall-back position during a cyber attack. Especially in critical infrastructures such as water treatment and distribution systems, the ability to operate physical infrastructure manually means that the worst reliability consequences of compromise are no longer possible to bring about. While manual operations are generally not as efficient or cost-effective as automated operations, a manual fall-back means that a cyber attack that might otherwise have had unacceptable physical or societal consequences can be reduced to an attack that has only consequences for business efficiency. Insurance companies are much happier compensating businesses for extra employees and overtime pay than they would be paying for class action lawsuits because of injuries to the public.

Decades ago, manual operations with analog controls and safeties were how all physical operations were designed. Today, manual controls and capabilities are seen by many as backwards looking. Engineering teams are often proud to report to their stakeholders that all those archaic manual controls have finally been removed in the most recent systems upgrade, and that physical operations have finally, irretrievably been brought into the world of modern, efficient computer automation. However, given recent requests from government authorities to revive the ability for manual operations, these perceptions are all changing. Increasingly, a manual operations fall-back position is seen as a valuable cyber risk mitigation.

Returning to manual operations is, however, easier to talk about than to bring about. Many modern factories and industries no longer have the analog gauges, dials, switches, and indicator lights that technicians can use to understand and control physical processes. Modern valves and semiconductor switches may no longer have any handles or mechanism that allows technicians to operate them manually. Retrofitting "modern" designs with the manual capabilities has a cost.

And – even when a physical process has all the controls and indicators needed to operate manually, this does not mean that the workforce has the knowledge and skills needed for such operation. If manual operations are to be a credible alternative for a water system or a smelter, the workforce needs to be trained and practiced for such operations regularly. Some water treatment systems for example, have instituted a "manual operations day" once per month

– on a set day each month, all the control computers are turned off. The team then gathers and interprets what analog information they have, makes the decisions the computers would have made, and then drives out to switches, valves, and other actuators to carry out those decisions manually. All water quality testing falls back to a manual mode as well.

Now, manual operations are not suitable for all industrial processes. Some processes are so complex, or so fast, that it is no longer physically possible for people to operate them manually, no matter how well trained those people are. In some industries, such as some kinds of consumer goods manufacturing, the cost of the finished product is enormously important. In these industries there is often no point in producing product unless it can be produced in a maximally efficient, minimal cost, fully automated manner – inefficiently produced product costs so much that there is no hope of profiting from producing that product.

When manual operations are possible and useful though, they can be a powerful fall-back position, especially for critical infrastructures. Developing and maintaining the ability to fall back to manual operations has some cost, but also has the benefit of material reductions in risk, especially in critical infrastructures, and in industries like smelting, where emergency shutdowns can lead to extremely expensive equipment damage. In these circumstances, an organization with a proven manual-ops capability should be able to find a cyber insurance provider who recognizes this reduced risk and rewards the organization with materially reduced policy costs.

Secure Operations Technology

Secure Operations Technology[12] (SEC-OT) is an OT-centric methodology that differs qualitatively from the SPR and CCE methodologies above. With SPR, when unsafe conditions arise, physical mitigations engage, and the physical process is shut down. Similarly, with CCE, when dangerous conditions are detected, CCE's physical and digital protections engage to shut down the physical process before damage can be done. And a capability for manual operations ensures that, during cyber emergencies in those industries and enterprises where such control is possible, physical operations can continue in a degraded, and less efficient mode.

SEC-OT is different from these approaches in that, if we recall, our goal for managing OT cyber risks was to assure *safe, continuous, and efficient* physical operations, not to shut down our site or degrade into inefficient operations every time there is a cyber attack. And so, unlike SPR and CCE, SEC-OT is focused on engineering-grade approaches to *preventing* attack information from entering industrial control systems in the first place.

SEC-OT observes that all cyber-sabotage attacks are information – the only way for an OT network to change from an uncompromised to a compromised

[12] *Secure Operations Technology*, Andrew Ginter, 2018, Abterra Technologies Inc.

state is for attack information to somehow enter the OT network. The methodology is therefore focused on engineering-grade, physical controls over the flow of information, and especially over the flow of control information that might enter our industrial networks and put them at risk.

The methodology encourages practitioners to carry out an inventory of all incoming control / potential attack information. A complete inventory of incoming information paths is, by definition, also a complete inventory of cyber-sabotage attack vectors. Unlike enumerating attack paths, which for non-trivial control system designs can number in the billions, the number of attack vectors identified by a SEC-OT analysis typically numbers less than two dozen. The methodology then encourages practitioners to systematically, and wherever possible physically, control every one of those attack / control information flows.

The SEC-OT methodology is described in detail in Appendix B, and some parts of the methodology are coming up next as part of Chapter 5.

Cyber-Informed Engineering

In 2022, Idaho National Labs, working on behalf of the US Department of Energy, published the *National Cyber-Informed Engineering Strategy* [13]. Officially, the strategy includes five pillars:

- **Awareness** – Promulgate a universal and shared understanding of CIE,
- **Education** – Embed CIE into formal education, training and credentialling,
- **Development** – Build the body of knowledge by which CIE is applied to specific implementations,
- **Current Infrastructure** – Apply CIE principles to existing systematically important infrastructure, and
- **Future Infrastructure** – Conduct R&D and develop an industrial base to build CIE into new infrastructure systems and emerging technology.

In short, this means the strategy document is not a "recipe" for how to do CIE, nor is it a body of knowledge for CIE – the strategy is a plan to create that body of knowledge. In the judgement of this author, the SPR, CCE and SEC-OT methodologies must all become essential elements of the CIE body of knowledge, as must the network engineering and risk management concepts in Chapters 5-8 of this book.

At this writing, there is a very large and very active community of interest participating in regular virtual meetings, interacting with Idaho National Laboratories and DoE personnel to help define the CIE body of knowledge, raise awareness, and otherwise support the five pillars of the strategy. In these meetings, CIE is frequently described as having two big objectives – teaching the engineering community about conventional OT cybersecurity approaches

[13] *National Cyber-Informed Engineering Strategy (CIE)*, 2022, US Department of Energy

and applying engineering techniques to mitigate cyber risk to physical operations. Much of the discussion on these meetings is about engineering, but the plan is very clearly to address both sets of needs.

The CIE strategy and the emerging body of knowledge are widely seen to be a very good thing, applying powerful engineering tools and approaches to the task of addressing cyber risk to physical operations, in addition to conventional cybersecurity mitigations. There is however, one point of debate that is worth mentioning here: the strategy emphasizes several times how important it is that engineering approaches and engineering designs be applied to the task of addressing cyber risk very early in the life of development projects, because adding such design after the fact is difficult or impossible.

In this author's best understanding, this is a mistaken perception. Would the same thing be said about safety? Imagine that the engineering community discovers a new kind of metal fatigue that was very likely to cause aircraft to disintegrate in flight, in the very near future. In this imaginary scenario, would the aviation community "shrug their shoulders" and conclude that it would have been nice to know about this failure mode when the aircraft were being designed and manufactured? Or would the community, world-wide, ground all aircraft that might be affected until they could be inspected for symptoms of this new kind of fatigue, and those symptoms mitigated? It does not matter that this new kind of risk was poorly understood and poorly addressed in the original design of the aircraft. When safety risks are unacceptable, we act to address them.

The same is true of cyber risks and of the CIE methodology. Addressing cyber risks early in a project tends to cost much less than addressing those risks late in a project, but address those risks we must, when the risks are unacceptable.

Summary

The NIST CSF describes a complete cybersecurity program as consisting of measures classified into five pillars:

- **Identify** – people, responsibilities, systems, assets and more,
- **Protect** – prevent compromise or consequences of cyber attacks,
- **Detect** – measures to discover attacks in progress,
- **Respond** – measures used by practiced incident response teams, and
- **Recover** – erase systems, apply backups and otherwise restore systems to normal operation.

Most of these solutions are not deterministic. Engineering-grade solutions are defined as those that deterministically eliminate unacceptable consequences of defined attacks for a predictable period of time, no matter how the threat environment evolves over that time. Not all problems have engineering-grade solutions available, but some solutions and engineering-grade approaches that do exist include:

- *Security PHA Review* – using unhackable mechanical and analog safety systems to protect human life,
- Manual operations – override computer control manually, generally at increased cost when the computers become untrustworthy,
- *Secure Operations Technology* – prevent shutdowns and inefficiencies due to cyber attacks on OT systems by deterministically preventing large classes of attacks, and
- Resilience via Manual Operations – operate physical processes manually, most likely in a degraded mode, when cyber automation has been compromised and can no longer be trusted.

The NIST CSF makes no mention whatsoever of safety engineering, manual operations, SEC-OT, or other engineering-centric approaches. That said, cybersecurity programs such as those inspired by the NIST CSF are essential to both IT and OT security. Security engineering and engineering-grade solutions are powerful tools for managing cyber risk to operations in addition to the NIST CSF.

A new Cyber-Informed Engineering initiative from the US Department of Energy is setting out to create a body of knowledge for applying powerful and long-standing engineering techniques to the protection of public safety and national security in the face of cyber threats, for teaching the engineering community about cyber threats and traditional OT cybersecurity mitigations, and for teaching IT teams about how to engage with engineering teams to take advantage of powerful engineering mitigations that do not exist in the OT cybersecurity space.

Chapter 5 – Network Engineering

Network engineering is a body of knowledge focused on designing networks to reduce or eliminate information flows that could include cyber attacks, especially those flowing into OT automation networks. In this chapter we survey network engineering techniques.

Note that this is the most technical chapter in the book before Appendix B. If you get bogged down in this chapter, please skip the bits that are slowing you down and move on. You do not need to understand every point in this chapter to make sense of the rest of the book.

An important component of network engineering designs is the difference between control information and monitoring information – a difference we saw highlighted in Chapter 1. In many cases, compromised or malicious control information can have catastrophic consequences, depending on the physical process and the details of the control system. Network engineering is focused on controlling the movement, volume, and other characteristics of control information.

Monitoring vs. Control

Before we go further, we need to define terms a bit more strictly. Many practitioners reading thus far in the text will start arguing that tampering with monitoring data can lead to unacceptable consequences. For example, consider a cyber attack on a gasoline pipeline, an attack that forges monitoring data, reporting that pressure in the pipeline has dropped to almost zero, and that the motion of fluids in the pipeline has stopped completely. In these circumstances, the pipeline operator must very quickly shut all outlet valves in that section of pipeline, so that a negative pressure condition does not arise, drawing fluid back into the pipeline that is not supposed to be there. This is a problem when, in fact, the pipeline is still pressurized and flowing. By persuading the operator to suddenly close valves in a pipeline in full service, attackers introduce the potential for those operator actions to trigger a hydraulic hammer and subsequent pipeline rupture. In this scenario, what appears to be tampered monitoring data has caused an unacceptable consequence. In hopes of clearing up this confusion, we define:

- **Monitoring Data** – data passing out of a higher-consequence network, into a lower-consequence network, and
- **Control Data** – data passing into a higher-consequence network, from a lower-consequence network.

In the pipeline example, there is no lower or higher-consequence network. The HMI the pipeline operator uses is, by design, able to control every aspect of the pipeline. The HMI sub-network is as consequential as the PLC sub-network. In the pipeline example, all the PLC and HMI data is *control system* data, whether it represents reported values or operator commands, because the data has not passed through a consequence boundary. The point of network engineering is to design networks so that there *are* consequence boundaries, so that we do not need to protect every network in our enterprise as if it were a safety-critical network. This means of course, that when control data enters a more consequential network from a less-consequential and less-secured network, that control data must be subjected to serious scrutiny.

Firewalls Are Not Network Engineering

Before looking further at network engineering techniques, however, let's look at firewalls - the workhorse of IT network segmentation. Why are firewalls not engineering grade? The answer is that firewalls are porous to control information. Firewalls have a very important role in segmenting industrial networks but cannot be used universally for such segmentation. Understanding the intrinsic limitations of firewall technology is important to deciding where firewalls fit into network architectures, and where they do not.

Terminology first: firewalls are used at the boundaries / perimeters of Internet Protocol (IP) networks, and 99% of the Internet consists of three things:

- **Hosts** – which are the sources and destinations of IP messages,
- **Routers** – which are specialized computers that look at every message they receive on one network connection, consult routing tables and other mechanisms to figure out what is the "best" way to get this message to its destination host, and push that message out to another network connection, and
- **Connections** – the wires, fibres, microwaves, and other technologies that carry IP messages between routers and hosts.

In this simplified view of the Internet, all network firewalls are routers. Yes, firewalls do more than routers do, but deep under the hood, all firewall devices forward network traffic from one network to another.

More properly, firewalls are routers with filters – the filters are software components that look at each message and try to answer the question "is this message allowed?" The filters might compare the source IP address, TCP port number, destination address and port in the message to a set of rules saying which combinations are allowed vs not. The filters might ask if the message matches any patterns in a database of known attack patterns for messages, and if so, conclude that the message is *not* allowed. The filters might do "deep packet inspection" or other things. The filters might even change the message – encrypting it, decrypting it, or doing Network Address Translation (NAT) to change IP addresses and port numbers. Fundamentally though, once a filter is done with a message, the filter renders a verdict. If the original or a modified version of the message is allowed, the filter subsystem hands the message to the router subsystem in the firewall, and the firewall forwards the message to its destination network.

The most common way, therefore, for attacks to breach a firewall is for the attack to persuade the firewall software that the attack messages are allowed. Perhaps the simplest way to do this, on IT networks, is to persuade a user to download malicious software. Most IT firewalls are configured to permit all outgoing connection requests, such as requests from deceived users to connect out to compromised websites. Slightly more sophisticated attacks convince a user, who is allowed to log into industrial systems through a firewall, to disclose account and password information. The attacker then uses these credentials to log in to the industrial systems, right through the firewall. More sophisticated attacks might hijack legitimate sessions or use DNS spoofing to launch "man in the middle" (MiM) attacks to defeat encryption or even two-factor authentication mechanisms. Firewalls are also vulnerable to many other kinds of attacks, including:

- Exploiting software vulnerabilities in the firewall software,
- Stealing credentials needed to log into firewalls themselves as a firewall administrator and then reconfiguring the devices to allow all connections and packets, and
- Deceiving ICS insiders into carrying attack software (control information) into the industrial network past the firewall, malware that subsequently connects out to the IT network or to the Internet through the control system firewall. This malware then enables remote control of compromised ICS equipment from the external network.

This last attack pattern can be disguised in many ways. One method in widespread use embeds communications with Internet-based command and control centers (C2) inside of legitimate Domain Name System (DNS) requests. More generally, C2 communications can, in theory, be steganographically encoded in *any* communications through a firewall with an external service. In practice, this kind of attack communications is encoded this way in the most sophisticated of cyber attacks.

More fundamentally, as evidence that firewalls are porous to attacks, we need look no further than today's ransomware plague. Ransomware attacks have compromised IT networks in countless businesses. Each of those IT networks was protected from the Internet by a firewall, or sometimes by multiple layers of firewalls. Thus, pretty much every ransomware attack ever reported breached at least one layer of firewalls to reach the network the attack compromised. In short, firewalls alone are not engineering-grade solutions at consequence boundaries.

Firewalls do, however, have many important functions in industrial networks. Firewalls simplify industrial networks by confining different kinds of traffic to different sub-networks or zones within industrial systems. Firewalls can also slow or stop the movement of many kinds of attack messages between networks. In industrial networks, firewalls are frequently deployed to segment:

- "North – South" traffic passing between lower-numbered and higher-number Purdue Model zones,
- "East-West" traffic passing between control, monitoring, and other zones, and
- Traffic exchanged with third-party supported subsystems such as HVAC systems and self-contained "skids" or cabinets provided by equipment manufacturers with their physical equipment.

Pretty much all industrial operations use firewalls for internal segmentation of the industrial networks, and of the enterprise networks. Firewalls, however, are not engineering-grade protection.

EPRI Industrial Internet

One example of an engineering-grade technique for enabling monitoring of industrial networks without the possibility of malicious control of such networks was documented by the Electric Power Research Institute (EPRI) in 2018. The technique was documented in the context of the question "how can we safely use cloud-based predictive maintenance systems in our most important power plants?" but the technique is more broadly applicable. The technique physically separates monitoring and control networks, so that Internet-based compromise of monitoring networks does not impact plant control systems.

The technique is most easily understood by example. Imagine that we operate a modern, natural-gas-based power plant. The plant has six large gas turbines, each turning a generator to produce power. A problem with all turbines, and indeed with all rotating equipment, is friction. Friction causes wear, and in gas turbines vibration and heat anomalies are symptoms of wear. As the owner and operator of these very large, very expensive, and very long lead-time turbines, we would very much like to maximize the expected life of the turbines, while minimizing maintenance and repair costs. To this end, we have a contract with the turbine vendor – the world's experts on these turbines.

The vendor operates a cloud-based expert system that gathers vibration, heat anomaly, and other data from all turbines under warranty and support. The expert system draws conclusions about when and what kind of maintenance each device might need so that we can derive the greatest value from the turbine over its operating life. The expert system uses real-time monitoring data from each turbine – hundreds of vibration, heat, and other sensors are attached to each turbine sending data through the Internet to the cloud-based vendor.

The risk: if an attacker compromises the cloud-based vendor, then that attacker can send messages back into the computers that are monitoring all the turbines connected to the cloud service. These attack messages might take the form of incorrect settings, malicious firmware downloads or buffer-overflow-style attacks that take over the computers monitoring the turbines. If the attacker can take control of the monitoring computers or "edge devices," then the attacker can pivot their attack through those computers to attack and take control of other systems in the power plant. Such an attack has the potential to cause all the affected plants to shut down, or cause damage to the turbines. The EPRI solution:

- Carry out an engineering study of the Industrial Internet computers and sensors (edge devices) that the vendor proposes to install on the turbines for monitoring purposes.
- Have the engineering team consider, if the monitoring equipment is completely compromised, are the compromised computers physically or electrically able to issue any instruction that would in any way control the turbines, or any other physical process in our power plant?
- If there is *any way* for compromised monitoring equipment to *control anything*, under any circumstances, then reject the equipment – demand that the vendor supply something less dangerous.
- If the proposed equipment proves physically unable to control *anything, ever,* then carry out a study of the cloud-based predictive maintenance system and the plant's own turbine monitoring and control systems. If falsified data enters the cloud-based system, what is the worst possible consequence?
- If the worst possible consequence is an acceptable business consequence – e.g., prematurely scheduled maintenance wastes money, or delayed maintenance increases the cost of the next maintenance cycle – then continue.

The bottom line? If we reach this point in the evaluation process, then we have determined conclusively that there is no way for compromised monitoring equipment or a compromised cloud to bring about an unacceptable physical or business consequence. The turbine monitoring equipment is therefore safe to deploy *provided* that we do not deploy the equipment on the power plant's control network. Instead, we deploy the monitoring system on its own physically separate monitoring network and connect that monitoring network out to the vendor's Internet-based cloud system, through a firewall or three. Alternately, many Industrial Internet edge devices nowadays have built-in SIM cards that allow the devices to connect to the cellular Internet directly, without any intermediary networks or devices.

In such a configuration, what happens if the turbine vendor's cloud-based predictive maintenance system is compromised? In the worst case, the monitoring computers are taken over and maintenance is mis-scheduled. Even if the attacker takes over the monitoring computers in our power plant, that compromise gives the attacker no advantage in terms of attacking the plant's control networks. To use the compromised monitoring-only edge devices to pivot into the control networks, the attacker must pivot from compromised devices back out to the Internet, to find a way back into our power plant from the Internet somehow. But the attacker could do that anyways. Deploying the monitor-only equipment on a physically separate monitor-only network that has no communications path back into our control network has not increased the risk of unacceptable consequences.

More fundamentally, what we have done here is introduce equipment and communications into our power plant that enables safe cloud-based monitoring of our physical process. We have introduced technology and communications that permit monitoring information to leave our plant without introducing any path for communicating *control information* to any equipment that is physically or electrically able to control the physical process.

Consequence Boundaries

The EPRI approach is great when it fits our needs, which it does some of the time. More generally however, the OT monitoring data that we need for business automation in our IT systems and cloud systems comes from control-capable equipment and networks. Given the intrinsic limitations of firewalls and indeed of all other software-based security mechanisms, is it sufficient to use one or more layers of firewall, software security and intrusion detection systems to connect control-capable equipment directly or indirectly to IT networks and the Internet? Well, it depends – the key question is one of consequences.

Consider for example, a small factory producing leather shoes. The factory might employ 20 people, operating 30 machines. The machines cut, emboss, shape, stitch, and glue leather, among other activities, automatically, and at high speed. The machines have moving parts. A yellow line is painted on the floor around each machine, cautioning employees as to the minimum safe distance to stay away from each machine while it is operating. When parts of the machine break or wear out, and they always do, there are physical switches that turn off the sources of electric power or compressed air that power the machines. On some machines there may be levers that drive pins into gears or rollers, physically locking those components into place so that the machines can no longer move. Those physical switches and levers have locks on them.

When a technician needs to diagnose or repair a machine that has malfunctioned, they move one lever to turn off the power or compressed air, move another to drive the pin into the gears, and then put padlocks on the levers. They put the keys to the padlocks into their pocket. Now the technician can safely reach into the machine, or if necessary, crawl into it, without fear that the machine will start moving. With these physical protections in place, no error on the part of the factory operator can turn the machine back on at an unsafe moment. Not even a cyber attack can deliberately turn the machine back on. All sources of power to the machine have been physically disabled, and the moving parts of the machine have been locked in place.

In this shoe factory, if a cyber attack sends malicious control information into the computers controlling the physical equipment, what is the worst that can happen? The machines might stop producing shoes. They might start producing shoes of poorer quality than the factory needs. The factory might need to lay its workers off for a few days while cyber experts erase all the computers and controllers in the factory and restore them from known-good backups. The factory might suffer costs due to production losses and due to the cyber experts they had to hire on an emergency basis. The factory might need to declare *force majeure* on one or more customer contracts to avoid lawsuits. The factory's reputation as a reliable supplier might suffer.

These worst-case consequences of cyber compromise are all business consequences. For many of these consequences and costs, we can buy insurance. These consequences are very similar to worst-case compromise of the factory's IT networks.

Contrast this with a passenger rail switching system. In modern rail systems, safety systems are almost completely computerized. Computers signal the locomotives whether it is safe to proceed onto the next section of track or not. Computers switch trains between parallel tracks. Worst-case compromise of these safety systems is collisions of passenger trains and mass casualty events. These consequences are completely unacceptable.

Which brings us back to our question. Is it safe to connect the control network in the shoe factory with the factory's IT network and indirectly to the Internet through one or more layers of firewalls so that we can enable modern business automation? Is it safe to connect the rail switching system to the IT network and indirectly to the Internet through layers of firewalls to enable business automation?

The difference here – what we see in the rail example, but not in the small shoe factory, is a *consequence boundary* – a connection between two networks with materially different worst-case consequences of compromise. We see these boundaries in some industrial processes, but not in others. We sometimes see these boundaries in government and classified military network as well. For example, the worst-case consequence of organized crime stealing the names and locations of people in a witness protection program can be unacceptable. At consequence boundaries, it is not safe to use only firewalls or layers of firewalls and other security software. At consequence boundaries, we need unbreachable, engineering-grade protections.

Optimizing Criticality Boundaries

Defining a consequence boundary can be challenging. Yes, if we have a network of Safety Instrumented Systems connected to the Internet, that connection point is very clearly a consequence boundary where we must deploy engineering-grade protections, but no fool puts their safety systems on the Internet. In widely used cybersecurity-based designs, safety systems and even reliability-critical systems are buried behind many layers of firewalls and intervening networks. In the worst case, as we look at networks closer and closer to our most critical systems, each network we look at becomes somewhat more consequential. There may not be a clear network boundary where there are completely acceptable worst-case consequences on one side of the boundary, and completely unacceptable business consequences on the other side.

This very common problem is in fact a cleverly disguised opportunity to reduce the cost of our network engineering measures. The goal of network engineering is to control flows of information into high-criticality networks strictly and deterministically. All such flow controls will have some kind of business impact, large or small. Network engineering protections will have minimal impact on our designs and businesses if we can deploy these protections at network boundaries where there is "naturally" very little incoming control data. When we have many network boundaries to choose from, we can choose a location that minimizes impacts. Better yet, choosing to designate as a consequence boundary a network connection that needs very little incoming control information maximizes the security benefit of the engineering-grade protections.

In practice, the network boundary most often selected to implement engineering-grade protections against incoming attack information is the so-called IT/OT interface. Some exceptions:

- Many discrete manufacturing practitioners regard PLC networks as "OT" and regard pretty much everything else, including the Manufacturing Execution System (MES) as "IT." The problem is that during the manufacturing process, the MES must send very detailed commands to PLC networks, very frequently. A more natural fit for engineering-grade protections is generally at a network boundary "above" the MES – between the MES and the rest of the IT network.
- Some industries, such as the rail industry, do not yet use the term "operational technology networks" and have many kinds of networks exhibiting fine variations between serious business, reliability, and safety consequences. In such industries it may be appropriate to deploy engineering-grade protections at more than one boundary.

Design principles to help us choose consequence boundaries that *both* maximize security benefits and minimize costs include:

- All cyber systems able to cause unacceptable consequences when misoperated *must* reside on networks protected with engineering-grade protections at all connections to external networks.
- Deploying network engineering at network boundaries through which very little control information passes maximizes security benefits and minimizes costs.

- There are times when we can reduce control information flows and network engineering costs at consequence boundaries by pulling non-critical systems into more-consequential networks. This is safe to do, *if we protect all systems* in consequential network every bit as thoroughly as we protect the most critical and most consequential systems in those networks.
- Control data entering a critical network through any medium should be abstract enough to enable easy checking for safety, ideally human checking for safety. This is easiest to do when abstract representations of control data are designed to make unsafe configurations impossible to represent. See the "Abstraction" Section below for details.
- Control data entering the critical network should use media, formats and communications mechanisms that are as different from outbound monitoring data as possible[14]. This makes it more difficult for attackers to establish a round-trip command-and-response loop that involves the control data flow.

The only exception to the rule "all systems in a critical network must be secured to the same extent as the most critical system in the network" is when nested networks are protected to engineering grade as well. For example, in a power plant, the entire DCS controlling each generating unit is often reliability-critical, and within that network, there may be several safety-critical sub-networks. If the safety systems are themselves protected from the DCS network by engineering-grade protections, then only the safety systems need to be secured to the standard of safety systems, and the DCS can be secured as a reliability-critical system. If on the other hand the safety systems are, for example, connected to the DCS through only a firewall, then all the systems within the DCS network must be secured as thoroughly as the safety systems, because the safety systems are the most critical components reachable via pivoting paths in the high-consequence network.

The "different media, formats and channels" rule bears expanding as well. Especially when designing new control systems, automation engineers are well advised to thoroughly separate monitoring information flows from control information flows. For example:

- Use the popular MQTT protocol to report monitoring data from critical networks out to Internet-based cloud services but send abstract instructions back into those critical systems via text messages to human operators who filter the information *through their brains* before picking up the mouse and acting on the critical network. Do not send those instructions back to the process through the same MQTT protocol.

---

[14] Analogous to the "least common mechanism" design principle from Salzer and Schroeder's design principles: https://en.wikipedia.org/wiki/Saltzer_and_Schroeder%27s_design_principles

- Use the OPC protocol or a process historian to communicate process data to optimization applications but send optimization instructions back to critical networks in simple files read by highly vetted parsers, for example short XML files that let the optimization application choose between safe states to optimize production or quality. Do not send those instructions back to the physical process via the same OPC or historian data points.

All this said, security practitioners in organizations "starting from zero" frequently find that none of this discussion makes any sense, because their networks have no boundaries. A pharmaceutical plant, for example, might contain only one network, separated from the Internet by a firewall. This network hosts everything – safety systems, control systems, batch historians, accounting systems, sales laptops, and the Wi-Fi network that guests connect to when visiting the site. If every CPU in this network is compromised in the worst possible way, then the consequences are unacceptable – hundreds of millions of dollars in production losses or even produced pharmaceuticals that have been tampered with silently to render them ineffective or even toxic. By the criteria above, this entire network demands engineering-grade protections, but such protections will dramatically interfere with business processes. Purchasing people cannot browse suppliers' websites through engineering-grade prevention of incoming information from the Internet. Salespeople cannot pull email through such protections.

The solution is obvious – we need network segmentation. We need to identify similar kinds of computers, with similar functions, security needs and communications needs, and group them into their own sub-networks. This is what the Purdue Model does. This is a big part of the IEC 62443 standard and in fact every other industrial security standard in existence. And when doing this classification and characterization of our networks, we should be especially aware of communications patterns – if we are able to separate our systems into networks with minimal communications between networks, then we are creating network boundaries that are maximally able to take advantage of strong network engineering techniques.

So – having defined network engineering and consequence boundaries and having seen the EPRI approach as one example of network engineering techniques, let's consider some other examples.

Hardware I/O Interfaces

The US Department of Defense (DoD) *UFT-4-010-06 Unified Facilities Criteria (UFC) Cybersecurity of Facility-Related Control Systems* standard describes another kind of engineering-grade protection. The standard describes two conventional Programmable Logic Controllers (PLCs), or analogous measurement and control devices deployed at the IT/OT consequence boundary. The digital and analog outputs of one device are connected to the inputs of the other device, most commonly by what is known as a 4-20mA current loop. These loops are used to signal analog and digital values. For example, a current loop might be configured to convey a 0-100% value range. In this case, a current flow of 4mA might correspond to a communicated value of 0%, a current of 20mA might correspond to a value of 100%, with the other values in between. Most PLCs can signal such values with up to 10-12 bits of precision. Such connections are practical for communicating up to several hundred discrete digital or analog/numeric values continuously between otherwise separate IT and OT networks.

The benefit of this kind of communication is that when these kinds of PLCs or other signalling devices is that malware cannot propagate across these kinds of connections. These 4-20mA connections propagate digital (1/0) and analog (numeric) values, not network messages that can be misinterpreted, or that might trigger messaging parsing vulnerabilities and other exploitable software defects. That said, any analog signals entering more-consequential networks are still control data. Having no ability to inject malware through analog signalling is an advantage, but the meaning of the signals themselves, and the scrutiny those signals must receive in the more consequential network are still issues. We revisit this topic in the section on Abstraction below.

Note that most modern PLCs can superimpose the Highway Addressable Remote Transducer (HART) messaging system on these analog signals. HART must be disabled on these consequence-boundary connections if we wish to prevent messaging vulnerabilities from propagating malware into OT networks.

Also – in the absence of HART signalling, in theory at least, attack information can still be steganographically or otherwise surreptitiously encoded in analog and digital signals, for example by making very small changes in the timing of when these analog signals change. In practice, such malicious signalling is only possible when there is already malware or other software in the destination network that can interpret these signals. If an industrial control system is not designed to encode additional data into hardware I/O and has not already been compromised with malware seeking to communicate in this way, then it is very difficult to imagine a vulnerability or other malfunction of the protected industrial system that would let malware propagate through this kind of analog communications.

In practice, despite the DoD standard, this kind of hardware signalling is not in widespread use. This author has seen only two uses of this kind of signalling outside of DoD applications:

- When generating power, “peaking” power-plants must respond to signals from a generating dispatch center or other authority to, every few seconds, generate a bit more power or a bit less, to match changing power grid load conditions. In a large plant for example, a half dozen analog signals can communicate new power generation setpoints every few seconds for each of the half-dozen generating units in the plant.

- In water treatment systems, the most cautious sites communicate information about the status of SIS to the main SCADA system using analog signalling, without connecting the SIS to any IP network.

Note that in the peaking plant example above, there is at least a theoretical risk of an attacker manipulating the content of the analog control signals in the less-consequential network. A peaking plant producing too much, or too little power can, in theory cause short but wide-spread power outages or rotating blackouts. The most robust design for such plants uses the generating dispatch center's signals as advisory and is deeply suspicious of large, sudden changes in such signals. In the safety system signalling example, the signals improve efficiency but have no material impact on safe operations. The analog signals allow HMI software to show SCADA operators whether and why a safety system has shut down physical operations – no tampering with these signals on the HMI network can alter the operation of the safety system.

Air Gaps

Air gaps are engineering-grade protection but are very much misunderstood. Definitions first: the term "air gap" is old – it stems from the days when wireless communications were not ubiquitous and the only way to communicate information online was through copper wires or optical fibres. In those days, an air-gapped system was one without any such online communications mechanisms – the only way to exchange information with such a system was to write the information to disk or tape and carry the storage medium across the "air gap" into or out of the protected system.

The confusion about air gaps? Today, the term "air gap" is used by some industrial security practitioners to mean a system that cannot route Internet Protocol (IP) packets directly from that system to the Internet. These practitioners for example, consider a control system connected to an IT system through a firewall to be air-gapped when the firewall contains no rule permitting packets to flow from the control system to the Internet – the rules permit only communications with assets on the IT network.

Such a design is clearly not an air gap in the original meaning of the term – online information can flow from an external network – the IT network – into the "air-gapped" network. Attacks from the Internet can reach IT hosts directly, and having compromised one or more of those hosts, can pivot into the "air-gapped" network. Misusing the term this way greatly confuses discussions around air gaps.

When used in the original sense of the word, the risk reduction benefits of an air-gapped industrial automation system are clear. Because all cyber-sabotage attacks are information, and because there is no online path to send information into or out of a truly air-gapped system, there is no way to send online attacks into such a system. True air gaps are powerful, engineering-grade protections for industrial networks.

A second confusion around air gaps is that, while such gaps may have been commonplace many decades ago, these gaps all but vanished 30 years ago, in the late 1990's. The confusion: many older practitioners or senior managers are not aware of this fact, because they last saw their systems close up 30 years ago. For example, a large power generating utility recently brought a wide array of cybersecurity vendors in to an internally organized "show" so that utility employees and management could become better aware of cybersecurity solutions that were available in the marketplace. After the presentations and demonstrations were finished, what happened? Senior management in the utility decided that, thank you, there would be no follow-up. The utility was at no risk because all its power plants were air-gapped, and so none of the demonstrated cybersecurity technologies or programs were warranted at the utility's facilities.

A year later, some of these same vendors received calls from a service provider for that same power utility, asking the vendors to re-engage with the utility about their solutions. The vendors of course complied, but asked the question "Why?" What value were any of their technologies to air-gapped facilities? The answer from the service provider was that, in the intervening year, the provider had carried out security assessments on all the utility's plants. In fact, the senior management was mistaken, and *none* of the plants were air-gapped any longer – they had not been air-gapped for decades. At the plants, business automation of various kinds, from predictive maintenance to central analysis and optimization, to cloud-based "big-data" crunching, had long-since resulted in connecting industrial to IT networks through firewalls, and the utility was now in serious need of a serious cybersecurity program.

A third kind of confusion around air gaps stems from marketing programs by industrial firewall vendors. Some vendors in the early 20-teens observed that USB sticks were the single biggest cause of common IT malware entering industrial systems – malware which subsequently had to be erased from those systems at some expense. These vendors further argued that the most sophisticated attack on industrial systems was the Stuxnet attack which propagated between sites on USB sticks, lending additional credibility to the argument that USB sticks were dangerous. These vendors argued that because of the risk, USB sticks should be banned from all industrial sites, and all required information flows should be enabled by and protected via the vendors' own firewall products. These vendors neglected to mention that:

- The most effective cyber attacks on both IT and industrial systems were online attacks – RATs that gave remote attackers continuous, interactive control of compromised equipment in industrial networks,
- The low-tech malware coming in on USB sticks almost never caused production shutdowns or other unacceptable consequences, and
- The Stuxnet malware which did cause physical equipment damage at the one site the worm targeted, flowed easily through IT/OT firewalls once the Stuxnet worm was loose on an IT network.

These firewall vendors did a disservice to the cause of industrial cybersecurity by persuading a great many industrial security practitioners to eliminate any true air gaps that remained in their designs, thereby exposing their industrial networks to powerful targeted attacks. Attack tree analysis shows that the level of technical sophistication required to carry out an attack via a RAT is several orders of magnitude less than that required for autonomous malware. Autonomous malware presupposes detailed knowledge of the target, which would otherwise be derived via the RAT. Furthermore, autonomous malware must be extremely sophisticated to adapt and maneuver around whatever defenses are found in the target network.

On the other hand, while air gaps are powerful engineering-grade protection for high-consequence networks, air gaps have a big disadvantage over connected networks. The disadvantage is not the risk of USB keys – USB key / removable media control programs and technologies are both affordable and practical. The disadvantage is that modern business automation relies very much on timely and reliable access to OT data. The reason that most industrial air gaps disappeared in the late 1990's is not security, but efficiency. It does no good to produce power or gasoline or transportation services if those products are so expensive that the target market cannot afford to purchase them. Ever since the 1990's, owners and operators have been installing more and more business automation that saves money by using OT data to make money-saving business decisions.

The bottom line? Air gaps are powerful security tools, but we should not believe air gaps exist at any facility without a connectivity audit, and we should not expect to be able to re-introduce air gaps into our sites in any but very special cases, because online access to industrial data is so important to modern business automation.

Today, air gaps are used routinely only for isolated CPUs, such as are found in today's drills, saws, sanders, and other power tools. Air gaps are also used routinely in very specialized circumstances, such as for some protective relays and safety instrumented systems – systems that exchange very little information with external systems, and whose consequences of compromise are truly unacceptable. And air gaps are used in scattered examples of pretty much everything else – not commonplace, but not unheard of.

Unidirectional Gateways

Unidirectional gateways are the most common kind of engineering-grade protection deployed at consequence boundaries. The NIST 800-82[15] standard defines the gateways as:

[15] *NIST SP 800-82 Rev. 2 Guide to Industrial Control Systems (ICS) Security*, Keith Stouffer, Suzanne Lightman, Victoria Pillitteri, Marshall Abrams, and Adam Hahn, 20126, National Institute of Standards and Technology.

Unidirectional gateways are a combination of hardware and software.

The hardware permits data to flow from one network to another but is physically unable to send any information at all back into the source network.

The software replicates databases and emulates protocol servers and devices.

In other words, the hardware requirement above specifies engineering-grade unidirectionality. In practice, the gold standard for unidirectional gateways is optical isolation. The best unidirectional hardware consists of at least two circuit board. The first has a fibre-optic transmitter – a laser – on-board. The second contains a fibre-optic receiver – a photocell. A short piece of fibre-optic cable connects the two circuit boards. This hardware enables the transmitting side of the device to send (monitoring) information to the receiving side, but it is not physically possible to send any (control) information back into the sending side of the device. There is physically no laser in the chipset on the receiving circuit board, and even if there were, there is no photocell in the sending board. When oriented from the OT network to the IT network, the hardware enables monitoring information to leave the OT network, and no control information whatsoever can enter the OT network through the device.

Unidirectional gateway software makes copies of servers. The software on the OT network side of the device logs into OPC servers, historian databases, relational databases and other industrial data sources and asks for all the new data – data that has arrived or changed since the last time the gateway asked. The gateway software converts that data to the one-way formats and protocols and pushes it through the unidirectional hardware. On the receiving side of the gateway, software logs into an identical server – if it is an AVEVA PI system on the inside, it is an AVEVA PI system on the outside, and if it is Oracle on the inside, it is Oracle on the outside. The software inserts or updates the data into the destination server. Now external users and applications can use the replica servers normally – sending queries and receiving responses. The replica servers are synchronized to the source servers, typically sub-second. Whatever answers the source / industrial servers would have provided to the queries, the replica servers also provide.

This gives the external network and users access to industrial data, without providing access to the industrial systems. The unidirectional hardware means it is no longer possible to send queries from external networks into industrial servers to put those servers at risk. The unidirectional software, though, means that external users and applications no longer *need* to send queries through the one-way hardware into the industrial network, because all the data *that is allowed to be shared* from the industrial network to external users, is already available on the external network.

A special case of this hardware-enforced unidirectional replication is when the servers in question are comparatively simple, such as OPC servers, or Modbus PLCs. In this case, there is generally no need for the unidirectional gateway to log into a replica server on the destination / enterprise network to insert data. Instead, unidirectional gateway software can simply emulate the servers. With OPC replication, the gateway software logs into and gathers OPC tags and values on a regular basis – say once per second – from the industrial OPC server. The software converts that data to the one-way formats and protocols the one-way hardware uses. On the enterprise network, the gateway software is a standards-compliant OPC server. The gateway software keeps the data in memory and waits for an OPC query from an external user or application. When the query arrives, the gateway responds to the query the same way as the source OPC server on the industrial network would have responded. In this sense, the gateway emulates the original data source to the external network – providing the same answers to the same questions as the original would have provided, entirely on the enterprise network.

These kinds of unidirectional gateways are engineering-grade protection and are deployed routinely at consequence boundaries. No cyber attack originating on an external network, such as from the IT network, or from the Internet beyond the IT network, is physically able to pass through the gateway to put industrial operations at risk. The receiving circuit board in the gateway has no laser – it physically has no ability to send information into the OT network. This is deterministic, empirically verifiable, engineering-grade prevention of propagation for online cyber attacks.

Note that since unidirectional gateways are deployed at consequence boundaries, and that connections between SIS networks and any lesser network constitute a clear consequence boundary, one might imagine that the most common deployment scenario for unidirectional gateways is to protect Safety Instrumented Systems, deep into a Purdue Model / IEC 62443 set of layered, firewalled networks. This is not so. Once most sites decide to invest in engineering-grade protections, those sites almost always deploy the gateways at the IT/OT criticality boundary. This means that the gateways provide engineering-grade protection from IT-based and Internet-based attacks, not only for the safety-critical systems, but also for reliability-critical systems that are essential to keep physical operations running, even if IT systems are compromised.

Note also that few modern automation systems can run indefinitely without any external information. Anti-virus systems need new signatures daily, refineries, food producers and even mines need new production orders a couple of times per day, and peaking power plants need new production setpoints every few seconds. In addition, control system software needs to be updated occasionally, especially for security updates. How is any of this possible through an outbound-only unidirectional gateway?

The short answer is that it varies. Unlike a firewall, where almost every question is answered by the least secure, one-size-fits-all answer of "open another TCP port or three," most of the questions above have different answers, tailored to the specific business need:

- Most sites using unidirectional gateways have someone at the site move anti-virus updates into the automation AV server manually, once per day, on a write-once CD. This move happens only after the updated signatures have been tested on a test bed that contains a copy of every piece of software in the automation system, to ensure that the updates do not contain an error that incorrectly quarantines essential software.
- The same is true for new production orders, but only after the orders have been visually inspected to confirm that they are ASCII-only XML files with no obvious formatting anomalies, such as extremely long elements.
- Most unidirectionally protected peaking power plants use either a hardware I/O mechanism to communicate production setpoints, or an inbound unidirectional gateway (see Opposing Gateways, below).
- Security updates and new versions of control system software do not come into sites with engineering-grade security at all frequently. Such updates are generally deployed first on a heavily instrumented, unidirectionally protected test bed and tested extensively before deployment. The test bed is instrumented not only to detect potential threats to safety and reliability in the new software, but to detect potential threats to security as well. This testing is generally between a weeks-long and a years-long process. At the end of this process, again, approved and tested new software is generally carried into the protected automation system on write-once CDs.

More generally, these scenarios are examples of the second of two big hurdles that most practitioners come across in the course of understanding unidirectional gateways. The first stumbling block is roughly "That can't possibly work," and the second is "Oh it *can* work but look at my needs – too bad it can't work *for me*."

The first hurdle "That can't possibly work," arises when practitioners familiar with firewalls see the gateways. Such practitioners often conclude that the gateways are some sort of "unidirectional firewall." These practitioners know that the TCP/IP protocol is the workhorse of the modern Internet, they know that almost all TCP/IP communications are query / response, which means that if queries cannot penetrate the gateway hardware into data sources, then there is no way that responses will come back to the external users and applications who need access to the industrial data.

Explaining server replication to these practitioners generally gets them over this first hurdle – unidirectional gateways are not routers. Instead, the gateways pull data from the industrial side and on the IT side, push the data into replica servers for use by external users and applications. Users who need access to industrial data do not need to send queries through the gateways into industrial data sources, because all the data that is allowed to be shared with the enterprise is already in the enterprise network, in the replica servers.

The second hurdle *"It can't work for me,"* has to do with business scenarios and network designs that either need, or seem to need, control information to enter a high-consequence network. The examples above are only a few of the scenarios addressed in this author's earlier book *Secure Operations Technology* (SEC-OT). That book documented twenty unidirectional network design patterns – patterns that address common business needs such as the anti-virus update and other examples above. Many of these designs are surprises to practitioners who see them for the first time – common modes of using unidirectional gateways do seem a bit counter-intuitive to firewall practitioners.

For example, most firewall practitioners believe that remote vendor support is impossible through a true unidirectional gateway. In fact, such support is enabled at perhaps one third of unidirectionally-protected sites in the form of "remote screen view" (RSV) capability. Remote screen view involves a software component that sits on one or more workstations in a protected industrial network – most commonly the engineering workstations in that network, not HMI or other constantly used workstations. When there is a problem at the site, an engineer enables RSV and uses the engineering workstation to log into the affected machine – one of the HMI workstations for example, that might be showing an unusual error message.

The RSV software works vaguely like the Windows-standard Remote Desktop tool – it takes pictures of the screen of the engineering workstation and pushes those pictures through the unidirectional hardware. On the external network, the software is a web server. Vendor support personnel remote into the web server and see a video feed of the engineering workstation screen. The vendors, however, are not able to send any keystroke or mouse movement information into the industrial network, because the gateway hardware prevents any such information flow.

Instead, the vendors pick up the phone and talk to the engineer sitting at the engineering workstation. The vendors can see the engineer working to diagnose and resolve the technical problem. The vendors can give real-time advice, such as "no, don't click on that – that's the communications diagnostics – yes – two buttons down – that's the system diagnostics."

The vendors see the process as one of supervising personnel at the industrial site throughout a complex correction, ensuring that the correction is carried out according to the vendors' processes and procedures. The engineer at the site sees the process differently. Whose HMI is this that has malfunctioned? It is not the vendor's. Keeping the HMI and the entire industrial process running is the responsibility of the engineers at site. Those engineers want to know what the vendor has done to the site's systems. The engineer using RSV sees the process as one of supervising the vendor, to be sure that site personnel understand what the vendor has done to the site's systems. Unidirectional RSV ensures that both needs are met.

RSV is used routinely for "untrusted" vendor support personnel – people who are not "insiders" at the site, people who have not been through the site's criminal background checks and security and safety training programs. Different solutions are used for trusted insiders and for continuous interactive remote-control scenarios. All twenty unidirectional network designs and the heart of the SEC-OT methodology are reproduced for your convenience in Appendix B.

Note that firewall practitioners also, often, ask if a "unidirectional firewall" might serve the purpose of separating monitoring from control information. In fact, there is no such thing. Once a TCP/IP connection is established through any firewall, that firewall forwards messages for the connection in both directions.

Opposing Gateways

One of the most confusing unidirectional design patterns in Appendix B is the opposing unidirectional gateways design: one gateway is oriented to send monitoring information out of an industrial network, and second is oriented to send control information back into that same network. The design is used when there is a need for some kind of control information to trickle into unidirectionally protected sites. The peaking power plant example in the Hardware I/O section above is one such example.

Perhaps a better example is a mining scenario currently under consideration by an automation standards body. Shovels in modern surface mines can hold up to 800 tons of ore, and in practice, no two shovels of ore are the same. Modern mines sample and analyze the contents of each shovel of ore while the ore is in a massive truck, on the way to the mine's primary processing facility. The mine sends large amounts of data about the load into a cloud-based optimization service. That service analyzes the shovel/load, applies a lot of machine learning and other mechanisms, and comes up with an optimal plan to process that shovel of ore. A few seconds or minutes later, this plan is expressed in the primary processing facility as hundreds of PLC registers and values being changed to process the ore optimally. Cost savings from this process range up to 30% of the total operating cost of the facility.

A unidirectional gateway sends the sampling data from the mine into the cloud, and a second gateway is oriented to send control information from the cloud back into the mining control network, providing greater protection than a firewall:

- The powerful targeted attack pattern – where an adversary sends attack commands into a compromised host from a C2 on the Internet – does not work through an inbound unidirectional gateway. In theory, it is possible to send attack commands in through the inbound gateway, but no command results or other feedback can come back through that gateway.
- Stolen passwords or two-factor credentials cannot be transmitted through the inbound gateway to put physical operations at risk – the gateway transmits optimization data, not remote access sessions.

- Vulnerabilities in the externally exposed gateway software can impair or corrupt data transfer through the device, but exploiting such a vulnerability does not give the attacker the same leverage as exploiting a firewall vulnerability. With a firewall vulnerability, in the worst case the attacker escalates privilege within the firewall, resulting in a bypass of the firewall and enabling interactive remote control of the OT system. With a vulnerability in the inbound gateway's external software, the unidirectional hardware still works. To reach into the industrial network, the attacker must find a second vulnerability in the software running on the industrial side of the gateway as well, and even with such a vulnerability, the attacker is working "blind" with no feedback as to the effectiveness of their attacks.

Note that to bring about these benefits, we need to be careful with the deployment of the two gateways:

- Unidirectional gateways replicate servers – they do not forward network traffic like firewalls do. When setting up inbound and outbound gateways, do *not* be tempted by vendors who forward network messages or TCP/IP payloads through one of their "unidirectional" devices, and forward responses to those commands back through the second "unidirectional" device. Such a configuration offers very little security value – attack commands can be sent through the one device, with feedback from the attack sent back through the other device.
- Do deploy the unidirectional gateways to replicate servers in each direction. And as much as possible, deploy the gateways as "differently" as possible – to make it as difficult as possible for adversaries to set up command and control loops through the gateways. Ideally, replicate different kinds of servers or devices in each direction – e.g., replicate historian tags, values, and timestamps outbound, and anti-virus signatures back in.
- Deploy the gateways on different sub-networks within the industrial network – sub-networks that are not able to route IP packets to each other.
- Deploy the two gateways so that they have different endpoints of communications in the industrial network, and in the enterprise network.

Again, at consequence boundaries, opposing gateways are safest when they are designed as "differently" as possible, with as much physical and conceptual "distance" between the gateways as possible. To be stronger than a firewall at such a boundary, the opposing gateways must make establishing a command-and-control loop close to practically impossible.

Abstraction

Deploying the opposing gateways in this way has material security advantages over a firewalled, encrypted and DMZ'ed design, but the system as a whole still may not have engineering-grade protection. Consider the mining example above.

If worst-case misoperation of the mine's primary processing PLCs can result in unacceptable safety or environmental consequences, then a compromised cloud system or compromised Internet connection can still cause a dangerous set of PLC commands to be sent through the inbound unidirectional gateway. To address this risk, we might consider hosting the cloud/AI system within the mine's industrial automation network, and not out in the cloud where the system is vulnerable to Internet-based attacks. Such local hosting may be possible but has costs and limitations. This class of optimization application is often most effective when it has access to large amounts of data from many mines and from many primary processing facilities. For maximum effectiveness, these mines really do need to send the output of the cloud system back into the processing facility as control information.

To address this risk, we need to define or restrict communications through the gateway to combinations of values and settings that are known to be safe. One can imagine a validation-checking step that looks at all the hundreds or thousands of PLC values and settings coming in and tries to determine whether the settings are likely to result in unsafe conditions. In practice, such testing systems are very difficult to design so that:

- They are not easily confused, and
- They are comprehensive as to the unsafe conditions they prevent.

A more secure and reliable system is one that uses a high degree of information abstraction – *sending control information into the industrial network in a very simple format, that is very easily verified for safety, both by humans and by software.* In the mining example, the control information could be encoded as a standard document schema, such as an XML or JSON schema, designed to express safe variations of primary processing conditions. For example:

- If a crusher has a safe operating speed of between 0.3 and 0.7 cubic meters per minute, do not send a "cubic meters per minute" setpoint through the gateway for the crusher, send a number between zero and one, with zero meaning the minimum safe speed and 1.0 being the maximum.
- If a tilted rotating drum has only two safe positions, send the instruction to the drum through as the string "low" or "high."
- If a kiln has a safe operating temperature range but can safely exceed that range by up to 300 degrees for the first ten minutes of every load, code each load's temperature instruction as two 0-1 values, one for the first ten minutes, and one for the rest of the hour.

Instead of sending the processing system hundreds of PLC values and timestamps and scratching our heads as to whether these values are safe, a process engineering team in this example has determined the safe operating modes of the processing facility and the control instructions are encoded as abstract points within that "space" of safe settings.

A syntax checker on the external network then verifies that the incoming commands comply with the XML or JSON or CSV or other schema describing allowed values. Any failures to comply are logged as errors and rejected. A second syntax checker repeats the process on the internal network. Any failures identified inside the primary processing network represent misconfigurations that defeated our first level of filtering – such misconfigurations are again rejected and logged as high-priority errors and very likely attacks. And finally, the twice-validated control instructions are passed to an MES or batch manager or comparable system in the mining network to be translated into PLC values and communicated to the devices controlling the physical process.

This is a concrete example of network engineering's focus on the difference between control and monitoring information. An attacker tampering with monitoring information that goes out to the cloud can at worst confuse the cloud. A confused or maliciously compromised cloud can at worst communicate an unprofitable configuration for the primary processor back into the industrial system. This is an acceptable business consequence, for which we can generally buy insurance, not an unacceptable safety or environmental disaster or equipment-damaging consequence.

Dependencies and Resilience

Dependencies on IT systems are one reason that so many ransomware attacks result in outages of physical operations. Ransomware attacks impair Internet-exposed IT systems and networks much more commonly than those attacks reach into and impair OT systems. If continued physical operations depend upon IT systems that ransomware has impaired, then physical operations cannot continue. These dependencies are called out explicitly in the *US TSA Security Directives 2022-02C* and *1580/82-2022-01* for pipeline and rail operators, respectively. The TSA directives establish requirements for the nation's most important rail systems and oil, gas, and petrochemical pipelines. For critical OT systems, owners and operators must:

- Implement segmentation designed to prevent operational disruption to OT systems if IT systems are compromised,
- In support of that goal, identify all OT dependencies on IT services,
- Review all domain trust relationships, including OT trusts of IT domains, and develop policies to manage those trusts, and
- Design OT networks so that they can be isolated from IT networks during incident response procedures.

While not stated explicitly in the security directives, the ability to separate OT and IT networks in an emergency can enable OT systems to continue operating through an IT emergency, but only if OT dependencies on IT networks and OT trusts of crippled IT domains do not impair that very desirable ability to operate independently.

If we wish to operate our OT systems through an IT security incident, then while it can be very difficult to eliminate all OT dependencies on IT systems, we cannot simply ignore those dependencies that remain. Instead, we must recognize that IT systems that are essential to continued physical operations are in fact reliability-critical components. These reliability-critical systems may be hosted on what we think of as the IT network instead of the OT network but must be managed and secured as if they were OT systems. For example:

- If a pipeline depends on a custody transfer and billing system in IT, we could modify our customer contracts so that if we must declare *force majeure*, custody transfer billing enters an "approximation" mode. The OT system continues operating the pipeline, caching all billing-relevant data in a historian or other repository until the billing system recovers and can reconcile accounts.
- If a container shipping business depends on the ability to print container routing information for truck drivers, then consider hosting the entire tracking system on a virtual machine, keeping a known-good copy of the VM stored where attackers cannot reach it, and logging container tracking transactions to write-once media. Then if the IT network fails, then we can promptly restore the tracking system and replay the transaction logs to restore functionality.
- If a factory needs new production orders and specifications to execute against when the current production run is complete, then keep a queue of 7-10 days of such orders stored in the OT system – enough to keep the factory working during any required emergency clean-up of the IT network.

More generally, what we see in some of these cases is not only two critical networks – a safety-critical OT network and a business-critical IT network – we see three networks. The third is a reliability-critical network that is often mixed up with other IT assets. In the pipeline and factory production order examples above, we were able to redesign our automation systems so that the custody transfer and order processing systems are no longer reliability critical. In the container shipping example, we change how we manage the container tracking system – we stop managing it as any other IT system and start managing it as a reliability-critical network.

To be effective in managing the tracking system as reliability-critical, we need to apply the TSA approach to the tracking network as well – be wary of allowing the tracking network to rely on IT resources that may be compromised, be wary of sharing trusts between the container tracking network and the IT network, and so on. It does no good to restore the reliability-critical systems to an uncompromised state if they, in turn, still depend on Active Directory or other IT services that are still crippled.

The word "resilience" is often used when looking at these dependencies between safety-critical and reliability-critical networks. In the container tracking example above, we might deploy unidirectional gateways at the IT/OT interfaces on ships and cranes to prevent any online attack from migrating from a compromised IT network into the safety-critical OT networks. If the IT network is compromised though, we must shut down the movement of containers when the tracking system fails. If we can bring the tracking system back within hours of failure, and we can bring the container movement system back to full capacity an hour or two after that, then the result might be regarded as an acceptable worst-case outage of only a few hours.

"Resilience" proponents might cite this example as an example of resilience – where the container shipping system "springs back" into operation after a brief outage, even while the bulk of the IT network is still compromised. Be aware though – while this kind of reliability-critical dependency analysis can result in improved resilience, there is no silver bullet. A petrochemical refinery, for example, takes a minimum of 10-12 days to go from a full stop to 100% of production again. Any IT dependency that triggers even a five-minute complete shutdown of the facility incurs this start-up cost of losing 5-6 full production day equivalents as the refinery transitions from a dead stop to 100% production again over 10-12 days.

Summary

Network engineering is focused on deterministic protection against cyber attacks that reach through networks and across the Internet to put physical operations at risk. Network engineering techniques are generally applied to protect the most consequential networks, and most of the techniques focus on consequence boundaries, which are connections between the more-consequential networks and less-consequential networks. Firewalls are used routinely within IT networks and within industrial networks, connecting networks at very similar levels consequence. Firewalls are not strong-enough nor deterministic enough protection to be considered network engineering solutions. Network engineering techniques include:

- The EPRI IIoT methodology – connect monitor-only IIoT devices safely to the Internet by hosting them on a network with no physical or logical connection to industrial control networks,
- Hardware I/O interfaces – use analog signalling to communicate a small number of values across consequence boundaries, without risk of malware or remote atta commands taking over the connection,
- Air gaps – an "old school" solution that may still apply to the very most sensitive SIS and related networks, and
- Unidirectional gateways – hardware that can send information from OT networks to IT networks and the Internet but is physically unable to send any attack information back into OT networks.

When remote control of physical operations from the Internet is essential, as is starting to be the case with AI-enabled cloud control, *simplicity and abstraction* are key. The communications mechanisms, media and encoding involved in such control must be designed in such a way as to be unable to express dangerous or unacceptable sets of control instructions.

Identifying, reducing, eliminating, and *managing* OT dependencies on IT networks and services is an important part of network engineering. Very often OT cyber risk programs have a goal of continued physical operations, even if some or all of an IT network is compromised, such as by ransomware. The strongest protections in the world from cyber attacks entering OT networks will fail to meet this goal if continued physical operations in any way depend on IT systems or services that have been crippled. When some IT systems supply reliability-critical services to OT systems, a subset of network engineering techniques can be applied to those IT systems to improve OT resilience.

Chapter 6 – Cyber Design Basis Threat

To recap: the engineering profession has been managing risks to public safety for over a century, cyber threats are becoming more pressing every year, and engineers have powerful tools available to manage physical risk, in addition to cybersecurity tools available to IT practitioners. Engineers, however, do not wave their hands and mutter vaguely when addressing risk and answering the question *"how much is enough?"* – engineers have strong empirical and mathematical models that they apply to worker safety, public safety, and other unacceptable risk scenarios.

Cyber risks do not fit these models. In this chapter we dig deeper into the nature of cyber risk, why "intuitive" models of risk fail, and what is a more accurate model of cyber risk. We wrap up by using that model to support using cyber Design Basis Threat (cDBT) directives as a robust way of drawing conclusions about risk tolerance and communicating those decisions throughout an organization as direction to project teams answering the *"how much is enough"* question.

Standard Terminology

While this chapter is not a general introduction to risk and risk management – readers can find many such treatments in other texts – we do introduce a few very standard risk terms here. Please skip this section if you know this stuff already.

A risk management process generally includes a handful of steps and sub-steps executed in a cycle. The most important steps, whether executed by a board of directors or by an individual contributor, include:

- **Assess** – understand what risks an organization, team, or project face and how important / serious each risk is,
- **Respond** – decide what to do about each risk, and then do it, and
- **Monitor** – continue to watch the risk environment, track the effectiveness (or not) of the risk response measures that have been implemented, and generally collect data relevant to the next iteration of the risk management cycle.

When choosing how to respond to specific risks, individuals, teams, and organizations most often choose one or more of:

- **Eliminate** – change physical processes, networks, automation systems or other elements so that the risk no longer exists –sometimes through physical changes and sometimes through changing the physical process, also known as *inherently safe* designs,

- **Mitigate** – make changes that reduce the risk, for example by deploying software-based security products and controls that reduce attack opportunities – this is the classic "IT-grade" response,
- **Transfer** – find a third party willing to assume or share the risk, most often by purchasing an insurance policy, or
- **Accept** – do nothing further about the risk.

Risk we accept is called residual risk. If a risk that an organization simply accepts is realized, then the organization suffers the consequences. As a rule, it is neither possible nor practical to eliminate all risk – there is always residual risk that we must accept. Which risks are reasonable to accept is the topic of Chapters 7-8.

The Nature of Cyber Risk

Cyber risks are both similar to and different from other kinds of risks that businesses manage. A key similarity: the common goal of directors, executives, and engineers is not to eliminate all risk, but rather to take *reasonable* risks when those risks are *necessary* to the mission of the enterprise – for example maximizing shareholder value, maximizing service to a community, or other missions. After all, if minimizing risk were the overriding goal, most businesses could simply sell their operations and put their investors' money into government bonds.

A key *difference* between cyber risks and other risks? Answering the question "what is reasonable?" is singularly difficult for cyber risks. Computing and communications technology generally and the nature of cyber attacks specifically have been evolving rapidly for decades, and that evolution shows no sign of slowing. Rapid evolution of both threats and targets means that our understanding of "reasonable risk" and "due care" are changing rapidly as well. Most businesses and business leaders struggle to keep up.

A second difference is that far too few enterprises explore deeply enough the question "what is necessary?" One reason for this blind spot is ROI calculations that attackers carry out. Developing attack tools and attack technology takes time, talent, and money. Attackers, like any other businesspeople, must decide which cyber technologies to target with their investments. The problem is that, while new business automation technologies are invented pretty much constantly, only a tiny fraction of those technologies come into widespread use. Investing in attack tools for a particular technology makes sense for most attackers only after the technology comes into widespread use.

This means that by the time many new attacks hit us, most of us have spent up to a decade developing business processes and other infrastructure around how we deploy and use our new computer automation technologies. When we then come under attack, our first instinct is to try to find a "band-aid" mitigation, a security fix whose vendors claim they "solve" the problem without changing anything else about how we do business. This is because, by the time we are attacked, we have come to regard our business automation and configurations as "necessary" to our business. These "band-aid" products and approaches are rarely as effective as we need them to be.

Comparatively few organizations ask how we might adapt our new automation or make small adjustments to our business processes so that the most consequential new risks are eliminated outright. In the case of OT cyber risks, these small engineering-grade adaptations tend to be both far more effective and far cheaper than mitigation.

Governance

Who is responsible for managing cyber risk? As with other kinds of risk management, responsibility for cyber risk management is generally spread very widely throughout an organization. Responsibility for risk in most organizations starts at the highest levels – with the board of directors. Most boards, however, do not themselves design their organizations' cybersecurity programs. The board is ultimately responsible for managing risks and participates directly in management of the most serious risks to the business, but most often delegates much of the process. For example, the board decides who should be the organization's CEO, and delegates a great deal to that CEO.

Boards generally do remain involved in managing strategic risk – risks whose worst-case consequences pose material threats to the viability of the business. For example, almost all boards remain involved in managing the most consequential financial risks – the risk that the CEO or other executives so materially misrepresent the finances of a business that the very existence of the business is put at risk. Most boards manage this risk by hiring independent auditors to assess the financial position of the business and comparing the report of the auditors to the report of the CEO and other executives. The problem with cyber risk is that in many businesses, worst-case consequences of compromise have become strategic risks, but boards have not noticed, much less become actively engaged in managing those risks.

This process of risk management overall is part of "governance" and is generally defined[16] as:

1) Providing strategic direction,
2) Ensuring that organizational mission and business objectives are achieved,
3) Ascertaining that risks are managed appropriately, and
4) Verifying that the organization's resources are used responsibly.

Ascertaining that risks are managed appropriately, breaks down further into:

---

[16] *NIST SP 800-39 Managing Information Security Risk*, 2011, National Institute of Standards and Technology

a) Establishing and implementing a risk executive function,
b) Establishing a risk management strategy, including the determination of risk tolerance, and
c) Developing and executing organization-wide investment strategies for cybersecurity.

Many of these functions in most businesses are delegated through the CEO to other executives and managers throughout a variety of business functions. Project managers are generally responsible for managing business, cyber, physical, and other risks to their projects. Compliance managers are responsible for ensuring compliance with regulations, including cyber regulations, for different business functions in different geographies. And engineering teams tend to be responsible for managing physical risks due to the physical processes they design – risks to public and worker safety, to the environment, and to other stakeholders.

And finally, individual employees and contractors within these organizations have a role to play too. As a rule, every individual in enterprises large and small needs to be trained as to their role within these larger risk management programs and needs to carry out their part for the programs to be effective. Examples of individual responsibilities across the spectrum of physical and cyber risks range from being aware that websites and email attachments may be fake and malicious, to wearing the mandated personal protective equipment (PPE) such as steel-toed boots and hard hats, to calling out and reporting individuals who "tailgate" through physical security checkpoints.

All this is easier said than done. In large organizations especially, responsibilities for risk management are most often spread so widely that the organization struggles with communicating risk management priorities effectively from the top to the bottom of the organization through many layers of management and struggles correspondingly to communicate new risks and poorly addressed risks back up through the organization, through those same levels of management. This is especially true of cyber risks, in both directions, because the threat environment is changing so quickly.

Modelling Risk – Classic Formula

Engineers and risk management professionals use mathematical models when looking at risk. Most risks in most risk registers, are modelled as:

$$Risk = (consequence \times likelihood)$$

For risks that are random and for which there is good historical data or a solid theoretical foundation, this formula is a good fit – think tornadoes or random equipment failures. In this formula, the consequence is the cost of an incident and likelihood is the probability of such a consequence being realized within the next 12 months. The resulting risk is an estimate of "annual loss expectancy" – the average amount of money the business should expect to lose in the next year due to this threat. This risk model is very familiar to most board members and even to engineers.

An important aspect of the model – "likelihood" is another name for "probability." This model assumes that risk is a random process, with significant risk events having a small, but non-zero probability. In most cases, for most risks, it is physically impossible to reduce the likelihood to zero. How would we reduce the likelihood of an earthquake for example?

In the world of engineering, safety engineers use much more detailed versions of this kind of probabilistic model to manage the risk of human errors and equipment failures that lead to worker casualties or other unacceptable outcomes. Most often, equipment failures cannot be eliminated entirely – physical equipment wears out. Thus, safety engineers using these models must always ask what frequency of worker injuries or fatalities constitute acceptable "mission losses," because in a world of probabilities, risk can rarely be reduced to zero. This acceptable loss threshold may be set by consulting the board, by consulting local safety regulations, and/or by consulting the local engineering professional association or other sources.

Safety engineers then calculate the expected failure rate of physical safety mechanisms at the site – over-pressure valves, flare stacks, containment berms and other mechanisms and devices. Failure rates for such equipment are often modelled using a "bathtub" curve, based on the design of the device or extensive testing of the device. Equipment failures for a lot of equipment more likely to occur early in the life of a safety device, where manufacturing defects become evident, and late in the life of the device, as it starts to wear out and reach the end of its useful life. Failures in the middle of the expected life of the device are less likely. Engineers also know how often these devices are inspected and tested, and thus how long it takes to detect the failure of a device. They also know how long this equipment takes to replace or repair if it is found to have failed.

Safety engineers also have historical data as to how often malfunctions or misoperations of some dangerous part of the refinery trigger a safety device. Safety engineers can combine all this knowledge mathematically to predict whether safety goals for a physical process, such as a power plant or refinery, can be met. Given all this, the engineers can then calculate: given how often we have safety incidents, and given the age of every piece of safety equipment in every dangerous component of the refinery, how likely is it that we will suffer an injury or fatality at the site due to a safety incident in the next year? Or in the next century?

When safety goals cannot be met by a particular design, those same engineers recommend changes. The most common change is simply to deploy additional mechanical safety systems. If three over-pressure valves on a catalytic cracker do not provide a high-enough degree of reliability for the safety system, consider deploying another one or two such valves. Probabilities multiply. Very loosely – ignoring bathtub curves, time-to-repair, and other details – if a single safety device has a 1/100 likelihood of failure in a given year, then three devices have a likelihood of:

$$(1/100)^3 = 1/1,000,000$$

in the year and five such devices in parallel have a likelihood of:

$$(1/100)^5 = 1/10,000,000,000$$

This *risk = (consequence x likelihood)* model works when we have reliable historical data as to the likelihood of an adverse event. In the world of cybersecurity, we have such data for only so-called High-Frequency, Low-Impact (HFLI) events. For example, a large organization might have as many as several percent of their employees every year accidentally install common malware that hijacks their web browsers. The cost of each such event might be one or two days of downtime for that employee, and a few hours effort by an IT person erasing their machine and restoring it from backups. In scenarios like these, we can substitute frequency for likelihood:

Risk = consequence x frequency

This model is problematic for High Impact, Low Frequency events (HILF). How many times in the last decade has the entire North American or European power grid been crippled by a cyber attack? Such an event has never occurred in all of history. So, what likelihood should we assign to such an event? That something has never happened does not mean it will never happen – especially in the rapidly changing world of cyber attacks. But – any probability that we assign to the risk is fiction. Business decision-makers are very reluctant to make spending decisions based on fictional numbers. Thus, most risk managers estimate cyber risk with qualitative scores:

- Consequences are approximated with one of five ratings: very low, low, moderate, high, or very high.
- Likelihood is similarly approximated.
- The resulting risk is also represented qualitatively with ratings such as: low, moderate, or high.

Boards and other senior decision-makers are then presented with a matrix with consequence on one axis and likelihood on the other. Those decision-makers approve a risk ranking that populates boxes in the matrix.

The organization expects to spend more money and effort addressing the highest-ranked risks, and less on lower-ranked risks. This qualitative approach to modelling cyber risk is widely documented and widely used. The very serious problem with this approach is that, with rare exceptions, modern cyber attacks are deterministic, not probabilistic. This means the likelihood matrix is a very poor model of the risk of such attacks and can lead to serious risk management errors.

Likelihood (threat occurs and results in adverse impact)					
Very High	Very Low	Low	Moderate	High	Very High
High	Very Low	Low	Moderate	High	Very High
Moderate	Very Low	Low	Moderate	Moderate	High
Low	Very Low	Low	Low	Low	Moderate
Very Low	Very Low	Very Low	Very Low	Low	Low
	Very Low	Low	Moderate	High	Very High
	Level of Impact				

Table (1) Likelihood and Impact Matrix from NISTIR 8286[17]

For example, imagine a ransomware attack that targets an automobile manufacturer and cripples a factory or three. Incident response teams spring into action, erasing all the affected computers and restoring them from backups. Now imagine – however unlikely this may seem – imagine that the victim organization brings the affected factories back into production and *changes absolutely nothing* in their cyber defensive posture. And finally, imagine that exactly that same ransomware attack targets exactly the same victim a week or a month later.

What will be the outcome of the attack? It is very likely that exactly the same attack, against exactly the same target/victim, will compromise that victim in exactly the same way as did the original attack. Deliberate cyber attacks are not like random equipment failures or even human errors and omissions. There is very little that is random about most cyber attacks. In safety engineering terminology, cyber attacks most always represent *design failures* of the system under attack, not *random failures*.

If an earthquake or tornado strikes an industrial facility, and the business survives the event with an acceptable amount of damage, then restoring operations and changing *nothing at all* may be a completely defensible course of action. Earthquakes and tornadoes are more or less random, and the fact that there was such an event today does not increase the likelihood of an earthquake or tornado occurring at that same site tomorrow. This is simply not true in the cyber world – to avoid an identical attack hitting us next week, and every week after that, we must change something in our defensive posture. Ignoring this reality and thinking of cyber attacks as random leads to repeated failures.

Modern Cyber Risk

More sophisticated organizations model deliberate cyber attacks the same way that they model deliberate physical attacks, such as terrorist attacks. Most such

[17] *NISTIR 8286 Integrating Cybersecurity and Enterprise Risk Management (ERM),* Kevin Stine, Stephen Quinn, Greg Witte, and R.K. Gardner, 2020, National Institute of Standards and Technology

organizations use some variation of the more complex equation:

$$Risk = f(consequence, intent, capability, c(opportunity))$$

Where:

- ***f()*** = "is a function of"
- ***Consequence*** = the qualitative and quantitative costs of a cyber attack,
- ***Intent*** = the degree to which a given adversary wants to compromise a given site,
- ***Capability*** = the tools, techniques, time, and other resources available to the adversary,
- ***Opportunity*** = all possible ways that a cyber attack can bring about the consequence, and
- ***c()*** = the attack capability needed to exploit each opportunity.

The function *f()* is not a simple multiplication like the classic risk equation, but something more like the sum across all adversaries and attack opportunities of:

$$f() = if\,(intent\ \&\ (capability > c(opportunity)))\ then\ consequence$$

That is: for a given adversary, if that adversary intends to attack us, and their ability to attack us exceeds the capabilities needed to exploit any attack opportunities that remains in our defensive posture, then the attack will succeed, and we will suffer the consequences.

Note that to be fair to the *NISTIR 8286* report, the report points out that likelihood is difficult to calculate. The report recommends a 5-point qualitative score for likelihood and recommends that factors including adversary capability and attack opportunities factor into the qualitative "likelihood" score. Nevertheless, the wording of the report still encourages decision-makers to think of cyber attacks as a random process. This works for HFLI cyber attacks, but not for HILF.

Also, while this approach for modelling OT cyber attacks is similar to the approach used to model terrorist attacks, there are hundreds or thousands of times as many cyber attacks in the world every year as there are terrorist attacks. One big reason for this is risk – not risk to the victims but risk to the attackers. Terrorist attacks are physical attacks where the attacker must be physically present to plant their bombs or fire their guns. All terrorists who carry out physical attacks put at least their liberty and often their own lives at risk in each attack.

With cyber attacks, our attackers can be sipping coffee on the other side of the planet when they attack us. Worse, depending on how hard they work at it, cyber attackers can make it very difficult for law enforcement and other authorities to determine who the attackers are. And even if authorities determine who the attackers are, there may not be international cooperation agreements nor other mechanisms in place that are sufficient to arrest and prosecute the attackers. Cyber attackers are from time to time identified and eventually sanctioned or arrested and convicted, but generally cyber attacks are much "safer" for attackers than are physical attacks.

Thus, while the risk formula for deliberate attacks is the same for terrorist cells as it is for ransomware criminal groups, we must not assume that because terrorist attacks are comparatively rare, significant cyber attacks will be rare as well. Again, cyber attack capabilities are evolving quickly, and the risk to attackers in launching attacks against us is low.

Back to our formula – let's look at each piece of the equation in turn.

Consequence

The meaning of the consequence term in the modern risk formula is essentially the same as the term in the classic formula. Consequence is an estimate of the nature and scale of the undesirable outcome that we seek to prevent. The most common mistakes made in dealing with the idea of consequence in our risk planning are failures of imagination. Too many practitioners:

- Measure or evaluate consequence in terms of what they regard as the "most likely" outcome of some kind of cyber attack, rather than the worst possible outcome, and
- Inadvertently omit serious undesirable outcomes, most often because they lack a detailed understanding of physical processes or automation systems, and so cannot predict what truly undesirable outcomes are possible.

Less frequently, security practitioners may over-estimate consequences of cyber attacks, because they are not familiar with unhackable engineering safeguards that are in place in the industrial process the practitioners are evaluating.

Intent

The intent of cyber adversaries is very difficult to model accurately. As a result, most experts simply assign a 100% or "true" value for intent. Intent may be possible to model accurately in a physical conflict, where for example a nation-state has gathered detailed intelligence regarding the intent and capabilities of an adversary nation or a terrorist group. This grade of intelligence, however, is almost never available to cyber defenders, hence the assumption that intent is constant.

Is this reasonable? Consider an analogy – imagine we are operating a large refinery – a multi-billion-dollar investment that routinely manipulates dangerous, high temperature, high pressure hydrocarbons. The facility has a fence around it, with guards, gates, guns, and video surveillance – all the usual physical security measures. We receive a report of a large hole in the fence, in the back of the facility where few workers ever go. We check it out. There is a hole big enough to drive a truck through. Looking through the hole, we see a dark alley with what look like heavily armed drug dealers looking back at us.

We are alarmed. We ask, "How long has this been going on?" The answer is that the hole has been in place for at least several years, possibly longer. We are told that intruders have been spotted entering the facility through the hole from time to time, but that we have always been able persuade them to leave again, without anyone being injured and without triggering a shutdown of the facility.

What do we do? Do we say "Oh – well that's OK then – if they haven't done any harm in the past, then they probably won't do any in the future?" Or do we say, "Fix that hole. Fix it now! And fire whoever's in charge of the security program!" The latter is our most likely response *even if* we have credible intelligence about the intent of each of the individual drug dealers and criminal organizations in the immediate vicinity. The alley we saw does not itself have a fence around it – anybody can walk into that area and then through that hole in our fence. Assuming we understand the intent of every person who has access to the hole in our fence is a mistake.

More fundamentally, human intent can change in a heartbeat, literally. From one heartbeat to the next a person skilled in the art who is watching TV or browsing the Internet may see something that inflames them and triggers a decision to launch a cyber attack at us. Cyber attackers may target a facility because they are unhappy with the facility, unhappy with the people associated with the facility, unhappy with the industry, or unhappy for some other reason. While public relations, diplomacy and other human-centric measures might serve to reduce "unhappiness" in our potential attacker population to some degree, these solutions are not reliable.

Attackers also target our facilities out of a profit motive, or for other motives. Legal deterrents, measures to make paying ransomware criminals more difficult, and measures to make laundering of ransom payments more difficult all serve to make ransomware attacks somewhat less attractive to criminals in certain jurisdictions, but again these measures are not reliable at present. The world is a big place. Legal deterrents and money laundering deterrents cannot reach across the entire planet, and it is unwise to base engineering designs on the laws of the moment in some other country. Engineering designs should rely on physical laws for safety and reliability, not human laws.

All that said, a significant minority of practitioners argue that at least for ransomware, intent can be modeled probabilistically. They point out that it is not yet the case that every physical industrial operation on the planet has been compromised by ransomware criminals. These experts will argue that intent should therefor be modelled as a fraction:

Intent = (number of sites targeted last year) / (total number of sites)

Should we accept their argument? Well, imagine that we do. Imagine that we are the security team responsible for a critical infrastructure site. Imagine that ransomware hits the site, and we suffer an emergency shutdown. The ransomware encrypted and impaired operations so quickly that our normal shutdown mechanisms did not work, and we had to carry out a "hard" shutdown.

The emergency shutdown damaged important equipment. It takes months and hundreds of millions of dollars to replace the equipment and bring the facility back online.

In the inevitable investigation that follows the attack, we are asked, "what happened?" We are asked by our executives, or by the board, or by the government. The truthful answer is, "Well, we knew that if a modern ransomware group came after us, that we would go down. We just didn't think that any of them would target us this year." If we tell the truth, we will be fired. This is the wrong answer – for many kinds of sites, not least critical industrial infrastructures.

But substitute a small shoe factory for the critical infrastructure site above. Is equipment damage in an emergency shutdown even possible for such a site? If the small shoe factory can suffer only acceptable business consequences because of such an attack, is a probabilistic intent reasonable? We revisit the question in Chapter 7 where we discuss Due Care, and to an extent in the sections on Design Basis Threat and Insurance below.

For many industrial sites however, most cyber risk practitioners attribute a value of "100%" or "true" to the intent part of the risk equation.

Capabilities

Attacker capabilities characterize the abilities of attackers, and the usual characteristics of attacker capability are:

- Time – that the attackers can spend attacking us,
- Money – that is available to hire professionals to attack us and to purchase powerful attack automation tools, and
- Talent – a knowledge of physical process, automation systems, cybersecurity systems and other systems we use in our industrial systems.

Nation-state militaries are generally considered to be the most capable adversaries, with essentially unlimited time, money, and talent to spend in attacking their victims. Nations all over the world are investing literally billions of dollars each in developing sophisticated cyber attack capabilities. Nation-state military organizations are unique in another way – these organizations tend to be the only ones who can coordinate physical with cyber assaults.

This occurs not just in open warfare, such as during the recent Russian invasion of Ukraine, but during peacetime as well. Military-grade cyber assaults can involve "sleeper" personnel who infiltrate target organizations as employees or contractors. Such sleepers are then uniquely positioned to do damage to an organization whenever the nation that placed them demands. Sleepers most often have passwords, permissions, and the trust of the victim organization. The sleepers generally also have the sophisticated attack tools backed by the cyber knowledge of the nation-state who is using the sleepers in their attacks.

Now, very few of the world's many industrial enterprises and smaller power utilities, such as water utilities and other "lesser" critical industrial infrastructures, very few believe that they will ever be the target of a nation-state attack. These organizations believe that they are not important enough in global affairs to warrant the attention of a nation state.

One problem with this thinking is that nations with massive investments in cyber attack capabilities have the means to focus their attacks on a far wider set of targets than most security practitioners understand. An even bigger problem with thinking that nation-state attacks do not apply to smaller organizations is ransomware criminal groups. The most sophisticated of ransomware groups are using attack tools and techniques that less than five years ago were used exclusively by nation states. Worse, nation-state attack groups and ransomware groups sometimes cooperate. In some jurisdictions, ransomware criminals are tolerated, provided they attack only facilities in "undesirable" target countries. In countries under economic sanctions, ransomware groups are state-supported and used to generate foreign currency for the sanctioned regime. For these and other reasons, we often see attack tools and techniques "leaking" from the nation-state sphere into the criminal sphere.

Ransomware groups are indiscriminate – they attack everyone with money. They attack victims large and small, provided they believe they can turn a profit on the attack. The tools and techniques that we see nation states using against each other today, we should expect to see ransomware groups using against everyone with money, within less than a handful of years. We all need protection against sophisticated attacks.

More generally, attack capabilities from the mundane to the arcane are important to understand. This is why security practitioners attend conferences such as Black Hat – to stay abreast of the very latest attack tools and techniques that have been observed in use, in the wild. Attacker capabilities are, however, not something that are easy to control. Trying to control nation states' and criminal groups' abilities to create powerful attack tools is beyond the ability of engineering and enterprise security teams. Trying to control the distribution of these powerful tools in underground economies and via the Internet is similarly beyond the ability of engineering and security teams.

When designing security systems to protect industrial automation whose worst-case consequences of compromise are unacceptable, designers should interpret our adversaries and their tools and other capabilities as a "load" that a security design must bear, reliably, for a set period of time. To do this, engineers must forecast the evolving capabilities of our adversaries and create designs robust enough to defeat those capabilities reliably as far into the future as practical. Forecasting attack capabilities is both possible and practical. Unlike motivation and intent, attack capabilities evolve very slowly, and pretty much all attacks are eventually discovered. When discovered, there is a very good chance that the attack tools and techniques will eventually be reverse-engineered and published, so that other victims can defend themselves against similar attacks in the future. Tracking and predicting attack capabilities is possible and practical, but controlling those capabilities in our adversaries is neither.

Opportunities

The "opportunity" factor in the modern risk equation is closely related to the "consequence" factor. For a given consequence, the opportunity factor is the sum of all possible ways that a cyber attack can bring about the consequence to some degree of confidence. We use the word "opportunity" here instead of "vulnerability," because too many security practitioners are confused about the definition of "vulnerability."

The term "vulnerability" is generally defined in one of two ways in the cybersecurity world:

1) **Vulnerability** – a software defect or design defect that can be exploited to compromise an asset or system, or
2) **Vulnerability** – a flaw or weakness in a system's design, implementation, or operation and management that could be exploited to compromise the operation of the system.

Definition (2) is more general than (1). Definition (2) is comparable to the definition of "opportunity," but (1) is not. The more general (2) definition is used in the *ISA / IEC 62443-1-1* standard. Most practitioners do not realize this, and therefore misinterpret the 62443 standards, thinking that all vulnerabilities described in 62443 can be corrected by patch programs – applying new software versions, patches, or security updates to eliminate the software defects. Far too many security programs therefore spend more effort and money than is warranted on patching and security updates, thinking that fully patched systems are in some sense "invulnerable."

"Attack path" is another concept that is closely related to opportunity. An attack path is a sequence of actions and events that an attacker can use to bring about a specific undesirable consequence. Attack paths may involve software, design, or other defects, may involve stolen credentials, or may involve only misplaced trust in an insider with passwords, permissions, and malicious intent. Attack trees are the set of all possible attack paths through a target system that an adversary can use to bring about a specific consequence. Attack trees can be very large – up to billions of attack paths for unacceptable consequences in a typical, large industrial process. Organizations who want to develop comprehensive attack trees as part of their risk modelling inevitably use attack tree software[18] to manage these very large data sets.

Risk managers sometimes use attack trees, and sometimes use more qualitative assessments of all attack paths that might lead to an undesirable outcome. Managers use these tools because they need to understand the capabilities that attackers need in order to carry out these attacks. Often, what

---

[18] *Attack Tree-based Threat Risk Analysis,* Terrance R. Ingoldsby, 2021, Amenaza Technologies Limited

risk managers need most is an accurate assessment of the *minimum* capabilities that an attacker needs to bring about unacceptable consequences. Attack trees are one way to find these minimum capabilities. Qualitative analyses by experienced practitioners may also find these attacks, but risk missing the truly simplest of attacks to which we are still exposed.

Cyber Design Basis Threat

In any risk management system, there is residual risk – risk the organization simply accepts – if the risk is realized, the organization suffers the consequence. How much cyber risk to industrial operations should reasonably be accepted is addressed in the next chapter. Cyber Design Basis Threat (cDBT) is a way to express and communicate acceptable risk in the form of risk tolerance statements. In an organization using the modern capabilities-based formulation for risk, risk tolerance statements are expressed in terms of the capabilities of our attackers.

cDBT is an adaptation of the Design Basis Threat (DBT) term used in the world of physical security. In physical security, DBT assessments are often drawn up for targets of terrorist or military-grade attacks. These documents are most often classified, so practitioners should not be surprised if they have never seen one. The documents describe design criteria for protections at a physical site. Specifically, the documents include a description of the most-capable physical assaults that the target site must withstand reliably.

Such a document for a nuclear generator might include, for example, a requirement that each reactor's containment dome withstand a direct impact by the largest commercially available passenger jet fully loaded with fuel without incurring a significant radiological discharge. Such a document for a nation's embassy in a hostile country might include a requirement that the embassy withstand an attack by a terrorist force of no more than 8 people armed with hand grenades and submachineguns, but not necessarily a line of tanks driving down the street shooting holes in buildings.

A cyber design basis threat (cDBT) similarly describes the most capable adversary that a site is required to defeat, and with what level of confidence. Examples of such statements include:

- No cyber attack operating exclusively across the Internet without the help of deliberately cooperating insiders in our organization, shall be able to bring about a material safety incident, cause material damage to essential equipment, nor bring about any interruption to physical operations.
- Cyber attacks shall not be able to bring about safety incidents at all, nor shall they be able to bring about production outages of more than ten days, more than once every three years.
- Cyber attacks causing production outages shall be impossible to launch by insiders using hacktivist-class attack techniques with access only to IT networks.

- The quality and coverage of logging and monitoring of OT networks, systems and facilities shall be sufficient to assure that insiders who commit material acts of sabotage can be prosecuted and convicted with a very high degree of confidence.

The degree of confidence specified in the cDBT statements is important. A tolerance directive such as "once every three years" is instruction to the security team to track the evolving threat environment, asking questions that include:

- What fraction of sites like ours is attacked by each grade of adversary, and how often?
- How are sites that are breached defended, vs sites that are not breached?

Government and industry Information Sharing and Analysis Centers (ISACs) can provide some of this information. The goal for a "once every three years" cDBT is to stay ahead of the threat environment "just enough" to achieve the goal.

What cDBT and degrees of confidence are appropriate to different kinds of business? We address this question in Chapter 7 where we discuss due care obligations.

cDBT and Risk Assessments

Many organizations engage third parties on a regular basis to carry out OT cyber risk assessments. This best practice is intended to bring "fresh eyes" to a site from time to time, to see if elements of the risk equation have changed, and to have some chance of seeing problems that previous assessments by different teams have missed. Unfortunately, many of these assessments look almost exclusively at IT-style risk indicators such as:

- How many machines are not at the latest patch / security update level?
- How many systems have weak passwords, shared passwords or have not had their passwords changed recently?
- How many systems have weak security provisions configured and enabled?
- Is anyone watching logs to see if there is password guessing, port mapping or other "attackers knocking on the door" activity going on?

These assessments result in a report filled with findings, most of which the requesting organization was aware of already. This is the kind of report has value for OT sites with acceptable consequences of compromise – sites that are managed as IT networks. This report has limited value for network-engineered sites whose consequences of compromise are unacceptable. At network-engineered sites, it is very difficult for cyber attacks to gain entry to critical OT networks and systems. For example, that an air-gapped safety system, locked behind many layers of physical security, has a password that has not been changed in a long time represents only a very small risk. In critical systems with a defined cDBT, useful assessments answer the questions:

- Is the design and implementation of the cyber risk management program sufficient to defeat all attacks below the cDBT specification, with the required degree of confidence?
- If so, is the program materially stronger than the designed cDBT specification? I.e., can the cDBT specification be restated in stronger terms and still accurately describe the existing security program?
- Given this cDBT as implemented in our risk management program, what are the simplest attacks "above the line" – attacks not defeated reliably, nor required to be defeated reliably?

The last question is important to any site wishing to assess and understand residual risk. The simplest attacks with unacceptable consequences that a risk program does not eliminate, or defeat, are a large part of the site's residual OT cyber risk. The site should look at those attack scenarios and ask whether they are still acceptable. If they are not, then the site needs to redefine their cDBT risk tolerance directives and update the security / risk management program correspondingly.

Insurance

Changing gears for a moment – a tool that can increase our tolerance for risk is insurance – transferring the risk to a willing third party, the insurance agency. While substantial and unpredictable production outages due to cyber attacks might constitute an unacceptable risk to a small business, if most of those losses are recouped through insurance, then the risk may well become acceptable.

In recent years, however, the business of cyber insurance has changed dramatically and continues to evolve. The trigger for many of these recent changes was the NotPetya attack in 2017. The attack impacted hundreds of victim organizations and caused an estimated $10 billion USD in damages, with significant insurance payouts. The largest payout was a $1.4 billion USD claim by Merck Pharmaceutical against their insurer Zurich Insurance. Zurich disputed the claim, arguing that since four governments had identified the threat actor behind the attack as an agent of the Russian government, and the attack was linked to the Russian invasion and annexation of the Crimean Peninsula, then the attack triggered the nation-state exclusion clause in the insurance contract. The courts disagreed and awarded Merck the claim. Zurich appealed. The appeals court sided with Merck Pharmaceutical.

This insurance claim and others triggered the UK regulator that governs the entire Lloyd's syndicate to pass two new rules. The first – insurers are no longer permitted to provide "silent coverage" for cyber attacks. In the past, large industrial and other clients could routinely purchase multi-billion dollar "general damages" policies that covered damage to equipment and facilities for any reason – i.e.: "all risks" – except only those specific risks the policy excludes. Such clients could also purchase multi-billion dollar "general liability" policies that cover lawsuits from all risks, excepting only specific risks that the policy excludes. The first new rule said that in all such "all risks" policies, insurers must include a clause that excludes consequences of cyber attacks. No new policy in the covered insurers, including the entire Lloyd's syndicate, could include "silent cyber" anymore – no "all risks" policy could include cyber. The result of the rule is that today, if a client wants to purchase coverage for any consequence of cyber attacks, they must purchase a separate cyber policy to cover those consequences and attacks.

The second rule the regulator passed limited coverage that syndicate members were allowed to offer in cyber-specific policies. Policies could not provide more than about $200-$250 million dollars in coverage. This is far less than the billions of dollars in coverage that large institutions are accustomed to in their general damages and general liability policies.

A third rule the regulator passed more recently was to exclude coverage for nation state attacks – Lloyd's syndicate members no longer cover events like NotPetya. Many insurance policies have long excluded "acts of war" and it was this clause that Zurich tried to use to negate Merck's $1.4B claim. The courts ruled that even though NotPetya was a nation-state-sponsored attack, it was not an act of war. Today, the Lloyd's syndicate requires members to include language in their policies excluding coverage for all nation-state-sponsored attacks, not only acts of war.

At this writing, all these rules apply only to the Lloyd's syndicate and not (yet) to other insurers. The Lloyd's syndicate, however, is a leader in the field of specialized insurance. Other insurers and other jurisdictions are watching the situation and watching the Lloyd's decisions very closely. If these policies work for the Lloyd's syndicate, other jurisdictions and insurers are very likely to enact similar rules.

Another factor to consider with insurance is that such policies generally protect the business, but not the society. This may be unacceptable to operators of critical infrastructures.

Imagine for example that the lights go out all over the Northeast United States for five days because of a cyber attack. Citizens and businesses in the affected region suffer enormously. Seventeen governors declare states of emergency. At the end of the five days, the lights come back on throughout most of the region. The CEO of the power utility that suffered the cyber attack which triggered the outage makes a live public statement on television and streaming media. The CEO accepts responsibility for the outage and apologizes. "We are very sorry to have been the trigger for this disaster and we feel very deeply for the hardships that everyone has had to endure in recent days. But – but – I want to reassure the nation that throughout this entire, horrible experience, my company – this utility – has not suffered one red cent of losses because we have insurance."

He would be lynched. Insurance is entirely the wrong message and the wrong response to a critical infrastructure outage. Yes, businesses need to purchase insurance, but critical industrial infrastructures cannot rely on insurance. Such infrastructures are seen by their societies as having a deep responsibility to their customers and to the society at large to keep their infrastructures running. Insurance is not enough for critical infrastructures, for military installations, and for any other industrial facility whose operation is essential to society.

Another factor when considering insurance: the world's largest businesses self-insure. When the Deepwater Horizon platform failed in the Gulf of Mexico and caused a massive oil spill, clean-up costs and lawsuits added up to tens of billions of dollars in costs. Note that this was not a cyber attack – the example here is one of self insurance. British Petroleum did not call on an insurance agency to pay for the clean up. The business paid out of their own pocket, resulting in a one-time nearly $70 billion reduction in their quarterly profits. Profits were back on track the next quarter.

The world's largest businesses do not need to purchase insurance and so might conclude that they are not affected by these changes in the cyber insurance industry. But think about it – insurance companies are experts on risk. If an insurance company concludes that a specific risk is too big to insure, is it reasonable for private business, however large, to simply accept those risks to their shareholders? Due care means doing whatever any reasonable person would do in the circumstances. If certain kinds of cyber risk are too big for a growing number of insurers, then are they truly reasonable for businesses to self-insure against? Especially when there is an alternative? When those risks could be materially reduced or even eliminated outright through modest investments in security engineering?

Summary

Engineering-grade designs use an engineering perspective of risk when deciding *"how much is enough?"* Risk management does not seek to eliminate all risk but seeks to take *reasonable* risks when *necessary* to achieve the mission of the enterprise. Since all efficiency improvements can be argued to be necessary, most OT cyber risk management reduces to the question, "what is reasonable?"

Strategic risks are those that threaten the continued viability of the organization. In publicly traded companies, material risks are those risks that any reasonable investor might consider as grounds to change their estimate of the valuation of the business. Boards of governors and senior executives must manage strategic and material risks.

Cyber risk is deterministic rather than probabilistic – the same attack on the same target a second time almost certainly results in the same outcome as the first attack. This means that while likelihood is a good metric for random risks, such as hurricanes and earthquakes, likelihood is a poor fit for HILF cyber risks. A better fit for such risks and attacks is:

Risk = f(consequence, intent, capability, c(opportunity))

Where:

f() = "is a function of"
Consequence = the qualitative and quantitative costs of a cyber attack,
Intent = the degree to which a given adversary wants to compromise a given site,
Capability = the tools, techniques, time, and other resources available to the adversary, and
Opportunity = all possible ways that a cyber attack can bring about the consequence
c() = the attack capability needed to exploit each opportunity

The term "vulnerability" is often used instead of "opportunity." This is very confusing. Most practitioners understand "vulnerability" to mean a software defect that can be exploited, and that is addressed through patching or security updates. Attack "opportunity" is a more general term for any aspect of a system that might permit an adversary to compromise the system.

Cyber Design Basis Threat (cDBT) is a way to use this model of risk to express deterministic limits. A cDBT directive describes the types of attacks that must be defeated deterministically – for example:

No cyber attack operating exclusively across the Internet without the help of deliberately cooperating insiders in our organization, shall be able to bring about a material safety incident, cause material damage to essential equipment, nor bring about any interruption to physical operations.

Defenders must design their protective systems to meet their cDBT goals. Risk assessors must render a verdict as to whether a system being assessed meets its cDBT goals. Risk assessors should also provide their clients with a sampling of the simplest cyber attacks above the cDBT line – not defeated to engineering-grade standards. Since nothing is ever completely secure, there will always be such attacks, and it should always be possible to describe samples of these attacks.

Finally, insurance is how businesses transfer risk. Since the NotPetya incident in 2017, insurance for physical damages or liability due to cyber attacks has become much harder to purchase. Many insurers have decided to limit payouts for physical damages and liability due to cyber attacks to dollar figures much smaller than the costs of a worst-case compromise of many industrial sites.

Chapter 7 – Due Care

In this chapter we start to pull it all together, looking at how to decide what risk tolerance directives are reasonable, determining what kind of protection should be applied to specific systems in specific organizations, and what residual risks are acceptable – in short, answering *"how much is enough?"* The unifying concept here is "due care" or "due diligence." Both terms are defined as "doing what any reasonable person would have done in similar circumstances." To a lawyer, the two terms are very subtly different:

- Due care is immediate, for example, putting on a hard hat when entering a work area, while
- Due diligence is longer term, for example analyzing risks and buying hard hats for the workers.

In practice, only lawyers care about these subtleties and the two terms are most often used interchangeably. In the discussion that follows, we use the simpler term "due care" universally to refer to what any reasonable person would do, no matter the time frame.

A word of caution: what a judge, jury or other authority may regard as reasonable is likely to differ somewhat from person to person, and more importantly, is changing constantly over time as technology changes and as cyber threat actors become more capable. Worse, due care obligations can be colored by hindsight – once a jury sees that a certain attack caused a disaster or other serious consequence, that jury might conclude that any reasonable person should have foreseen the possible outcome, even when in the day no standard of practice hinted at the possibility.

To protect organizations and individuals from liability, unfortunately, cyber risk management programs must anticipate what judges and juries will regard as reasonable. This also means that to exhibit due care, cyber risk programs must either change constantly in response to new threat information, or these programs must have anticipated the evolution of threats in system designs that may then change more slowly.

All this is one reason that many engineering teams are very concerned about cyber risk, their responsibilities, and their liabilities regarding risk. Cautious teams are working hard to deploy affordable engineering-grade protections for unacceptable consequences as universally as is practical, so that no matter how the technology or threat environment evolves in the future, their defensive designs will continue to be effective. Similarly, cautious teams are working to use attack trees, audit reports, table-top exercises, and other mechanisms to assess and document cyber risks and their decision rationale as thoroughly as practical. Courts, regulators, and government investigations generally do not require perfection, but they generally appreciate thoroughness, even when imperfect.

Network and Attack Connectivity

The first step towards due care in the design of automation systems is to determine the criticality of the networks involved in our designs. We measure criticality in terms of the worst-case consequences of compromise of a network.

Networking is important both because all non-trivial industrial sites involve networked equipment, and because these inter-connected networks are how hacktivists, ransomware criminals and nation states prefer to reach into our automation systems and misoperate them. All cyber sabotage attacks are information. The only way that an automation system can change from an uncompromised to a compromised state is to have attack information enter the system. And there are only two ways that information can be moved: online and offline. Offline information movement is when information is encoded into a physical medium, such as a USB drive, a laptop hard drive or even a human brain, and that medium is physically carried into the vicinity of the automation system, with the attack information transferred from the medium into the system. Online information movement is when there is no medium being physically carried around – information flows through wires, fibres, photons, or more exotic signalling mechanisms.

By far the most common way of communicating cyber-sabotage attack information is online communications. Attackers reach through the Internet to remotely exploit software vulnerabilities, or exploit firewall or application misconfigurations, or deceive insiders into downloading malware, or steal remote access and other credentials – all to gain a foothold on a network. This foothold is then expanded into taking remote control of a computer on the IT network. The attackers then *pivot* – they use the compromised machine to search for passwords and other credentials, and they use the compromised machine and/or those credentials to attack other machines. With control of another machine, the attackers pivot again, most often eventually pivoting through IT/OT or other firewalls deeper into networks to gain access to more heavily defended targets.

The lesson here is that in engineering terms, all connected equipment is at essentially the same level of security / protection from pivoting attacks. This is certainly true for Internet Protocol (IP) connected devices – attackers routinely pivot from one machine to another in IP networks, even through intervening firewalls. For example, a back of the envelope calculation suggests that over nine thousand businesses were compromised by ransomware in 2022[19]. By far

---

[19] The *Federal Bureau of Investigation Internet Crime Report 2022* reports 2,385 ransomware complaints. If less than half of incidents are reported and the USA accounts for less than half of incidents worldwide, then total incidents are greater than 4 x 2,385 = 9,540.

the most common infection vector for such attacks was via email, phishing attacks or otherwise through the Internet. In the vast majority of attacks, the ransomware penetrated the firewall deployed between the IT network and the Internet. Ransomware penetrates firewalls routinely. In engineering terms, the only safe assumption is that essentially all IP-connected networks and systems are sooner or later reachable from each other via attack pivoting paths.

When it comes to non-IP protocols, such as serial-based or other more exotic industrial protocols, pivoting might still be possible, or it might not be. It would take a serious security investigation of the protocol and its software implementation to rule out the possibility of pivoting through any given serial protocol. On the other hand, *even if* an expensive, exhaustive investigation proves that attackers cannot pivot from a compromised IP-connected computer through a serial connection into another PLC or industrial device, the compromised IP-connected computer can almost certainly use the serial connection to control, operate and *misoperate* the industrial devices. Such control is after all what these serial industrial protocols were designed for – to enable higher-level automation computers to monitor and most often also control connected industrial devices.

Connected Networks

Again, the first step towards due care for cyber risk in the design of automation systems is to determine the criticality of the networks involved in our designs. Criticality is associated with the worst-case consequences of compromise of any device or set of devices on the network. This is the first step towards due care, because worst-case consequences of compromise of any element of a network determine the strength of the security measures that due care demands we apply to the entire network – the complete set of computers that can be reached by an attacker pivoting throughout the network.

An example before we go further – consider the computers that automate passenger rail systems. Operators sitting in a central control room use a SCADA system to monitor where trains are, and to give orders to switch the tracks every few seconds or minutes so that different trains and passengers are routed to different destinations. Safety computers connected to the switches have information about whether the next track is occupied, and issue emergency stop commands to trains that attempt to cross into an occupied segment of track.

A casual examination might suggest that the worst-case consequence of a cyber attack on the safety systems is a collision that kills or injures many passengers. That casual examination might further suggest that the worst that can happen if the SCADA system is taken over is that trains are told to enter segments of track that are currently occupied, and the safety system will then stop the trains. The consequence of compromising the SCADA system would seem to be a reliability consequence – the trains stop running, not a safety consequence – a mass casualty event.

The key question in this evaluation: “Is there a pivoting path from the

SCADA system to the safety system?" If, for example, the SCADA system routinely exchanges messages with the safety computers to (a) check that those computers are still working properly and (b) understand if those computers have detected an unsafe condition and stopped one of the trains, then there may very well be a pivoting path that lets an attacker who has taken over the SCADA system use that system to attack and take over the safety computers. Unidirectional gateways, analog signalling and other network engineering techniques could safely send status information into the SCADA system, without the risk of attacks pivoting into the safety systems. Putting a network interface on the safety systems, or serially connecting the safety computers into a networked computer, introduces pivoting paths. If a pivoting path exists, then the worst-case consequence of compromising the SCADA computers is that this compromise pivots and in turn compromises the safety computers, bringing about a mass casualty event.

The worst-case consequence of compromise of any computer or network is the worst-case consequence of any device reachable by a pivoting path from the computer or network in question.

At this point, an astute reader will observe that if attacks can pivot through firewalls (and they can), and if most industrial networks are deployed on IP networks separated from each other and from the Internet by firewalls (and they are), then the entire industrial / OT, IT and Internet networks are a single network connected by attack pivoting paths (and they are). Thus, if due care demands that the worst-case consequences of compromise on our automation networks determine the security program that must be applied to all computers reachable through pivoting paths (and it does), then the worst-case consequences of compromise of most of our industrial network determine the security program that we must apply to the entire Internet. This is of course, nonsense – due care cannot demand that we secure the entire Internet.

The above paragraph is a concise summary of the essence of the problem: when worst-case consequences of compromise in our automation networks are unacceptable, then we must either use engineering-grade designs to reduce those consequences to acceptable levels or we must redesign our networks or otherwise deploy engineering-grade mechanisms to reliably interrupt pivoting attack paths originating on the Internet. This is again, because of course we cannot secure the entire Internet.

Network Criticality

So, hold that thought for another few paragraphs. Before we look at solving the problem, we should first finish the job of figuring out how much trouble we are in by classifying our networks. To do this we must first identify our networks so that we know what we are classifying. This may seem difficult. Even if we have a cabinet of wiring diagrams of how all fifteen thousand CPUs in our refinery or power plant are connected, how many networks do those wiring diagrams constitute? What exactly is a network, and at what level of granularity are we classifying our networks?

Most industrial sites choose to classify as few networks as possible. After all, if network criticality determines the security measures that we must apply to each network, then how many different security programs do we want to be managing at the site? If we already have our hands full with one program and are thinking that maybe two and three programs are probably too many, then surely dozens of networks and associated security programs are pointless to consider.

This is sound reasoning. As a result, most industrial sites start with the obvious – two networks, the IT network and the OT network. Now we must determine the worst-case consequences of compromise for each. An engineering team might be able to list these outcomes in painful detail: this boiler could blow up, that catalytic cracker might start leaking and cause a fire or explosion, or the lights might go out all over the US Northeast for 6 days. In the end, however, these details rarely matter. The security program appropriate to a network tasked with preventing a boiler from blowing up and killing someone is little different from the program for a network tasked with preventing a cracker from catching fire and killing someone. Most of the time, the significant differences between networks in terms of compromise can be captured by identifying consequences as either:

- Safety consequences – worker injuries and casualties, environmental damage, and threats to public safety,
- Reliability consequences – interruptions of service for critical national or local infrastructures, such as power outages, boil water advisories, lack of any drinking or sanitary water in a community, and transportation interruptions big enough to impair the delivery of food or other essentials to population centers, and
- Business consequences – leaked PII lawsuits, shareholder lawsuits, financial losses, costs of emergency clean up for compromised equipment, and other "business" costs.

Due care demands that all network designers must answer one question about the magnitude of these consequences: are the worst-case consequences acceptable? For example:

- If the worst-case safety consequence on an aircraft engine manufacturing network is a robot breaking a worker's arm somewhere in the factory, once every few years, then the business might legitimately conclude that because such injuries can occur anywhere – with a worker falling down a flight of stairs at home in a moment of inattention for example – these consequences constitute an acceptable business risk.
- If the worst-case reliability consequence of compromise of a gasoline pipeline SCADA system is a half-day unscheduled outage of the pipeline,

the business might legitimately conclude that, since both gasoline consumers and gasoline producers have multi-day storage capabilities, and since such pipelines undergo routine half day outages for maintenance several times a year, then infrequent half-day outages due to cyber attacks are an acceptable risk.

- If the worst-case consequence of a small shoe factory is the cost of incident clean up and a few overtime shifts to make up lost production, the business might legitimately conclude this is an acceptable risk.

Of course, depending on the design of the systems and networks, worst case outages may be much worse. For example:

- If the worst-case consequence of compromising aircraft engine manufacturing robots is subtle defects in the engines that lead those engines to fail during flight with a full load of passengers, or
- If the worst case for a gasoline pipeline is a combination of pump and valve operation that leads to a "hydraulic hammer" rupturing the pipeline in the middle of a population center, or
- If the worst-case consequences for a shoe factory is the release of concentrated and easily evaporated toxins that the factory uses to prepare, color, or otherwise treat leather,

then we have a different situation. In all these cases, engineering teams might conclude that the consequences are unacceptable. To this end we introduce terminology: when risks are unacceptable, we use the word "critical:"

- Safety-critical networks are pivoting-connected networks whose worst-case consequences of compromise are unacceptable safety incidents,
- Reliability-critical networks are those whose worst-case consequences are unacceptable production or service outages, and
- Business-critical networks are those whose worst-case consequences are unacceptable monetary losses, corporate valuation losses, reputational losses, or other business losses.

One could argue that the categorization above is not broad enough, because extreme events are possible. When the Chernobyl nuclear generator core exploded (*not* a cyber attack, but an example of a worst-case consequence), tens of thousands of people were exposed to life-threatening amounts of radiation, and hundreds of square kilometers of land became uninhabitable for centuries. When the Deepwater Horizon platform sank off the coast of Mexico (*not* a cyber attack), there was widespread environmental damage. Clean-up costs for British Petroleum were estimated at $69 US billion dollars. That such extreme events are possible is undeniable, but such events change little in terms of network designs. The computers tasked with controlling physical processes in such a way as to prevent these extreme events demand engineering-grade protection against pivoting attacks, just as the computers tasked with preventing lesser but still unacceptable consequences.

In the Chapter 8, we will look at insider risk and offline data flows. For now, we focus on network engineering for pervasive, nation-state-grade Internet-based threats. When engineering-grade network designs prevent all network / pivoting attacks from external networks, online pivoting attacks from the Internet become impossible. This prevents both unacceptable consequences of compromise and extremely unacceptable consequences. And it means we do not have to secure the entire Internet.

Every CPU Compromised

A very important point is worth repeating here. The single most common mistake we make in classifying industrial automation networks is failing to consider the worst-case consequences of compromise. To determine the criticality of a network, we must assume that every last CPU in the network has been compromised. We must assume that every computer in the network is issuing the worst possible instructions at the worst possible moment to the physical process. These are the consequences that our defensive posture and risk management measures must address.

Note that this definition of consequence may seem counter-intuitive – why should the worst case determine required protections? Why should we ignore our existing defensive measures, detection systems and incident response capabilities into account when evaluating consequences? The answer is that it is the worst case that *determines* the protection we should put in place for a network or system. We can consider existing defenses when evaluating how much more or possibly how much less we should defend an existing target, but the worst case determines *total required* protection.

Even in the small shoe factory example, the automation network can be treated as a business network if and only if the very worst outcomes possible, even if every CPU in the network is compromised, constitute acceptable business consequences. If the worst case is an unacceptable safety consequence, then even the small shoe factory's automation network is safety critical. If the worst case is that most of the equipment in the factory is damaged beyond repair and the factory is down for 6 months as the equipment is replaced, then the worst case is reliability-critical, not a business consequence.

What determines criticality is not what we might imagine is the most likely or most credible attack. Criticality is not determined by what statistics show is the most probable attack historically. Criticality is determined by the worst that is *possible*.

What is Acceptable?

Back to the question of determining the criticality of our networks. At this point in our analysis, we have identified some networks and determined their worst-case consequences of compromise, and we are asking the question, "are these consequences acceptable?" You might ask – "Is this the right question?" Is the question "Are these risks reasonable?" not the right question to ask instead? After all, consequence is only part of the *Risk = f(consequence, intent, capability, opportunity)* equation – why does worst-case consequence alone determine network criticality?

The answer has to do with pervasive threat. Ransomware is the pervasive threat to all computer networks and the organizations that rely on those networks. Ransomware actors are well funded and are using tools, tactics, and practices (TTPs) that trail nation state TTPs by less than five years. Nation state militaries and intelligence agencies, as well as ransomware groups, are targeting organizations all over the world with the most powerful of attack tools and techniques, from the comfort of their offices on the other side of the planet. For almost all businesses, predicting the specific intent of these adversaries in a useful time frame is not possible. If a network is exposed to a pivoting path of attacks from the Internet, then it is reasonable to expect that sooner or later, a nation-state-grade adversary, whether it be a true nation state or merely a ransomware group using nation-state techniques, will target the network with the most capable of attacks, which risks bringing about worst-case consequences.

So – if intent is impossible to predict and we must assume worst-case remote attack capabilities, then the question of risk and reasonableness reduces to factors of consequence and attack opportunity. Said more plainly, the question we must address with network-based attacks reduces to whether or not we must apply engineering-grade network designs and defenses to the task of preventing the consequences. For unacceptable consequences / critical networks, we must apply those techniques. The rest of the time we can choose to apply them or not, depending on perceived costs and benefits. Given these factors, the following are some rules of thumb for engineering and business decision makers re: acceptability of worst-case consequences. In most cases:

- *Loss of life is unacceptable*: imagine the headline "Ransomware Attack Causes Explosion That Kills 6 People." Ransomware threat actors target everyone with money – this is a predictable, sophisticated threat. Network engineering and other security engineering techniques are widely available, widely understood and are not prohibitively expensive. A failure to use easily available and widely understood engineering techniques to prevent on-the-job deaths in the face of a predictable and pervasive threat will be seen by the courts as a failure of due care. Said the other way around: threats to the lives of workers due to the possibility of remote attacks demand a security engineering response. Nothing less is good engineering.
- *Threats to national security are unacceptable*: Every nation is responsible for defining its own critical infrastructures, which generally include the most important parts of power grids, pipelines and other energy infrastructure, the biggest water treatment and distribution systems, and the transportation systems that are essential to large population centers and military

preparedness. Each nation defines which providers and utilities are essential to national security and provides these utilities with standards they are expected to uphold in terms of acceptable downtime, if any, for their parts of the nation's infrastructures. Cyber threats whose worst-case consequences could impair critical infrastructures for long enough to constitute a threat to national security demand a security engineering response. Nothing less will be seen as good engineering.

- *Environmental damage*: This is a more difficult decision. How much damage to the environment will be seen by society and by the courts as acceptable, resulting only in clean-up costs being charged to the offending business, vs. unacceptable? In the Deepwater Horizon disaster (not a cyber attack), criminal charges were brought against British Petroleum. As a rule, any threat of remote cyber attacks able to damage the environment seriously enough to trigger criminal charges demands a security engineering response.

And when in doubt, prudence dictates that we deploy engineering-grade protections. After all, the cost of such protections and designs differs little from the cost of conventional IT-grade cybersecurity programs. As security engineering practices become more systematic and more widespread, courts, governments and societies at large will almost certainly come to judge increasingly harshly any designer or operator who could have prevented a serious incident with engineering-grade designs but failed to do so.

What is Reasonable?

Given that we need to use engineering-grade designs to address cyber risks in networks whose worst-case consequences of compromise are unacceptable, does it follow that we can use IT-grade protections everywhere else? It does not.

Consider an automobile manufacturer where a ransomware attack cripples four large factories for four days. These factories are working at capacity, with 24x7 shifts scheduled producing one thousand vehicles per day per factory. A four-day unscheduled outage costs the plants and all their supply chain 16,000 vehicles less production than scheduled in the quarter. If the average of these automobiles sells for $30,000, this is a loss of revenue of roughly a half billion dollars.

For a large automobile manufacturer, such a loss is not likely to drive the business to insolvency, but the question remains, was that loss preventable with an engineering-grade security program? And if it was preventable, then was it reasonable for the business to deploy only IT-grade protections? If shareholder lawsuits are brought in this circumstance, then the courts may decide that engineering-grade protections would have been reasonable and find against the manufacturer.

As ransomware and other cyber attacks with material consequences become widespread, there will be more and more such incidents and lawsuits. Powerful security engineering techniques are something that will increasingly need to be considered even for networks whose worst-case consequences are acceptable safety-wise and reliability-wise but are material business-wise.

Table-Top Exercises

A table-top exercise is often useful to determine what risks are reasonable. Prepare an attack scenario with material consequences. This is easier said than done – credible attack scenarios are more than the technical bits and bytes of the attack with corresponding alerts presented (or not) to the SOC. These scenarios also include real or simulated interfaces to local and national cybersecurity and law enforcement authorities, regulators, simulated leaks to the press, inquiries from the board of directors, banks, partners, and customers, and so on. Businesses carrying out a table-top exercise will often use external providers for these exercises – providers who study the details of the business and use their experience in responding to incidents at similar businesses to put credible, detailed, and comprehensive scenarios together.

With an exercise defined, assemble a team to respond to the hypothetical incident. The team should involve representatives of every team that would be involved in a real incident, including salespeople fielding customer inquiries, partner management people fielding supplier and partner inquiries, marketing people fielding inquiries from the press, finance people interfacing with banks and investors, and so on. Run through the scenario. The contractor provides the hypothetical inputs and responses from the technology and from external partners, customers, press and so on. The team responds to these inputs according to their incident response plans. There are two key outputs from such an exercise:

1) The obvious – do our incident response plans work, and if not, how can we fix them? These exercises are recommended routinely to test incident response capabilities.
2) Less obvious – repeat the exercises a few times over the course of a few years and our response plans should start to work. Now evaluate – if the scenarios result in our business suffering a hypothetical multi-million, half billion, or multi-billion-dollar loss as a result of this kind of cyber attack, are our defenses reasonable?

Ask the team – if this attack had really happened, and we respond as planned, and we suffered this loss, would we change any of our defensive postures because of the event? For some businesses and some scenarios, the answer is "no change." The business will suffer an acceptable loss. The insurance company will have compensated us. The insurance company may order some small change in our defensive posture. After this kind of event, the business is most likely to execute on a security awareness training refresh for employees, and make sure that we are executing on all the security measures we have assured our insurer we are executing on and carry on.

For other businesses or other scenarios, the opposite will be true. The loss in the scenario may be so large that insurers will not cover it. The losses may involve lost customers, new government regulations, or other "reputational" damages that insurers will not cover but will have substantial and material impacts on the business. After such a loss the business would almost certainly invest to strengthen its engineering and cybersecurity measures for OT cyber risk.

Which brings us back to the "what is reasonable?" question. We know that because of a certain kind of cyber incident, the business will almost certainly decide to materially strengthen its defenses. Knowing this, is it reasonable to wait until we suffer such an incident before strengthening our defensive posture?

Well – what would we do for other kinds of threats? What if the exercise were for a hurricane, not a cyber attack? If we discovered because of the exercise that a hurricane hitting our facility would cause us material business losses, losses that could easily have been prevented with a modest investment of some sort, would we invest in better hurricane defenses? Or would we wait for the inevitable hurricane and suffer the losses before investing in better protection? Many people will say that no, delaying the investment is not reasonable. If we can see a problem with our preparedness that will sooner or later lead to an easily preventable material loss, fixing that problem now, before the loss, is the reasonable approach.

All that said, never waste a crisis. If your business *does* suffer a material cyber breach, that loss is very likely to trigger a wave of investment in at least cybersecurity tools, methods, and preparedness. When this happens, use the opportunity to allocate funds and invest in both cybersecurity *and* engineering approaches to reduce or eliminate the most important classes of cyber risk to physical operations. That a business *should* have anticipated these losses and invested pre-emptively in engineering and cyber designs and defenses does not mean your business *did* so. Every crisis is an opportunity to invest in reasonable and appropriate protections.

Determining Criticality

Determining the criticality of a given network can be difficult, and not only when it comes to deciding whether potential losses are reasonable. For example, in an early CIE exercise, participants were given a description of a small city's electricity distribution system, networks and automation. When it came to characterizing network criticality, the IT security and SCADA security practitioners involved in the exercise expressed frustration. They were not able to determine what worst-case consequences were for most of the networks under consideration.

This kind of frustration occurs frequently, not only in training exercises. Cybersecurity practitioners very often have none of the engineering expertise, insights, nor information needed to determine worst case consequences of compromise. Security practitioners often do not know what safety or equipment damage consequences are possible in the physical process. Once these practitioners are told what is possible, they often will not know which safety, protection and control computers are relevant to these consequence scenarios. When safety and protection engineers are involved in the exercise, they can explain what consequences are possible in the physical process, and they may even know some of the computers involved in controlling dangerous processes. However, very often these same engineers do not know what cyber attack scenarios are credible, given a specific set of networks and automation. A fair amount of discussion and even cross-training may be needed to be confident of a criticality determination. This is a new kind of skill the world needs.

Even with all the training in the world, often nobody in the room in a criticality evaluation will know enough to put an answer together:

- In many smaller organizations, some or all engineering functions are outsourced – the people who can answer questions about process safety, and about why a system was designed as it was, work for other organizations and engineering consultancies.
- In many organizations, "as built" engineering documentation is incomplete and knowledge of how and why the physical process and automation evolved over the course of decades is stored only in the heads of individual employees, some of whom have since retired.
- Even in large, well-staffed and very disciplined organizations, "black boxes" purchased as systems of systems from suppliers can pose difficulties. A large wastewater treatment organization, for example, may have installed a gas turbine to generate power from the methane harvested from anaerobic bacterial digesters. A large cabinet full of computers and other equipment is delivered by the turbine vendor to control the unit. The manufacturer assures the water utility that the computers in the control cabinet are "secure." What does this mean? Are there unhackable, engineering-grade protections in the cabinet? What is the worst-case consequence of misoperating the turbine? Manufacturers very often refuse to provide these answers.

And even in a world where complete design information is both available and current, the question of worst-case consequences is not something that current engineering practice demands be documented. For example, conventional power plants must synchronize their water, steam, and gas turbines with the power grid before connecting the generators those turbines drive to the grid. Connecting hundreds of tons of rapidly spinning metal to the grid out of phase leads to enormous stress – stress that very often is enough to tear the turbines to pieces. This is why manual procedures for power plant operators document very carefully how to assure synchronization before connecting a generating unit to the grid.

The problem here is that very often, this synchronization step is a manual process. There is no automation where the operator presses a button that says "synchronize and connect" – so there is no evident automation responsible for the consequence. Yet, if the automation is compromised and executes the commands the operator would have given to connect the turbine to the grid, and the attack carries out this connection out of phase, the turbine is destroyed. The only evidence of this possible outcome lies in the procedures manual used to train the operators. When considering criticality, does anyone in the room read all the operators' and technicians' procedures manuals?

Criticality evaluation errors can work the other way as well. At a recent security conference, I heard an expert describe a scenario for a small, 100MW natural gas power plant in North America. The security and engineering teams were asked the question "What is the longest unscheduled power production outage that the business should regard as acceptable?" After much debate, the engineering and cybersecurity teams agreed that 24 hours was the maximum acceptable unscheduled outage due to a cyber attack.

Digging deeper though, the risk team eventually interviewed the power utility's finance department. Those practitioners observed that the power plant was not deemed critical by NERC, the regulator, nor was the plant essential to any part of the grid's "black start" processes. In fact, the plant only produced power when both:

- The contracted price the plant received for electricity was higher than the combined cost of the fuel and other production costs of the plant, and
- The price of buying the contracted electricity on the spot was higher than the cost of producing the electricity themselves.

In practice, if the power plant suffered an unscheduled outage that could not be made up by other power plants in the power utility's portfolio, then the utility would be forced to purchase power on the spot market, no matter the price. In this scenario, the losses suffered by the utility would be only the difference between the cost of producing the power themselves and the cost of buying the power on the spot market. Looking at trends, projections and worst-case scenarios, the finance department concluded that up to a 30-day unscheduled outage was an acceptable risk to the business.

All this said, it is worth noting that equipment damage is a blind spot in many criticality evaluations. In any power plant for example, worker safety is a constant focus of attention, as is reliability – keeping the plant running to "keep the lights on" for the business and for society. Preventing damage to equipment, on the other hand, is most often the domain of a very small number of protection engineers who rarely visit the plant. Agonizing over whether a 24-hour vs 30-day unscheduled outage and reliability impact is acceptable or not is pointless when the worst-case consequence is in fact an $80 million turbine tearing itself to pieces and taking many months to replace on an emergency basis.

The conclusion here is that it can be difficult to determine what are the worst-case consequences of compromise for any given industrial network, and it can also be difficult to determine whether these consequences are acceptable. In the emerging CIE body of knowledge, determining criticality is a new body of best practices that must be assembled, and in fact may need to be invented.

In a real sense, however, none of this is news. Many parts of the engineering profession work with imperfect risk information routinely. In all such cases, engineers are required to make reasonable decisions, and whenever public safety is at risk, *reasonable* very frequently means *worst case*. For example, if the exact strength of a given formulation of concrete always falls within a range of values, but it is very difficult to predict exactly where in the range the strength of a given batch will land, then engineers designing a bridge with this type of concrete must use the weakest number in their calculations, because the failure of the bridge under load is unacceptable. When we consider network criticality, we can eliminate consequences when we have the information and expertise in the room to do so reliably. The rest of the time, we must assume the worst.

Defining Networks

With this background, we return to the question of what to do with criticality knowledge once we have classified our networks. Our network analysis always results in one of three outcomes:

- We have no critical networks – the design of our physical process and of our business is such that no worst-case compromise of automation equipment can cause an unacceptable consequence. In this case, we engage our IT teams, consider the demands of our insurers, and put suitable IT-grade mitigations in place.
- We have critical networks and appropriate network engineering designs already in place. There is no pivoting path from the Internet into safety-critical, reliability-critical, or business-critical networks. In this case, we continue to Chapter 8.
- We have critical networks and pivoting paths from the Internet into those networks. This is unacceptable, and we need to deploy network engineering techniques to mitigate the risk.

Chapter 5 looked at available network engineering techniques and how to select critical network boundaries to minimize costs and impacts on existing automation designs and business processes. Additional rules of thumb that can prove useful include:

- The SEC-OT methodology points out that it is not only pivoting paths that can communicate attacks. *Any* information flowing into a critical component risks compromising that component or causing the component to malfunction. In particular, serial communications are no panacea – especially when incorrect commands, values and setpoints can be communicated across those serial connections into devices that act on those commands and setpoints without question. Robust designs not only interrupt pivoting paths with non-routable communications, but such designs also minimize the amount of information entering critical networks and components, both by defining network boundaries at points of minimal information flows, and by protecting those boundaries with engineering-grade unidirectional flow controls.

- Safety is easily confused. Many practitioners assume that only SIS equipment is relevant to safety, but this is regularly contradicted in SPR PHA spreadsheets. Mitigations for safety incidents often include alerts shown to an operator with responses by the operator via the HMI software. Mitigations often involve PLCs and other computers that are not SIS equipment. As long as we rely on non-SIS automation to help mitigate safety incidents, the networks containing those PLCs and automation components are safety critical.
- Granularity is easily confused. Many practitioners assume that protecting safety-critical networks is more difficult than protecting reliability-critical networks and so these practitioners seek to define dozens of tiny safety "pond" networks in the bigger "sea" that is the plant-wide reliability-critical network. In fact, the most complex network engineering issues arise at criticality boundaries. The more boundaries we define, the more complex our engineering and security tasks become.

In practice, network engineering is network engineering, whether applied to safety-critical or reliability-critical networks. There are material advantages to defining a single critical network at a plant, encompassing essentially all industrial automation components and sub-networks. Such a single network minimizes the number of criticality boundaries and reduces opportunities for errors and omissions in applying security practices to networks.

Responsibility

Responsibility for the OT cyber risk decision process is a problem in many organizations:

- Engineering teams are generally held responsible for designing systems to address threats to worker and public safety, the environment, equipment protection and continuous operations, threats that include fires, earthquakes, explosions, human error, and deliberate physical sabotage.
- Enterprise security teams are generally held responsible for designing networks and security programs to protect corporate information from cyber threats.

Enterprise security teams often have neither the training nor experience needed to assess and address risks with physical consequences, and engineering teams often have neither the expertise nor authority within the organization to require network-engineering measures to address cyber threats to engineering domains.

The result is sometimes a turf war, and sometimes blind acceptance of risks that neither team nor anyone else in the business really understands.

It is vitally important that businesses bring together cybersecurity and engineering teams to determine network criticality, and to jointly design engineering-grade and network engineering solutions when needed.

Risk Tolerance Directives

Ultimately, the engineers designing physical processes, automation systems and networks will act on the assessments and decisions made above. And at some point, in the hopefully near future, issues of cyber risk and criticality will be widely understood within the profession, within the community of business decision makers and within the greater society, from government policy makers to courts and standards bodies. Until then and possibly even after, engineers asked to design critical systems should insist on having a written statement of what risks the business considers reasonable to accept. If leaders of the project or business are unclear as to what such a statement should contain, then engineers can certainly recommend the statement, but business leaders should sign off on the statement. This is especially true if the engineering team concludes that the business is asking them to undertake unreasonable risks.

Project leaders and middle managers might reasonably expect that their leaders will provide similar statements, in writing and signed. Risk tolerance directives issued by higher-level business leaders might properly be broader and more general than the directives used by specific projects, but risk tolerance directives are reasonable to ask for in any business.

Written cyber risk tolerance directives and cyber risk strategies not only place responsibility for unacceptable risks where that responsibility belongs, at the highest levels of the organization, but these directives can help to address issues with communicating risk tolerance within an organization. In private, senior business leaders often express concern that their priorities for addressing OT cyber risks are not reaching the rank and file in their businesses. Business leaders often see their concerns about safety, environmental and material equipment damage risks turn into action on only regulatory compliance by individual contributors many levels of management lower in the organization. Examples of high-level risk tolerance directives:

- The business shall design physical processes, automation systems and networks such that no Internet-based attack, pivoting through intermediate networks and systems, can reach safety-critical networks or systems.
- Production outages of up to 24 hours due to Internet-based cyber attacks are acceptable. Longer outages are unacceptable, including outages due to Internet-based cyber attacks damaging long lead-time equipment.
- Networks and systems shall be designed such that physical operations can continue at 80% of capacity or greater, even if all IT computers and networks are crippled by a cyber attack. OT systems shall be designed to operate in

this way for up to 10 days. IT networks shall be designed such that the functionality of OT-critical components can be recovered after a worst-case outage in no more than 7 days.

- All systems and networks that must comply with NERC CIP or other regulatory requirements shall comply with those requirements, without exception.
- It is unacceptable that a single, momentary lapse of judgement on the part of one employee, contractor, or visitor – such as clicking on a malicious link or opening a malicious attachment – will put operational safety or reliable physical operations at risk[20].

Note that a risk tolerance policy statement may contain multiple directives such as the ones above. Yes, individual contributors in the North American power sector must be aware of NERC CIP compliance obligations. But they must also be aware of other kinds of cyber risk to physical operations.

A note on compliance – it is often a mistake to focus risk tolerance directives exclusively on compliance. Regulators derive their authority from legislation, and very often that legislation has limited scope. In the USA for example, the Federal Energy Regulatory Commission (FERC) has a legal mandate to regulate certain industries and has delegated authority to the North American Electric Reliability Corporation (NERC) to regulate the reliability of the Bulk Electric System (BES) – the backbone of the North American power grid. As a result, the NERC Critical Infrastructure Protection (NERC CIP) cybersecurity regulations are focused exclusively on the reliability of the grid – the regulations say nothing at all about safety, and likely will never say anything about safety. Focusing tolerance directives exclusively on compliance obligations risks failing to address important cyber safety and other risk scenarios with unacceptable consequences.

OT Cyber Risk Audits

Senior management and boards of directors regularly use external auditors to inspect financial policies, records, and systems to reduce the risk that lower-level managers and employees are misrepresenting financial results, or outright stealing money from the business. For the next decade at least, similar audits regarding OT cyber risk are appropriate in many businesses. While the risk to directors and to the business in the OT cyber realm is not outright fraud and criminality, there are material risks that often justify an external audit, including:

- OT cyber threats are increasing rapidly, and there is a risk that even a well-meaning team has not kept up in their OT cyber risk mitigation plans.
- There are today and will always be far more IT cyber experts in the world than OT cyber experts. There is a risk of IT cyber experts migrating into OT

---

[20] *National Cybersecurity Strategy,* 2023, The White House

cyber risk management programs, misinterpreting what they see, and misapplying their experience and expertise in this critical space.
- There are perennial risks in communicating risk tolerance throughout an organization – with high level directives for safe and reliable operations being lost, misinterpreted, or replaced with compliance directives, as risk tolerance knowledge is passed down to individual contributors.

The role of external auditors should not be to examine every policy and every scrap of record-keeping, but rather to ask questions to gauge the robustness of the OT risk management program. These questions may include:

- Top down: are there company-wide OT cyber risk tolerance directives? Bottom up: if not, is every OT facility in the organization covered by a lower-level or more specific risk tolerance directive?
- Is there evidence that all OT networks have been recently assessed or re-assessed and had the assessment reviewed for criticality? Were those assessments or reviews carried out by individuals likely to have all the knowledge needed for an accurate assessment?
- Is there evidence that OT cyber risk management programs have been implemented that reflect these directives and criticality assessments? Have risk tolerance directives been "lost" in the course of communication with lower-level teams and individual contributors, for example by being re-interpreted as compliance directives?
- Have IT networks been evaluated for criticality as well as OT networks? Have IT resources whose compromise would have material impacts on physical operations been identified and those risks addressed as part of OT cyber risk management programs?
- Do these management programs reflect the latest capabilities in terms of both engineering-grade and IT-grade protections, with each kind of protection used to best effect?
- When these programs require on-going action or attention by engineering teams, security teams, contractors, employees, and other people, is there evidence that these contributors are aware of their responsibilities and are discharging them effectively?
- Have material residual risks been identified lower in the organization, and if so, were they communicated effectively through the management chain to individuals responsible for risk tolerance decisions?

Unfortunately, in most enterprises and industries at this writing, all these issues are problem areas that auditors are likely to find issues with, which only reinforces the necessity of auditing these programs. Worse, at this writing, almost no external auditors are familiar with engineering-grade protections or the principles and practices of network engineering, and comparatively few auditors have experience with OT cyber risk at all, though there are exceptions. None of these are reasons to neglect an external audit, but business leaders selecting an audit team would do well to explore the expectations, qualifications, and preconceptions of any potential audit team very carefully.

Squirrels, Hurricanes and Earthquakes

A common objection to doing anything about cyber risk to physical operations can be phrased in terms of squirrels and hurricanes: squirrels chewing through insulation currently cause more power outages than do cyber attacks. Hurricanes historically have caused more widespread equipment damage and power outages than cyber attacks. Earthquakes historically have caused more casualties at power plants and in power utilities than cyber attacks. Why then, does it make sense to spend any effort protecting against cyber attacks and their consequences, when we already accept these other risks?

Scale is part of the answer here. Squirrels cause power outages in distribution systems, not large generators or transmission grids serving dozens of cities. And – localized power outages in distribution systems are routine. Forget squirrels, most thunderstorms that come through any large city result in a handful of localized power outages that are generally repaired within a handful of hours. These localized outages are widely regarded as acceptable risks, even by the people affected. Installing systems that can completely prevent this class of outage would cost a lot of money and would therefore increase the cost of electric power by more than what the occasional short power outage costs consumers.

We must not, however, mix these analogies. Would we say, "well, squirrels get electrocuted routinely, so we don't need to protect our utility workers from electric shocks?" Would we say, "a hurricane can kill dozens of people, so we do not need to protect our utility workers from electrocution on the job?" No – when the costs of preventing unacceptable consequences is nominal compared to the severity of the consequence, reasonable people deploy protection, even if the protection is not able to address all possible causes.

And again, engineering-grade techniques are used more widely than only in safety-critical or reliability-critical networks. If expensive physical processes, such as the Merck Pharmaceutical $1.4B outage, are at risk, then business leaders and shareholders might well demand that engineering teams deploy engineering-grade protections to avoid those worst-case business outcomes, even if the consequences are acceptable to the business. The issue here is fiscal due care, not safety due care.

We accept material risks of hurricanes and earthquakes when we have no choice – when the cost of eliminating these risks doubles or triples our cost of operations. We accept superficial risks of squirrels and thunderstorms, because the consequences are acceptable. We will however be judged harshly if we accept material risks to save a vanishingly small fraction of our operating costs.

When to Start Thinking About Cyber Risk

A question many practitioners ask is, "When in the lifecycle of a major project should we start thinking about and planning for OT cyber risk?" In practice, many projects do not plan for OT cyber risk management until very late in the project, almost as an afterthought. And if a project is materially delayed or over budget, OT risk management can be set to the side and addressed late in the project or not at all, relying on second-phase or operational funding allocations. Sometimes the question is focused on these problems, and sometimes it is more academic, focused on how premature attention to cybersecurity and cyber risk management issues might "impair innovation" and so put the entire project at risk of failure.

The best answer to this question is with another question: "When do you start thinking about safety?" As a rule, we start thinking about and planning for safety very early in every large industrial project. Safety may not be considered as the very first step in a new kind of project or innovation – the innovation itself must first be created and proven, at least theoretically, to be viable. But no construction planning or actual construction starts until there has been a review for safety, and there is a clear understanding that we will be able to find a path to safe operation of the new process.

In today's threat environment, cybersecurity is essential to safety. If a new artificial intelligence or other initiative hold the promise to materially reduce costs, or increase quality or yield other benefits, yes, we must first carry out tests and investigations to prove the viability of the innovation. But no concrete plans or steps towards implementation can be taken until we have reviewed OT cyber risks for the project, and we have a clear understanding that we will be able to find a path to safe operation for the new invention.

Summary

Due care is doing what any other reasonable person would do in the same or similar circumstances. *Due care for OT cyber risk starts with addressing the pervasive threat – sophisticated ransomware criminals using nation-state TTPs across the Internet.* The engineering-grade conclusion with respect to these threats is that modern RATs and ransomware criminals risk pivoting their attacks throughout any IP-connected network, even passing through firewalls. *Engineers must therefore apply network engineering techniques to critical networks.*

Critical networks are those whose worst-case consequences of compromise are unacceptable. Worst-case consequences are the worst thing that could come about if every CPU in the entire system started issuing the worst possible instructions to the physical operation that the CPU is physically able to issue.

When evaluating network criticality, determining worst-case consequences of cyber attacks takes a lot of knowledge. Determining and tracking such consequences over the life of an industrial installation is something that must become part of good engineering, rather than repeating that work in periodic risk assessments.

Grouping assets and sub-networks into critical networks is somewhat simpler – most sites define a very small number of critical networks, often only one critical network – to simplify securing reliability-critical and safety-critical components. Non-critical components can be included in critical networks, provided that all components in all critical network are secured to the degree of the most critical component, because sophisticated attacks can pivot from less-critical to more-critical components.

As to what is acceptable vs. unacceptable, most organizations define:

- Loss of life is unacceptable,
- Threats to national security are unacceptable, and
- Environmental threats may or may not be unacceptable, depending on the nature and scale of the environmental impact.

Given that we must use network engineering for critical networks, can we use IT-grade protections everywhere else? It turns out this is not the case universally. One way to evaluate whether existing protections constitute reasonable due care is to carry out a table-top exercise. Use the example attacks above the cDBT line in the latest risk report to simulate a credible attack where unacceptable consequences are suffered. What changes would the team make after such an incident? Given that we can predict these outcomes and the changes we would make, is it reasonable to make those changes now in anticipation of the event? Most people would say "yes" – it is not reasonable to delay implementing changes you know you would make the first time you suffered an unacceptable loss.

Risk tolerance directives are cDBT directives issued company-wide and describe specific adversaries and consequences. For example, taking inspiration from the 2023 US *National Cybersecurity Strategy*:

> *It is unacceptable that a single, momentary lapse of judgment on the part of one employee, contractor, or visitor – such as clicking on a malicious link or opening a malicious attachment – will put operational safety or infrastructure essential to national security at risk.*

Just as boards of governors and other senior executives routinely engage the services of external auditors to address the risk of material misstatement of finances, businesses and executives should recruit the services of cyber risk auditors from time to time. These auditors must become familiar with security and network engineering techniques and must start evaluating businesses against the latest due care expectations.

Lesser decision makers within businesses must also become involved in managing the risk of cyber attacks causing unacceptable consequences. cDBT directives for project teams and engineering teams should be consistent with corporate directives and should come from personnel responsible for directly or indirectly managing teams who interpret and execute against the directives. These individuals and teams must begin considering cyber risk to operations at essentially the same time in the project lifecycle as the individuals and teams start thinking about safety.

Finally, we must be careful not to confuse our risk equations. That squirrels historically cause power outages more often than cyber attacks is not grounds to avoid protecting the lives of utility workers from cyber attacks.

Chapter 8 – Residual Risk

Once the risk of remote attacks has been addressed to a standard of due care, we must then ask:

- What cyber risk remains?
- How material is it?
- What must we do about it?

In OT networks with only acceptable consequences of compromise, the answer is often simple: it is often very reasonable to buy insurance, consistently implement at least the cybersecurity measures that the insurance company demands, and work with our enterprise / IT security teams. Enterprise security teams tend to be experts on managing cyber risks to business operations, and can provide advice as to what cybersecurity measures, if any, are needed over and above the minimum that an insurance provider or regulator demands.

Offline Attacks

For critical networks, where worst-case consequences of compromise are unacceptable, we must do more. Engineering teams and enterprise security must cooperate to understand what the risks are, and what measures are appropriate to address those risks. In short, we need to look at all the other ways an attack can occur, once network engineering has reduced the risk of pervasive, very sophisticated Internet-based attacks.

What risks and attack modes remain in critical networks after network engineering? Fundamentally there is only one way that an OT network or system can change from a normal to a sabotaged state – attack information must somehow enter the OT system. There are only two ways that cyber-sabotage attack information can move from outside the OT system to inside the system: online and offline data movement. Online propagation through different kinds of communications and network connections were dealt with in Chapter 5 and Chapter 7. Offline communications are where attack information is carried into contact with OT networks on physical media, including USB thumb drives, laptop computers, cell phones and many more. A reminder – offline communications also include the human brain – if a person has attack information, such as passwords and malicious intent, in their head, that person can carry this information into contact with OT systems and express that information to the system, such as through their fingers on a keyboard. In most cases, there are only three ways that offline attack information can be introduced to an OT system:

- Physical attacks – attackers may physically break into, walk into, or otherwise come into physical contact with industrial sites containing OT systems and networks, physically carrying attacks into the site.
- Well-meaning insiders, from employees to contractors to visitors at a site, may be deceived into carrying attacks with them into the site, or may make mistakes in deploying what they believe to be money-saving innovations into OT networks, "innovations" that are in fact powerful attack vectors, such as Wi-Fi access points.
- Malicious insiders, including disgruntled personnel, personnel compromised by nation states and criminal organizations, and "sleeper" agents planted into the facility long ago may have access or gain access to OT sites and systems.

The capabilities of insider threats and offline attack modes are more complex than the simple "ransomware criminals have access to nation state attack tools" equation in the network engineering arena. We explore the complexity in this chapter and look at what due care means in this more complex arena.

Autonomous vs. Remote Controlled Attacks

A key concept for understanding offline attack flows is the difference between autonomous and remote-controlled attacks:

- Autonomous attacks are malware that acts on its own, completely automatically, without second-by-second inputs from attackers, from insiders, nor from across the Internet.
- Remote control attacks are either attackers logging in to OT systems via remote access systems, or the ubiquitous Remote Access Trojans used by everyone from ransomware criminals to nation state espionage and sabotage agencies to operate their malware interactively across the Internet.

When looking at offline attack risks for critical networks, remote control attacks should not be possible if due-care network engineering techniques have been applied. This is good news, because common wisdom has it that sophisticated adversaries prefer remote controlled attacks. Remote-controlled attacks:

- Are simpler, because human intelligence can be used to analyze feedback and decide what are the most effective next steps in the attack,
- Are better controlled – ransomware criminals do not want to do damage to their reputation in the extortion "marketplace" by destroying information or operational capabilities when the victim has agreed to pay the ransom, and nation states generally desire fine-grained control of their weapons, so that those weapons can be activated when and to an extent that are indicated by evolving battle conditions, and

- These kinds of attacks are safer. Remote-controlled attacks minimize the risk to local agents who might otherwise be called upon to plant and/or give instructions to locally controlled malware.

The clearest example of this lesson that remote control is important for attacks is the NotPetya attack in 2017. Russia is accused of planting the malware in a Ukrainian tax package, which then auto-updated into hundreds of victim organizations. In practice, the alleged Russian attackers lost control of the worm. Yes, many businesses in Ukraine, the presumed targets of the attack, suffered major losses, but there was material collateral damage. For example, Maersk shipping, the world's largest container shipping company, went down for six days, an outage that delayed the shipments of Russian businesses as much Ukrainian businesses, and Maersk was and is not a Ukrainian-owned target.

Arguably, even the famed Stuxnet worm suffered from loss of control. Code in the worm that was intended to limit the spread of the worm contained a bug, allowing the worm to spread without bounds. Eventually, the worm spread to the point where it was reported and analyzed publicly. The presumed targets of the worm, Iran's nuclear weapons program, very likely benefited from the very public analysis and disclosures about how the worm operated. The Stuxnet worm was very complex, representing a huge investment in intelligence and technology, an investment whose value plummeted after these public disclosures.

Common wisdom or no, there currently exist at least three kinds of malware and attacks:

- Manually operated attacks and malware, the most common of which are remote-controlled across the Internet,
- Autonomous, indiscriminate "kill-ware" – malware such as NotPetya and Shamoon that indiscriminately erase or otherwise damage whatever systems they come into contact with, and
- Autonomous, targeted malware – malware such as Stuxnet that carry out very specific actions on very specific targets, doing almost nothing to almost anything else that the malware comes across.

Autonomous, targeted malware is widely regarded as much more expensive and difficult to create than indiscriminate kill-ware and remotely operated attacks. At this writing, most experts believe that ransomware criminals are not willing to invest the amount of money needed to produce capable, autonomous, targeted malware. While intent is difficult to predict generally, in this case most experts believe that nation-states are the only credible threats when it comes to this class of attack. Whether this common wisdom is correct, especially in the coming era of generative AI, is an open question.

Residual cDBT Directives

What constitutes due care when it comes to these offline and insider risks? As always, this depends on the industrial operation, its worst-case consequences of compromise, its regulatory environment, and other factors. That said, a cDBT risk tolerance statement that many industrial sites with robust OT cyber risk management programs use is:

No cyber attack shall be capable of producing unacceptable OT consequences, no matter how sophisticated that attack, without the deliberate cooperation of a compromised OT insider, and even with such cooperation, unacceptable consequences shall be impossible to bring about by any attacker less capable than a nation state.

This is a high bar. On one hand, this tolerance directive means nation states who are willing to invest in Stuxnet-grade attacks installed with the deliberate cooperation of malicious insiders are still a threat – such attacks are above the cDBT line. The directive also means that we require our organization and OT risk management program to reliably defeat pretty much any lesser attack. In particular, it means that our OT cyber risk program must address:

- Remote attacks – Network engineering sufficient to prevent any remotely initiated and operated attack from reaching a critical network – these attacks were addressed in previous chapters,
- Physical attacks – Techniques and technologies to reliably defeat disgruntled insiders, vandals, hacktivists, criminals, and other less-than-nation-state attackers who may have legitimate access to critical facilities, or who may physically break into those facilities carrying malware and/or malicious intent, and
- Autonomous attacks – Mechanisms to reliably prevent well-meaning insiders from inadvertently allowing autonomous attacks to enter our critical networks, even malware originating with nation-state adversaries.

Given the example cDBT directive, physical attacks by professional spies with nation-state support are out of scope, as are disgruntled or compromised employees cooperating with nation-state-grade adversaries. We look at what can be done to address these threats later in this chapter.

Physical Perimeter

Physical security is essential to both cyber and physical risk management. Large industrial sites, such as power plants and refineries, should be physically protected by sophisticated security personnel and systems: so-called "guards, gates and guns." Typical physical protections at large sites include:

- Fences and other barriers to slow down vandals, thieves and other attackers trying to enter a facility surreptitiously,
- Video monitoring and recording of the physical perimeter,

- Identity and authorization checks at gates, to provide a high degree of confidence that individuals who are entering a facility are both authorized and not impersonating authorized personnel, and
- Practiced incident response teams for physical security incidents where unauthorized people are found in the site.

Physical security experts generally understand these topics and mechanisms much better than do cyber experts, with one important exception – OT networks that extend through the physical perimeter. For example, an OT penetration tester tells the story of how their consultancy was engaged to try to break into an OT network at a large power plant. After some investigation, the white-hat attackers decided that the fastest way into the network was to try to enter the facility physically. As part of a deeper investigation of physical attack options, the attackers noticed that an office building just outside of the plant's security fence was being used as "overflow" office space – many plant employees worked in the building.

Further investigation on social media revealed that many of those "overflow" employees were engineers and technicians involved in maintaining, testing, and upgrading OT systems. A quick reconnaissance showed that physical security at the building was almost non-existent – the main door on every floor used by power employees was unlocked during business hours, with a receptionist asking visitors who they were, and who they wanted to see.

One of the penetration testers purchased a half dozen large pizzas and presented himself as a delivery person for one of the engineers with social media accounts. The receptionist gave instructions to the engineer's office and the attacker walked in. Walking through the empty hallway, the tester carefully opened doors into what looked like service closets. They continued this way, finding a small room containing computers, switches and a lot of wiring running into the ceiling. The penetration tester stepped into the room and pulled three Wi-Fi access points and cabling out of their backpack. The tester hid the access points in the ceiling crawlspace and ran cables to each of the three large switches deployed in the room. The tester then stepped back into the hallway, left the pizzas in the kitchen, and exited the facility.

Sure enough, one of the switches was part of the OT network. The attack team returned the next day with laptops in hand, bought coffees at the coffee shop on the main floor of the building, connected to the Wi-Fi several floors up and proceeded to log into the OT network to acquire the screen shots and the other evidence they needed to prove that they had achieved their contracted penetration objective.

The lesson here? Yes, the physical infrastructure of the power plant was protected by a sophisticated physical security perimeter and security systems. The cyber infrastructure, however, extended *through* that physical perimeter and was exposed to physical attack in less secured outside areas. This lesson and some other key lessons for interactions between physical security and cyber risk:

- When physical security protects the safety of the public from dangerous industrial facilities or protects the safety and reliability of those facilities from the public, OT automation systems critical to safety and reliability must be protected as thoroughly as the physical infrastructure.
- Whenever possible, critical OT networks must be entirely contained within a physical security perimeter – any extension out of the perimeter is exposed to physical attack.
- Furthermore, the computers and automation that are used to manage physical security, such as video cameras, door swipes, door locks, and visitor identification systems, must be secured from cyber attacks, at least to the level of the capabilities of physical attackers we are required to defeat reliably. Physical security is singularly vulnerable when access control and other automation are easily breached.

Combinations of the above make sense as well. Computers and networks involved in physical security and physical access control systems should not extend outside of the physical security perimeter either.

An emerging physical threat is drones, not least because in some jurisdictions it is illegal to interfere with even a malicious drone, since all drones are classed as aircraft. Given today's drone capabilities, we should not expose out of doors any USB ports, network ports nor other ways to transfer information into control systems, in any location that is conceivably accessible to drones.

Unstaffed Sites

Remote, unstaffed sites are more difficult to secure physically than central sites. Communications media that generally connects remote sites to central SCADA systems are outside of any physical security perimeter and so are more vulnerable to tampering. In addition, with a few tools and very little skill, attackers can simply cut through fences and shed walls, ignoring gates and badge swipe systems. Worse, in many remote sites, even if the intrusion is detected immediately, it can take tens of minutes or more before the first employees or law enforcement personnel arrive at the site.

In that time interval, attackers could physically access and misoperate computers at the site or could carry out a "leave behind" attack. Leave-behind attacks are straightforward to carry out at such sites and can be very effective. In a leave-behind attack, the attacker's motive is not to steal or damage anything, but to leave behind an attack tool, similar to the Wi-Fi router in the power plant penetration test above.

For example, electric utility substations are almost always small, unstaffed sites and many substations are very remote from anyone or anything else. Thieves routinely target substations to steal valuable copper. Note that it is a very bad idea to try to steal copper from a high-voltage substation – thieves routinely suffer electrocution and death during such thefts. Nonetheless, thieves routinely break into substations to steal copper. A moderately-resourced cyber vandal – a hacktivist – might take it upon themselves to cover their face and their car's license plate to defeat video surveillance, drive out to a distant substation and break in. They further break into the automation shed inside the fence they've cut through, taking care to smash all the video cameras in the shed.

Then they tape a laptop computer containing a "burner" SIM card under a shelf in the shed and connect the laptop to power and to a network switch. On their way out of the shed, they steal something – a computer or three, or an uninterruptable power supply, or some copper if they see it stored somewhere that does not seem energized. And they leave.

Incident responders arrive. An investigation ensues. The authorities conclude that the motive was theft, and they wrap up the investigation. A month later, the attacker returns and parks some distance away, with a directional antenna to gain access to the Wi-Fi signal. Or if the leave-behind was a laptop with a SIM card, the attacker can connect into the substation across cellular network, from anywhere on the Internet. Best practices to protect remote, unstaffed sites include:

- Video and other surveillance systems detect attacks in progress and minimize the time needed to dispatch response personnel,
- Passwords and two-factor authentication protect any exposed user interfaces at the site, so that attackers cannot simply walk up to a screen and start using it,
- Firewalls or unidirectional gateways at the remote sites and at the central SCADA site to limit communications that can be exchanged with the remote site,
- Firewalls or other technology to provide strong encryption for all communications between remote sites and other destinations, such as central SCADA systems, and
- Network intrusion detection systems deployed at remote sites to raise alarms when suspicious cyber activity is detected, during and after a physical intrusion. The very simplest of these kinds of alarms is arguably among the most valuable – alarms when new equipment is detected.

IDS sensors in remote sites and indeed throughout OT networks should be programmed to alert when unrecognized devices are connected to OT networks. All such alarms must be investigated to determine whether the new equipment was in fact authorized as part of an approved change process, someone mistakenly using unauthorized laptops or other computers on sensitive networks, a well-meaning engineer or technician deploying a new Wi-Fi access point or other unauthorized device to make work "more convenient," or in fact a cyber attack or leave-behind attack.

In addition, it is very useful when the communications systems used to connect to remote sites do not have the ability to connect the remote sites to each other. Many remote sites have no need to connect to each other, they need to connect only to the central SCADA system. Designing the communications system so that direct communications between remote sites is impossible prevents a leave-behind or other attack at a remote site from impacting other remote sites directly. In this design, all attacks from one substation to another must pass through the central site, which is generally more heavily defended and heavily monitored, and so more likely to result in attacks being detected or defeated.

In practice, engineering-grade central routing can be cost-prohibitive. Old fashioned modems and leased serial / telephone lines could do this, but with very limited communications bandwidths. Modern leased T1 and MPLS lines can do this as well but may not be available or may be cost prohibitive for the most remote of sites.

More generally, remote sites are problematic for more reasons than cyber risk. Attackers have been known to shoot holes in substation transformers, pole-top transformers, and transformer cooling equipment. Protecting remote power systems, pipeline system and other industrial systems from this type of physical sabotage is difficult and is beyond the scope of this text.

Transient Devices

Insiders can mistakenly carry cyber attacks into critical networks. Again, most modern attacks are Remote Access Trojans, and these widely used Trojans require connectivity with an external attacker to operate. These Trojans may be annoying because if they are introduced, we need to clean them out eventually, but they cannot carry out attack commands because they cannot penetrate network engineering designs to communicate with attackers.

Autonomous malware is still an issue however, and the example cDBT directive states that while deliberately cooperating insiders are above the cDBT line, deceived insiders are below the line, even when it is nation-state attackers deceiving the insiders. In practice, there are only three offline ways that autonomous malware can enter an industrial system:

- Via removable media, such as DVDs, thumb drives and USB hard drives, that "picked up" attack software in the course of using the media,
- Via computers that are in use for some purpose, such as laptops or cell phones, which have become contaminated with malware, or
- Via computers, media, or other components able to store information, that ere contaminated by the manufacturer or during the manufacturing process.

These latter attacks are a subset of the much-discussed category of supply chain attacks and will be dealt with later in this chapter.

Note that in theory other attack vectors are possible. For example, a complex QR code printed on a package of copper cable entering a power plant might be designed to exercise a zero-day vulnerability in a QR code reader in a tablet computer that is connected to the plant's OT network. In practice, such compromises can carry only very little information, and it is very difficult to put a credible autonomous attack malware together out of only a few hundreds or even a couple thousand bytes of information. Worse, most computers that use shipping information and are thus exposed to this kind of attack are hosted on business networks, not critical networks. On the other hand, while any such attack gives up the ability to activate, deactivate or control it remotely, it is still something to be aware of for the future.

Given our example design basis threat directive, we must assume that the malware on our media or computers can be very sophisticated, produced by nation-state threats. Our goal, therefore, must not be to be "smarter than the malware" – this may not be possible with a nation-state adversary. Our first goal is to, as much as we can, prevent this attack information from entering our critical networks in the first place. To this end, techniques from Chapter 4 of *Secure Operations Technology* are relevant, including:

- Train all employees, contractors, and other contributors that for our critical OT networks, external information is a threat more than an asset. Train our people not to connect to critical networks any physical media that has ever been exposed to external information sources.
- Physically disable all DVD drives, floppy drives, USB ports, and other ways to connect to external media on all automation devices that do not need such media to function.
- When removable media cannot be avoided – USB ports for example are the only way to change the programming of some PLC devices – use only media that are clearly labeled for use on OT networks only. Never share media between IT and OT networks.
- Have a pool of OT laptops or tablets when you need these devices for visitors or contractors. This equipment is configured offline, using original software media, and has never been connected to an IT network nor to the Internet.
- When possible, use software systems to prevent unauthorized media from being connected to or mounted on industrial equipment, and software systems to prevent sensitive OT laptops, tablets and other computers from recognizing IT network or Internet connections, even if the computers are accidentally connected to the wrong network.
- Use host IDS and network IDS systems to alert when foreign media and computers are connected to OT hosts and networks and follow up these alerts to understand why they occurred, and when appropriate, offer awareness and remedial training to employees using media and transient computers mistakenly.
- When complex incoming information is unavoidable, such as a manual anti-virus signature update, or a new version of control system software, deploy that information first to an engineering testbed. Such test beds are most often heavily instrumented to detect whether new software exhibits any defects or

behavior that might put critical operations at risk. Modern test beds are instrumented to detect suspicious behavior as well – for example, advancing the clock faster than normal to try to trigger autonomous time-bombs, inspecting network traffic very aggressively for anomalies, and so on.

The above mechanisms are intended to teach insiders about the dangers of all external information, and to develop and reinforce technology, behaviors and habits that simply do not permit attack information to propagate accidentally to critical OT systems and networks.

Note that with autonomous malware, OT intrusion detection / response / recovery systems deployed on critical networks are generally too late. By the time such systems detect anomalous malware carrying out an attack, the consequences of the attack have generally started to be realized. Autonomous attacks can be very fast. Intrusion detection, response and recovery systems still make sense to deploy, because we need to be aware of how much trouble we are in and when we need to shut down operations.

Disgruntled Insiders

Disgruntled insiders are almost never cyber attack experts, but these insiders do have passwords and physical access to systems that other attackers either do not have or must invest effort and sometimes physical risk to acquire. Common mitigations for disgruntled insiders include detailed monitoring as well as access management. We deal with access management first.

Thus far, we have said very little about this staple of IT cybersecurity: identity and access management (IAM). On a great many IT networks, IAM is code for "Microsoft Active Directory" (AD) – the system that manages passwords, identities, permissions, and many other aspects of modern Windows-based networks. While in many OT networks, most devices do not support Active Directory, and historically most devices did not support any sort of IAM, modern OT devices generally have some kind of support for IAM. Modern devices generally define at least a handful of roles:

- Administrator – able to do everything,
- Operator – able to operate physical processes using the automation, but not able to manipulate the automation in other ways, and
- Technician – able to initiate diagnostics, reboot devices, and carry out other tasks short of reprogramming the devices.

What exactly these tasks mean depends on the device – a serial communications aggregator is different from a process historian, which is different again from a leased spectrum wireless access point.

IAM is generally deployed for at least two reasons: to impair attacks by disgruntled insiders, and to reduce errors and omissions on the part of insiders. The latter is beyond the scope of this text – we are focused on the risk of cyber attacks, not on more general "cyber" risks that include:

- Insider errors and omissions using computers (rather than using wrenches or other tools),
- The potential for programming errors in critical systems leading to malfunctions,
- The fact that computer automation and controls wear out in different ways, and with different failure modes, than do analog systems,
- Concerns that even experts have a poor understanding of how artificial intelligence systems in self-driving cars or OT automation "learn" and what the limits and blind spots of such "learning" are, and so on.

Cyber risks are more than cybersecurity. That IAM addresses one of these issues – errors and omissions – does not mean that all cybersecurity mechanisms are relevant to all cyber risks. That said, IAM is deployed routinely to control somewhat the activities of insiders who may wish to use their cyber permissions and knowledge of industrial operations to cause harm.

Furthermore, IAM addresses only the least sophisticated attacks, and that only partially. For example, in any operation with material safety risks to workers, most often any worker who discovers a truly unsafe condition can trigger an emergency shutdown of some or all of the physical process. This might be with a button on an HMI, or a command typed to a device, or more commonly, a "big red mushroom button" – generally with an easily removed cage protecting the button from accidental activation. No amount of permission controls can prevent this threat – safety shutdowns must be triggerable at any time by almost anyone – password-protecting these emergency mechanisms introduces more failure modes than they address. IAM systems can also be bypassed with credential theft, with attacks that exploit software vulnerabilities, and with other attacks, such as the very technical Windows "pass the hash" attacks.

To address this risk, most critical sites deploy extensive physical and cyber monitoring systems. Video cameras record who triggers safety shutdowns. Audit logs record which command coming from which computer carried out which potentially dangerous function. Further, video recordings give us a clear idea of who was sitting at that computer when it issued the command, with IAM and other audit logs confirming who was logged in where when commands were issued.

This kind of surveillance does not prevent attacks but does deter them. Surveillance influences insider intent rather than capability. If surveillance records are used routinely in safety near-miss investigations, which occur regularly, then employees and contractors are reminded that everything they do is being recorded, for their own safety.

Supply Chain

The second way that insiders can be deceived into carrying autonomous malware into sites is supply chain attacks. Note that the term "supply chain" means many things to many people, and at this writing is still evolving rapidly. Currently supply chain means addressing questions and risks including:

- Are my suppliers trustworthy? Or can governments, criminals or others induce these suppliers to insert malware or remote-control hardware into the components they send to my organization?
- Are my suppliers secured? Are their manufacturing, transportation, and inventory management system such that malware or hardware components cannot easily be introduced into the products they ship without the supplier or anyone else noticing?
- Are my suppliers thorough? For every component, product, system, or system of systems they ship me, can they explain who manufactured every piece of it and assure me all those component manufacturers are in turn trustworthy, secure, and thorough?
- Are my suppliers transparent? Do they supply me with hardware and software bills of materials that I can use to verify that none of my product's components have known vulnerabilities?
- Are my suppliers doing business legally? Do they prohibit purchases from banned businesses, distributors and other businesses that are listed in various jurisdictions as fronts for terrorism or that channel money to terrorists? Can they assure me that the same is true for all their suppliers and those suppliers' suppliers?
- Are my suppliers immune? Are they immune to very sophisticated attacks such as the SolarWinds incident, where the supplier was all the above, and still the nation-state breached the product development system and silently inserted malware into the product SolarWinds was distributing?

All these and more are the modern supply chain, and the term continues to evolve to mean even more concerns and scenarios. And no, almost no supplier can satisfy the trailing "immune" requirement today.

The piece of this very big space that is the most relevant to critical OT networks is the fact that, no matter how autonomous malware or remote-control hardware may have been introduced into a product, we cannot let those attack components loose on our critical networks. For autonomous malware embedded in a product, it is vital that we test our incoming products thoroughly on our heavily instrumented test bed / sandboxes before we deploy the tested components on industrial networks. This is expensive, doubly so if we are to have an emergency repair capability. For such a capability, we need an inventory of already-tested components that we can use to replace on a moment's notice any production component that fails.

Wireless Hardware and Malware

Wireless malware is especially difficult. The conceptually simplest wireless attacks are signal jamming – sending a strong "noise" or other signal that interferes with normal wireless communications. Signal jamming is something that many security practitioners neglect as a risk – all the encryption in the world will not prevent a directional antenna from being left on a nearby rooftop to cripple some or all of a plant's wireless communications systems. When crippled wireless systems are essential to plant operations, a plant-wide shutdown is possible. Drones can also carry signal jammers into very close proximity with important wireless receivers and access points.

More generally, wireless tampering is an exception to the "network engineering prevents remote control" rule we postulated earlier. If a nation-state adversary can deceive an insider into activating malware on a device capable of wireless communications, such as any modern laptop or tablet, and the malware can take over the wireless communications capabilities, then the malware can enable wireless remote control for any attacker at least within range of a directional antenna, possibly much further. Directional antennae are routinely able to propagate attack signals over at least several kilometers.

If the wireless communications capability that the malware takes over involves a SIM card, the device can communicate straight out to the Internet over the wireless cell phone network. In this case, a remote attacker on the other side of the planet can operate the malware remotely. And with drones, there is no need to deceive an insider – a drone can carry a SIM-card-based remote control attack deep into a site to access Wi-Fi and other wireless access points, access points that site designers might otherwise have thought inaccessible to external access and tampering.

The wireless problem is compounded by the possibility that adversaries may design undesired wireless communications capabilities, or insert such capabilities surreptitiously, into products destined for critical sites. In this case, both the malware and the hardware are delivered as part of what appears to be a trustworthy product, only to activate later to provide attackers with remote control of the computer, pump, software, or other component they have provided us.

The world's most secure industrial sites are, for this reason and others, very skeptical of the safety of wireless communications. These sites generally forbid wireless communications at their sites. Their contracts forbid wireless components in hardware products that are supplied. They inspect computers and other equipment arriving at their sites for un-ordered wireless capabilities and chipsets. These sites routinely deploy wireless scanners to understand where and what kind of wireless communications are originating in their secure facilities.

Is this due care? This is currently being debated vigorously in many fora. The question of supply chain security shows little sign of consensus on the horizon. This, despite governments in some jurisdictions already passing laws and regulations about some aspects of this expanding "supply chain" issue.

A better answer perhaps is that whether this degree of paranoia regarding wireless communications is justified depends on the criticality of the site. Nuclear generators are different from small shoe factories. Where these extremes of consequence and non-consequence fit into the spectrum of due care paranoia is clear. Where other examples fit, such as large conventional power plants, large petrochemical pipelines, or small petrochemical pipelines, is an open question.

Engineering Discipline

In earlier chapters, we have used the word "engineering" to refer primarily to unhackable, physical approaches to preventing cyber sabotage or the consequences of cyber sabotage. The word "engineering" is used in many other senses in common usage, and one is very relevant to managing OT cyber risk. "Good engineering" is often used as a synonym for robust, disciplined designs for industrial automation. Design principles for disciplined systems engineering include:

- Deep transparency – document the interfaces, behaviors, operating assumptions, and structure of systems and components thoroughly enough for any engineer skilled in the art to look at the documentation and understand the system's capabilities and limitations, how the system might be misused, whether the latest new attack poses a credible threat to the system, and so on. This principle applies from the smallest components and libraries to entire automation systems of systems deployed at industrial facilities. EPRI for example, has a methodology based on such transparency and OSIsoft (now AVEVA) were pioneers in and champions for the methodology.
- Simplification – disable unused libraries, functions, services, and capabilities out of products, operating systems, and devices, because the greater the amount of code running in a product, the easier it tends to be for adversaries to find and exploit software vulnerabilities and other attack opportunities. Or better yet, remove the code / programs / configurations needed only by unused components entirely from systems.
- Spare capacity – design systems with spare network, memory, storage, processing, and other capacities, so that new and enhanced cybersecurity tools and systems can be added to existing systems without risk of exhausting resources and causing existing "brown field" systems to malfunction.
- "Secure by default" – while nothing can ever be "secure," purchase products whose security features are all enabled by default, leave those features enabled, and if you cannot, then deploy engineering-grade compensating measures to address product insecurities.
- "Secure by design" – while no software artifact of any significant size or complexity can ever be "secure" or completely free of defects, purchase products whose vendors can attest to having considered cyber risk and taken at least some measures to address risk from the beginning of their product development processes.

Said another way, a reliable system or component is one that does what it is supposed to do, in the specified environment the system is supposed to operate in, to a specified level of consistency. A robust system is one where: what the system is supposed to do and how it should do that is documented, testable and tested. A secure system is one that does nothing but what the system is supposed to do.

In general, engineers should exercise this kind of discipline when producing hardware and software products for automation systems. Systems engineering teams working for owners and operators should demand products of their vendors that are designed to meet the operating environment and reliability, robustness, and security needs of specific industrial automation systems. Systems engineers must then use those components to design and deploy automation systems that again, meet the needs of the site.

Security needs are difficult to quantify, because security is in principle a negative, not a positive. Proving that a system does only what it is supposed to do under all possible attack conditions is much more difficult than designing tests to demonstrate that the system does what it is supposed to do under all normal and emergency operating conditions. Enumerating all possible attacks is much more difficult than enumerating normal and emergency operating conditions.

A disciplined engineering approach to component, product, and system designs results in automation systems whose residual risks can be more reliably characterized, rather than only estimated using worst-case assumptions.

IT Tools for Residual Risk

A cDBT directive demands that we not only work very hard to eliminate as much as practical the possibility of attacks less sophisticated than the directive, but also that we do what we can above the line. As a result, essentially all physical operations with critical networks not only use cyber-informed engineering, network engineering and other engineering approaches to managing OT cyber risk, almost all use IT-grade protections as well:

- Patch programs make freely downloadable Internet attack tools harder to use for more capable insiders, by reducing the number of exploitable vulnerabilities inside critical networks,
- Anti-malware systems, both anti-virus and application control, deployed wherever practical, increase somewhat the difficulty of insiders introducing common malware silently into critical networks, either deliberately or accidentally,
- Automated asset inventories, bills of materials and known vulnerability analysis and prioritization tools can help automate the process of understanding where hidden software vulnerabilities may still lie, and the process of prioritizing compensating measures, patches or other remediations for those vulnerabilities, and

- Many other tools add security value as well, from filesystem scanners to device communications encryption to compliance managers to risk analyzing attack trees, depending on the nature of an OT network, its criticality, and other circumstances.

Generally, these tools and approaches are applied as universally as possible, given the constraints of the ECC discipline. For example, engineering workstations are generally not involved in minute-by-minute operation of critical networks, and so are able to be patched aggressively, anti-virus-ed aggressively and so on. This is because even if there is a failure of the workstation due to an incompatibility with a patch for example, the workstation being down for a day while it is rebuilt from backups has no effect on the safety or reliability of physical operations. Sometimes IT-style mitigations are applied more selectively – applied most aggressively on those parts or assets within critical networks that are the most exposed to external information, such as those PLCs that must have USB ports enabled for routine reprogramming.

Detect, Respond and Recover

Essentially all industrial sites with critical networks should use both engineering techniques, and to the extent applicable, the full spectrum of the *NIST Cybersecurity Framework* (NIST CSF). This includes the detect, respond, and recover pillars of the framework. Thus far, we have focused on the identify and prevent pillars of the framework, and this is the right thing to do for sites with critical networks. It takes time for human analysts to investigate alerts and conclude that a given set of alerts are a potential attack in progress. It takes time to scramble an incident response team. It takes more time for that team to further investigate and determine that yes, this is a real attack and not a false alarm. It takes even more time to interrupt the attack. For all this time, the attackers are in control of part of our automation, with the potential to cause unacceptable consequences.

Whether the detect, respond, and recover pillars take time or not, no critical site can afford to ignore those pillars of the framework. If an attack, however sophisticated or unsophisticated, penetrates our deterrent and preventive measures, it is vital that we discover that attack promptly and address it promptly. Much has been written about these pillars in the IT space by a great many experts – we reproduce little of that here. When applying these pillars to the OT space, we should keep in mind:

- ***IT-focused asset identification, compliance management, deep packet inspection and other technologies may not recognize or interact effectively with OT systems.*** Even when evaluating technologies that claim to "understand OT," be sure to ask about specific support for the products, protocols, network designs and other aspects of the site's OT systems. An

OT IDS with a deep understanding of only DNP3 and IEC 61850 protocols is not useful to apply to S7 and Data Highway protocols.

- ***Technology to detect attacks on OT networks is only the first step*** – SOC analysts must be trained to interpret alerts from these systems, since both the content of the alerts and their meaning tend to be unique to the OT system(s) being monitored.
- ***Modern OT attack tree tools can add value in the SOC*** – these tools not only model attack opportunities but can model defensive actions to understand how attack opportunities change when specific defensive actions are taken. This information can dramatically reduce incident response delays and can increase effectiveness by automatically recommending what are likely to be the most effective responses to a given attack stimulus.
- ***Incident response teams must practice in each kind of OT environment they will encounter,*** if the cure is not to be worse than the disease. A troop of responders descending on a site and stumbling around systems they are not familiar with often results in outcomes that add up to "I guess it was a false alarm after all, sorry I tripped your plant."
- ***The decision of when to shut down operations is a key aspect of OT incident response*** that has few analogies in IT space. Who is responsible for the decision, who is their backup if the responsible person is not available, what criteria should that person use for the decision, and how will this person acquire the information they need to evaluate the criteria – these issues all need to be documented and practiced. The alternative is chaos during any real or false-alarmed incident.
- ***Recovery and post-incident forensics often benefit from a tamper-proof forensic and backup repository***. Recovery for industrial sites differs from IT sites intensely in terms of the variety of devices and configurations that must be restored. Worse, recovery also depends on the confidence of the engineering team that all equipment has been restored correctly – confidence that is hard to come by if backups were missing or were taken from inconsistent dates and OT configuration versions.

And of course, recovery of operations can be delayed materially by several factors:

- In some industries and jurisdictions, regulatory approval is needed before operations can resume after an emergency shutdown,
- Repairs to, or replacement of, physical equipment damaged in the shutdown, either because of the attack or as a side effect of the emergency shutdown, can materially delay a restart,
- Some physical processes, once engineering teams are confident of their configuration, can start up comparatively quickly. Others take days or weeks.

For example, a power plant that was disconnected from the grid because of an emergency, but whose turbines and generators are still spinning, can be reconnected to the grid, generally within a matter of a day or two. Generators that shut down completely need to undergo a full cold start, which can take two to three times as long. Refineries generally cannot be taken from full stop to full production in less than 10 days. Rail systems, if equipment was not damaged, can generally go from full stop to full speed again within hours.

Government Programs

In the example cDBT directive, the risk of nation states compromising insiders is above the line, but most critical sites with this kind of directive do take steps to address the risk of compromised insiders, employees, contractors, and visitors. Such sites most often involve their government agencies in vetting and tracking these threats.

Governments generally have been dealing with insider threats in a great many contexts, for centuries. Governments very often have entire agencies, programs and infrastructures devoted to these kinds of threats. Governments routinely assist important sites in vetting proposed visitors and services vendors before they visit the site, tracking employees who may be accumulating gambling debts or other liabilities that make them more susceptible to criminal or government compromise, and vetting proposed new employees. None of these programs is fool-proof – in the worst case, we are looking at espionage and counter-espionage activities with enormous resources behind them. That said, involving government agencies in this kind of risk management generally makes resources and insights available to a site that would otherwise simply be out of reach.

Governments are also well known for sponsoring Information Sharing and Analysis Centers (ISACs). These are forums where members can confidentially share information about attacks that they have observed, suffered, or defeated. These are also forums where, given security clearances, government agencies may be willing to disclose classified intelligence they have developed, for example, information from sleepers or compromised insiders in ransomware criminal groups or other nations' intelligence agencies. Again, this is not information that protects a site second-by-second, but it is information that can be used to evolve OT risk management programs with a more sophisticated understanding of adversaries, their intent-of-the-moment, and their attack capabilities.

Summary

IT-class protections are important in almost all OT security programs. For example, if engineering has taken safety and equipment protection risks off the table, and the site in question is not reliability-critical, then IT style protections should be used throughout the industrial network mitigate cyber risks. For critical networks, even when network engineering has eliminated the ubiquitous risk of sophisticated remote-control attacks over the Internet, there is still the possibility of attacks arriving via offline means – compromised USB keys, laptop computers, insiders, and similar attacks.

A common cDBT example regarding USB keys and other offline threats for critical networks is:

> *No cyber attack shall be capable of producing unacceptable OT consequences, no matter how sophisticated that attack, without the deliberate cooperation of a compromised OT insider, and even with such cooperation, unacceptable consequences shall be impossible to bring about by any attacker less capable than a nation state.*

This is a high bar, and generally demands protections including at least:

- Physical security sufficient to keep amateurs and common criminals out of the protected facility, with the cyber perimeter of the critical network contained entirely within the physical perimeter,
- Video surveillance and network IDS systems sufficient to detect "leave behind" attacks,
- A combination of people, process, and technology sufficient to keep removable media, laptop computers and other transient media and devices from being carried into the site and connected to critical networks and equipment,
- Network and host IDS systems that alert on the use of transient media and devices,
- Video, computer, and other surveillance mechanisms visibly deployed and sufficient to protect other employees and the business from the actions of disgruntled employees,
- A supply chain security program, including detailed inspections of and testing of newly received hardware and software components before those components are installed on critical networks,
- Cooperation with government agencies to vet people who work at or visit critical sites, learn about the latest threats and defenses, and share intelligence with similar sites,
- Strict control over wireless communications on critical networks, and use of network engineering to protect critical networks when wireless communications are unavoidable,
- Deployment of cybersecurity tools such as identity and access management, encryption, and firewalls throughout critical networks to address residual insider risks, and
- Sound implementation of the detect / respond / recover pillars of the NIST CSF, as an additional line of defense.

The last point is important – detect / respond and recover are not engineering-grade protection, because they are part of a different NIST CSF pillar. Worse, because people are involved in these processes, there is no such thing as engineering-grade intrusion detection, incident response, or recovery processes. Monitoring our networks and security postures is nonetheless very important, even if it is imperfect. Having practiced incident response teams is important, even if every activation of those teams for a real cyber incident represents a material failure of our cyber risk management program. Having the ability to recover from a cyber disaster as quickly as the business and society demand is important as well.

Finally, even though governments cannot protect us from fast-moving attacks, governments have very valuable threat intelligence, information sharing and other programs from which OT sites can very much benefit. Governments tend to have powerful tools at their disposal for ferreting out compromised or disgruntled insiders.

Chapter 9 – Objection Handling

Having laid out examples of due care obligations in this space, we arrive at the question of objection handling. There are many people involved with OT cyber risk management, many with misconceptions, and many who may express those misconceptions as objections to the measures we looked at in the last two chapters. We have already dealt with some objections and fallacies: confusing compliance with due care for example, backwards-looking statistics versus worst-case analysis, and the risks of self insuring against risks that no insurance company will touch. In this chapter, we look at a few other common objections and how to refute them.

Rigidity

Many stakeholders complain that engineering-grade protections are inflexible or "rigid." If, for example, we learn that we can run our boilers safely and more profitably at three times the maximum pressure, and we have mechanical over-pressure valves deployed, then we need to replace the valves outright, or at least mechanically recalibrate them, to run the boiler in the new high-pressure mode. If we have unidirectional analog signalling between SIS computers and a DCS network in that same scenario, we need to walk over to the isolated SIS engineering workstation to change the SIS pressure setpoint – we cannot do it remotely. These stakeholders and even many IT security experts will argue that an ideal cybersecurity program is invisible and does not impact normal operations in any way[21]. Since many engineering-grade protections are less flexible than IT-grade protections, these stakeholders argue that engineering-grade solutions are less practical. At the very least, engineering-grade solutions often force us to travel to certain processes and automation systems and touch those systems physically, rather than do everything remotely from our home offices on the other side of the world, as we have tried to become accustomed to in the era of the COVID pandemic.

These people are right in terms of the facts they present in their argument, and even in their assertion that remote operations are desirable. They are right that, ideally, cyber risk prevention is as invisible as possible. It is only the conclusion that we should therefore avoid engineering-grade designs that is mistaken.

---

[21] *Good Security Should Be Invisible,* Rashmi Knowles, 2017, https://www.cioandleader.com/article/2017/02/17/good-security-should-be-invisible

Fundamentally, any measure that is effective in addressing cyber risk to physical operations *must* make *something* harder to do. Specifically, every such measure must make attacking automation and sabotaging the physical process harder to do. This will never change. In an era where cyber-sabotage attacks often use the same tools and communications paths as legitimate tasks, this means that cyber risk reduction measures *must* make those communications and tools much more difficult for attackers to use to carry out their sabotage, and sometimes this impacts normal operations as well.

This is less of a problem with security engineering than it is an opportunity for innovation. Some years ago, I heard an expert explain a vision for the Industrial Internet of Things (IIoT). In an ideal world, we would look around and see a problem to be solved or an optimization opportunity to be exploited in some part of an industrial system – say a catalytic cracker in a refinery. In this ideal world, we would go to our favorite IIoT distributor and buy 83 IIoT devices that were sitting in inventory at the distributor. We would connect those devices to the cracker and turn them on. They would automatically reach out to the Internet and rendezvous in a cloud system. They would talk to each other and to the cloud. They would figure out what the problem was, or what the opportunity was, and they would engage controls to solve the problem or exploit the opportunity. The entire solution is standard and interoperable. The entire solution is automatic. The entire solution is remote controlled and integrates seamlessly and automatically with the plant's remote operator sitting at head office on another continent.

In light of the concepts in this book, however, this description triggers many questions. What happens if the cloud is compromised? What if the remote operator station is compromised? What if the Internet is compromised? No wait – that's already happened. What if the device vendor is compromised?

Despite these questions, though, the vision is not wrong. The vision is a great vision. In some industries and physical processes, the vision simply works. In other situations, the real question is *how close can we come to this vision, safely?* The answer, in part, is that it very much depends on the physical process, on consequences, on what engineering-grade safety systems we have deployed, and so on – all topics we covered in this book. The answer, almost all the time, is that we can come very close to realizing exactly this vision, in a great many industries and circumstances. And we could come even closer if our automation or IIoT system or cloud systems were designed just a little differently.

Some of the rigidity of today's security engineering solutions is by design, and possibly even necessary. Some of it is not. Today's rigidity is tomorrow's business and product opportunity. As CIE and engineering-grade security designs become used much more widely and systematically, the market will demand more flexible solutions, to squeeze that last fraction of a percent of efficiency out of our physical processes. And vendors will respond to that opportunity with new products and new flexibilities *within* the security engineering discipline and mindset.

Confusing Windows with Doors

Another objection has to do with residual risk. Some argue that if there is any residual risk of unacceptable consequences, then what value is there in defeating sophisticated Internet-based attacks? For example, a sophisticated remote attack might damage difficult-to-replace high-voltage transformers at a large substation, but so might someone shooting holes in transformers. If the latter is impossible to prevent with engineering-grade protections, what value is there in deploying such protections against the former?

Part of the answer is that this is not usually the same adversary, with the same capabilities. Disgruntled insiders, for example, are not sophisticated adversaries, nor are lone shooters. Physical and cyber surveillance systems can often identify the people behind physical assaults, so that the responsible individuals can be apprehended and prosecuted. This is a strong deterrent for most individuals. None of this is possible for sophisticated remote attackers – these are not apples-to-apples comparisons.

Saying that since we cannot reliably defeat insiders or physical assaults, then there is no point in engineering-grade protections against remote attacks, is like confusing windows with doors. In some neighborhoods, would-be thieves walk through the neighborhoods turning doorknobs. If a door is unlocked, they run in, steal something, and run away. If a door is locked however, a determined thief can take a hammer to our windows, break in that way and steal things. Does anyone say that, because there is always a risk of a thief with a hammer, it makes no sense to lock our doors? Would any court say that insurers must pay out claims to policy holders who never lock their doors, because the risk of windows and thieves with hammers is always there? No – due care demands that we take reasonable measures to defeat pervasive threats, and that obligation is enormously more pressing when pervasive threats risk bringing about unacceptable consequences.

False Economies

Too many people ignore risk when they develop their return-on-investment (ROI) analyses. A small water utility, for example, might have a total corporate budget of only $10 million USD. The IT manager at that utility might come up with a spreadsheet that shows how a small investment in remote access technology will save the utility tens of thousands of dollars per year, by not paying vendors to drive to the utility when those vendors must work on the utility's OT systems.

The problem is that these spreadsheets ignore the cost of risk. Yes, the savings can be measured, and the savings are greater than the cost of purchasing and operating the remote access technology, but what of the risk? Does the utility have a quarter million dollars, or a half million dollars per year to spend on a cybersecurity program strong enough to provide even a semblance of protection from unacceptable consequences? Does the spreadsheet take this cost into account?

When such a calculation concludes that we would save money with remote access, this is a false economy. We appear to save money only because we have not considered all the costs.

It is a controversial position, but arguably small water utilities are much better off with old-school, engineering-grade air gaps than they are with remote access enabled. If we cannot afford the cost of the risk mitigation program, then we should not be undertaking the risks in the name of a false ROI.

Zero Trust and Encryption

Many practitioners and indeed OT cybersecurity vendors argue that we do not need engineering-grade security designs because zero trust will save us. What is zero trust? Everyone has a different definition. There is a formal definition, but it is long and, to most people, incomprehensible. One simple model for zero trust is to compare how a laptop's security works in a public coffee shop versus how a desktop works on a corporate network in an office building.

When we work for a big company and come into our office in the morning, we log into our desktop computer. The computer is wired into the corporate network that runs throughout a floor of an office building. If we need to print a report, we send it to the printer down the hall. The printer does not challenge us for our identity, and communications with the printer might not even be encrypted. Why? Because the printer "trusts" that all computers that are on the network anywhere on the floor are authorized to use the printer.

Contrast that with how a laptop behaves when we are on the move, connecting to the Internet in a coffee shop. If we want a report printed, we log in to the FedEx website, or a similar Internet service, upload our report, give the site our credit card number, and the report comes out on the printer at the provider's location down the street. Communications with the printing vendor are of course encrypted, so that nobody on the Internet can steal our report, our password, or our credit card number. The Internet is the prototypical zero-trust environment. On the Internet, nobody should or hopefully does trust anybody else, everything demands credentials, and all communications are encrypted.

Do these "zero trust" measures prevent our Internet-connected laptops from becoming compromised from time to time? Of course not – we can still download malware from email servers on to our laptops, we can still visit compromised websites that phish for passwords or exercise unpatched or zero-day vulnerabilities in our browsers – there are countless ways of being breached in zero-trust environments.

Zero trust has value, make no mistake, but it is no panacea. Zero trust has obvious value on the Internet, which is why we use it there pretty much universally. Zero trust has value on corporate IT networks, slowing down somewhat the spread and impact of malware or insider attacks. But zero-trust is not engineering-grade protection.

Worse, zero trust is singularly difficult to implement on OT networks, more or less because of key management. One could argue that password management is part of the problem as well, but really it is authentication that is the problem, and both passwords and encryption keys can be used as authentication. For simplicity, consider only encryption keys – the same arguments hold for passwords.

The problem with encryption is managing the keys, so much so that it is a truism in the industry that "encryption is the science of turning every problem into a key management problem." What is the problem? Consider a banking website with 12 million customers. How many encryption keys does the bank manage? A very small number – in theory it can be as few as a single key pair – the private key pair for the banking website. The ubiquitous TLS protocol has the bank use a pair of private keys to calculate a public key, and the bank then publishes the public key using a certificate. Clients all over the Internet connect to the bank website – the website proves it is who it says it is with the certificate, the client verifies the certificate with an Internet-based certificate authority, and the client then uses the public and private keys to negotiate an encrypted connection, so that, for example, other people in coffee shops cannot steal the bank's clients' passwords and bank account numbers.

This asymmetry – 12 million customers and only one web server demands only one key is characteristic of TLS – only the servers need keys. How many servers are there in an OT / industrial network? In such networks, most of the devices accept TCP connections, and so most of the devices are servers. We need a key for more or less every device. That's a lot of keys and certificates to manage. Worse, while non-critical OT networks may be configured to have access to Internet-based certificate authorities, critical networks should never be thus configured.

You might argue that we could use shared private keys instead and not public keys as TLS does, but this only makes the problem worse. With shared private keys, we need a pair of keys for each pair of communicating devices, not just one key per device. Passwords complicate the problem as well – if we use passwords as authentication, we should really have a separate password for each pair of communicating machines. If we use public / private keys as authentication, then we need a permissions system somewhere, to keep track of which machines with which public authentication keys are allowed to communicate.

This sounds like a lot of work. Can somebody not write a program to solve this problem? In theory yes, but in practice, we would need a universal key management standard or protocol for such a program to work. Currently, there is no standard protocol for managing encryption or authentication keys in industrial networks. Some vendors are starting to build their own key management systems, which means their tools work with their devices and not anyone else's. Power meter vendors for example, have sophisticated systems to manage encryption keys in what may be millions of meters in "smart metering" systems, but those key managers do not work on PLCs or protective relays.

A deeper problem is what to do when there is an issue with keys. For example, encryption keys are supposed to have a limited life, to reduce the chance that attackers have stolen private keys or have used supercomputers over the course of months to crack the private keys brute-force-wise. If keys have a limited life, what should we do if a key has expired? Refuse to connect to the offending device? What are the physical consequences of such refusal? Can key management omissions or errors cause our physical process to fail? What happens in the unlikely event that a key expires in the middle of a crisis – a safety shutdown? Does the physical process not shut down and remain in a dangerous state?

Again, zero trust has value, but is not a panacea, and there are difficult issues with implementing zero trust on OT networks, especially critical networks.

Summary

Physical risk is not a topic that most cybersecurity practitioners know anything about, and cyber risk is not one that most engineers know anything about. This can lead to confusion. Some objections and common answers:

Q: What good are engineering-grade protections against ransomware if people can still shoot holes in our infrastructure?

A: These are different adversaries and risks – we don't leave our doors unlocked, even if our windows are glass.

Q: Engineering-grade solutions are inflexible, and therefore cost more money to use than do IT-grade solutions.

A: When and where we use engineering-grade solutions is determined by consequences and risk tolerance directives. That these solutions are less flexible than less-secure IT-grade solutions is immaterial to that calculus. And in the long run, complaints about flexibility will inevitably lead to innovation, just as every other complaint from customers has led to innovation over the last 50 years of the automation industry.

Q: But my spreadsheet shows we would save $7,293.25 every year!

A: This is a false economy unless it considers the very difficult to estimate cost of increased risk of unacceptable consequences.

Q: Is zero trust engineering-grade?

A: Zero trust is how the Internet works. Does anyone on the Internet trust anyone else without evidence? No. Yet, have Internet services ever been compromised? Yes. Zero trust is a useful IT-class solution, not an engineering-grade solution.

Chapter 10 – Conclusion

So, how much *is* enough? In part, the answer is another question – how much of what? Addressing cyber risk to OT systems is (in some sense) a coin with two sides: engineering-grade approaches and IT-grade approaches. As a rule, we need both, pretty much everywhere. We engineer away as much risk as we can with physical and electro-mechanical protections, and we deploy IT protections to address the risk that remains.

How much of each do we deploy? Consequences determine the protections we require. Given that cyber attacks are more deterministic and repeatable than random, the question is not "what is the likelihood of a serious incident?" but rather, "what capabilities does an attacker need to defeat our defenses?" Given that many ransomware groups and other adversaries are using nation-state-grade remote-control attacks across the Internet, the question of *"how much"* for network-based attacks is determined pretty much entirely by worst-case consequences, because nation-state techniques can bring about those consequences, thus:

- Unhackable engineering mitigations are required when safety, equipment damage and environmental consequences are unacceptable. Businesses, workers, and the society all need these risks eliminated, to the greatest extent practical.
- In practice, we are only sometimes able to eliminate all unacceptable risks with process engineering. For example, rail switching systems are computer controlled and wireless, modern electrical equipment protections in the form of protective relays are all hackable software, as are Safety-Instrumented Systems, not to mention that lengthy downtimes of critical infrastructures are unacceptable threats to national security.
- This means that many times, we must also deploy network-engineering protection at network criticality boundaries, to prevent attacks from entering critical networks in the first place.

On the IT side, when consequences are unacceptable, we must look at offline attacks and the people and organizations who are our potential adversaries. How much do we trust our people? Are attacks *on our people* by our adversary credible, for example bribes, threats, or blackmail? We need to decide which classes of cyber attacks we need defeated reliably and issue cyber Design-Basis Threat (cDBT) directives that describes those attacks and attacker capabilities. Governments can help us here as well, with sophisticated threat intelligence about our adversaries' capabilities to target our personnel, and intelligence regarding how susceptible our people are to compromise.

In simpler cases, where engineering-grade designs have eliminated threats to safety, for sites that are not critical infrastructures, and where worst-case costs of compromise are acceptable losses, we have choices:

- We can choose to deploy network engineering mechanisms because they are cost-effective ways of reducing risk, or
- We can deploy IT-grade defenses exclusively, enjoying the added flexibility of software-based solutions, while at a somewhat greater risk of compromise.

In all cases, we should capture our decisions in cDBT directives and communicate those directives widely throughout our organizations, projects, and teams, to avoid common miscommunications, such as confusing compliance with required security.

Whatever we decide, it is important to document our decisions and how we arrived at them, and to revisit those decisions every year or two. The threat environment is evolving quickly, as are professional obligations and societal expectations. When documenting our decisions, it is important to preserve the evidence that we have considered all our targets across a broad spectrum of possible attacks, because, if there is a serious incident, then the courts and other investigators will give us credit for thoroughness of analysis, even if it turns out that our design was not strong enough to defeat a serious attack.

The big changes in the world of OT security that enable the clear decisions above are both changes in the threat environment and changes in our understanding of the role of engineering in the space:

- As cyber attacks with physical consequences continue to more than double annually, no reasonable person can continue to ignore cyber threats to physical operations.
- As threats to safety and national security become clearer, the role and obligations of the engineering profession in addressing cyber risk become clearer.
- As engineers become aware of their obligations and of the limitations of engineering-grade solutions, they become much more willing to engage with IT / enterprise security experts to deploy systems to address residual risks.

All these developments are very welcome to anyone who has followed the field of OT security for any length of time.

Appendix A Hacking Everything

Countless vendors claim to "solve the problem" of cyber risk to OT systems, but there is no "silver bullet." For every defensive posture, there is an attack than can breach it. The question is not whether we are secure or not, but rather how secure are we? Which attacks do we defeat reliably and deterministically, and to which others are we still exposed? Any vendor who claims to sell a "secure" product or service, or claims to solve the OT security problem, without first and very carefully defining precisely what problem the product or service "solves" is deceiving us. And even with careful definition, sometimes they still seek to deceive us.

In this appendix we review common security approaches and technologies. For each, we look at what it does, where and why it makes sense to use in OT environments, the limitations of the technology, and how to defeat it.

Caveat emptor.

Allow-Listing Systems

What they are: Allow-listing systems intercept operating system functions that execute software, restricting execution to a list of "known good" allowed software.

Where to use: Allow-listing systems are recommended for all industrial systems that tolerate this kind of protection. Allow-listing systems are seen as better fits for most industrial environments than anti-virus systems for many reasons. Most allow-listing systems do not need the regular, resource-intensive, full filesystem scans that anti-virus systems need. Allow-listing systems prevent the execution of all known software, including new attack software the system has never before seen.

Intrinsic Limitations: All allow-listing systems are software, with vulnerabilities known and unknown that can be exploited. Allow-listing systems generally intercept and check the validity of software as it is loaded into memory for execution. As such, these systems tend to be blind to over-the-network in-memory attacks. These systems can also be blind to scripted malware arriving as text files and executed by interpreters that are allowed to execute because they are needed in parts of the automation system. Allow-listing systems are also vulnerable during software / security updates. During such updates, new software must be registered as "allowed." Allow-listing systems are therefor vulnerable to attacks that masquerade malware as legitimate software during installation and update processes.

Anti-Virus Systems

What they are: Anti-virus systems are Host IDS systems with extra functionality to prevent writing malware to disk, loading malware from disk, executing malware or otherwise interrupt attacks in progress, hopefully before those attacks cause unacceptable consequences.

Where to use: Anti-virus systems are recommended for all industrial systems that tolerate or support these systems. Like Host IDS systems, however, many industrial devices do not support the installation of third-party software such as anti-virus systems or come with a built-in anti-virus system and support only that one. Many industrial systems cannot tolerate full filesystem scans and may not have been tested for safe and reliable operation with anti-virus functions intercepting system functions to understand what the protected host is doing that might be suspicious.

Intrinsic Limitations: All anti-virus systems are software, with vulnerabilities known and unknown that can be exploited. Signature-based anti-virus can only detect "old" attacks – attacks that vendors have seen already and for which signatures have been produced, distributed, and installed. Anomaly-based anti-virus can detect attacks that "look" suspicious with respect to the characteristics the built-in host IDS function is monitoring / learning. A big risk for anti-virus systems is false alarms – if a defective signature file is loaded into an anti-virus system, that system risks quarantining or otherwise interrupting the correct function of legitimate automation and operating system software.

Data Diodes

What they are: The US NIST glossary defines data diodes as hardware that is physically able to send information in only one direction. If you Google "data diode" you will find close to 100 vendors world-wide, with each vendor selling their product to their local government. Data diodes are used routinely to send data into classified government and military networks with no ability to leak national secrets data back into unclassified networks or the Internet.

Where to use: Data diodes are recommended at consequence boundaries that connect classified government or military networks where worst-case consequences of data theft are unacceptable, to unclassified networks.

Intrinsic Limitations: Good data diodes deterministically control the flow of network packets and network information – diodes do nothing about potentially contaminated USB drives or laptops, or cell phones being carried into OT networks. Data diodes are hardware-intensive solutions. Most diode vendors provide little or no software to go with their products, preferring to develop any needed software on a custom engineering basis for their government and military customers. What little software diode vendors do provide tends to have low sales volumes, which means the vendors are not able to invest in features such as web-based or graphical user interfaces. When diode vendors provide software with their products, that software – like any software – has vulnerabilities that can be exploited. On the other hand, even if such vulnerabilities are exploited, the hardware in true data diodes is still physically incapable of leaking government secrets.

Firewalls

What they are: Deep in the heart of every firewall is a router, because like routers, firewalls forward network messages from one network to another. Most firewalls are of course much more than routers – firewalls also contain software that looks at each message trying to pass through the router piece of the firewall and asks the question "is this message allowed?" If the software decides the message is allowed, it forwards the message, otherwise it most often drops the message. Modern / next-gen firewalls generally also have built in VPNs, IDS's, IPS's, and "deep packet inspection" that claims to understand many IT and sometimes OT protocols and let you craft rules such as "allow Facebook status updates, but do not allow images to be posted" and "allow writes to these Modbus registers, but not those."

Where to use: Firewalls are used most effectively between networks at the same level of criticality. That is: within industrial / OT networks, within business networks, and between business networks and the Internet. Properly configured firewalls can stop or slow down many kinds of online cyber-sabotage attacks that originate on external networks.

Intrinsic Limitations: Firewalls control the flow of network packets – they do nothing about potentially contaminated USB drives, or laptops, or cell phones being carried into OT networks. Almost all modern, popular firewalls are complex and easily misconfigured in ways that are difficult to detect. Firewalls are intrinsically software, with vulnerabilities – for evidence of this look at your favorite firewall vendor's website and count the number of security updates they've issued recently. Exploit these vulnerabilities and the protective function of the firewall can be subverted. There are many other ways that attackers defeat firewalls, for example disguising attacks inside packets that look legitimate to the firewall, so the firewall passes the attack through to the protected network. For evidence of how porous firewalls are, look at ransomware attacks. Almost all the hundreds of thousands of ransomware attacks that reach IT networks every year pass through the organization's IT/Internet firewall.

Host Firewalls

What they are: Host firewalls are firewall software built into hosts. Instead of routing allowed messages from one network to another, host firewalls inspect traffic, decide if it is allowed, and permit allowed incoming messages deeper into the host for processing, or allow messages to leave the host destined for various networks.

Where to use: Host firewalls are recommended on all industrial equipment, but can be difficult to apply to existing installations, and difficult to manage as communications needs evolve, typically very slowly, over time.

Intrinsic Limitations: Host firewalls control the flow of network packets – they do nothing about potentially contaminated USB drives or DVD media entering a computer. Host firewalls are software, with vulnerabilities. Many host firewalls come with built in network IPS capabilities, with all the limitations of those systems. Modern attacks, however, rarely exploit host firewalls. More commonly, these attacks are carried into compromised hosts inside of encrypted, allowed connections to other hosts, users, and devices – connections that the host firewall is configured to permit.

Host Intrusion Detection Systems

What they are: Host IDS look at files, memory, kernel calls and other characteristics of computers (hosts), looking for indicators of an attack in progress. Signature-based systems match host characteristics against rules / signatures looking for a match. When a match is found, an alert is generated warning of a potential attack in progress. Anomaly-based systems use "machine learning" to look at patterns of host / memory / CPU activity and raise alerts when unusual changes are detected in these patterns. Vendors compete on patterns, and common patterns include file names, contents, and hashes, unusual patterns of execution such as connecting to another process in debug mode, requests to the computer user to escalate privilege, installing software and especially device drivers and many other patterns.

Where to use: Host IDS are used much less commonly than host IPS systems, such as anti-virus and application allow-listing systems. Host IDS or IPS are recommended for all industrial systems that tolerate or support these systems.

Intrinsic Limitations: All host IDS are software, with vulnerabilities known and unknown that can be exploited. Signature-based IDS can only detect "old" attacks – attacks that vendors have seen already and for which signatures have been produced, distributed, and installed. Anomaly-based IDS can detect attacks that "look" suspicious with respect to the characteristics the IDS is monitoring / learning. Attacks that "look" normal can go unreported. False alarms / false positives are a bane of all anomaly-based host IDS systems. System administrators often need to "tune" IDS systems to eliminate false alarms. "Low and slow" attacks can defeat IDS as well – attacks that change the "normal" behavior of compromised assets over time so slowly that normal machine learning and false alarm elimination processes "tune out" the attack indicators. All IDS are also susceptible to alert flooding attacks, where the attacker creates a "noisy" distraction in another part of the business that creates many high-priority alerts while pursuing the attacker's real objective creating only a few low-priority alerts. And in the end, fast attacks risk bringing about unacceptable consequences despite IDS, because human or even automated incident response is too slow to prevent the consequence. Many low-level devices such as PLCs do not support the installation of third-party host IDS or run operating systems for which no such systems exist. Many parts of industrial control systems cannot tolerate the long file-system scans used by signature-based systems because of the performance impact of such scans, and critical systems may not have been tested for compatibility with arbitrary Host IDS or IPS systems.

Host Intrusion Prevention Systems

See:

- Anti-Virus Systems
- Allow-Listing Systems
- Host firewalls

Identity and Access Management

What they are: Identity and Access Management (IAM) systems manage passwords and permissions. On Windows networks, Microsoft's Active Directory products are the most widely used IAM systems. The term IAM can also refer to built-in users and permissions in software, hosts, and devices, not only external IAM services.

Where to use: Users, passwords and permissions are recommended for most industrial systems that tolerate such protections. Exceptions are equipment that is involved in or can trigger emergency shutdowns – as a rule, safety shutdowns must be triggerable by any person in an unsafe environment, whether or not they have or remember a password. Older systems such as PLCs, RTUs, and other embedded devices may support only one or a very limited number of users, permissions, and roles. Some systems, such as HMI workstations, have timing constraints that prohibit using operating system usernames, passwords, and permissions. Dangerous physical processes, such as petrochemical pipelines, can only be operated "blind" for a limited number of seconds before an emergency shutdown is required. It can take much longer than those limited number of seconds at shift change for the outgoing operator to shut down all applications and log out, so that a new operator can log back in and restart all the applications.

Intrinsic Limitations: All IAM systems are software, with vulnerabilities that can be exploited. Indeed, Active Directory (AD) systems are prime targets of remote-control attacks. The attackers find some way to steal AD administrator credentials or otherwise take over the AD server, create new accounts for themselves with universal access, and log in using those accounts to work their will upon the network of systems. IAM servers are not security tools – they are identity and permission *management systems* that urgently need to be secured.

Intrusion Detection Systems

See:

- Host Intrusion Detection Systems
- Network Intrusion Detection Systems

Intrusion Prevention Systems

See:

- Host Intrusion Prevention Systems
- Network Intrusion Prevention Systems

Network Encryption and Authentication

What they are: Encryption and cryptographic authentication are tools used to protect communications sessions from man-in-the-middle attacks. These are attacks where an attacker who has access to the communications system steals information, such as passwords, from the communications, or injects malicious commands into the communications, "hijacks" the communications session, taking the place of one of the endpoints, or otherwise impersonates a legitimate endpoint. Encryption is a mathematical algorithm that combines plain text with keys in such a way as to produce encrypted text that is indecipherable but can be turned back into the original plain text by a recipient with the right keys. Cryptographic authentication is a tamper-detecting "signature" that can be appended to messages, much like conventional error-detecting checksums.

Where to use: While there is a clear consensus that encryption and authentication are essential when communicating across the Internet, there is less consensus in OT environments. Some experts recommend that these cryptographic measures be deployed throughout industrial control systems, from the very lowest to the very highest levels. Other experts observe that this is most often impractical, because of the difficulty of managing encryption keys in these challenging environments. At this writing, practical key management tools for industrial networks exist in only very limited domains – there is no such thing as a cross-vendor, cross-platform encryption and key management tool that can be used for IP network communications, serial communications, and every other kind of communications in an industrial automation system.

Intrinsic Limitations: The simplest way to defeat cryptosystems is to steal the key information. More fundamentally, all cryptosystems are software and thus have vulnerabilities, both discovered and undiscovered. By far the most common way to defeat cryptosystems is neither of the aforementioned, but rather to compromise an endpoint of the encrypted communications and use that endpoint to pivot attacks inside of encrypted, authenticated communications to other devices the compromised endpoint can communicate with legitimately.

Network Intrusion Detection Systems

What they are: Network IDS look at network packets exchanged on a wire or fibre via a tap or exchanged within a managed network switch via a mirror / SPAN port. Signature-based systems match packet contents or sequences of packets and contents against rules / signatures looking for a match. When a match is found, an alert is generated warning of a potential attack in progress. Anomaly-based systems use "machine learning" to look at patterns of communications and raise alerts when unusual changes are detected in these patterns. Vendors compete on patterns, and common patterns include traffic volume, volume per type of connection, sources and destinations of connections, new / unrecognized equipment connected to the network, and which PLC or device registers are being read from or written to. Many Network IDS products have built-in asset inventory features.

Where to use: Network intrusion detection systems are recommended for most industrial networks and IT networks for that matter. We can only optimize what we measure, and so monitoring and measuring what is going on with network communications provides important insights. And if our protective measures fail, Network IDS gives us some hope of detecting attacks in progress and triggering incident response actions before we suffer unacceptable consequences.

Intrinsic Limitations: All network IDS are software, with vulnerabilities known and unknown that can be exploited. Signature-based IDS can only detect "old" attacks – attacks that vendors have seen already and for which signatures have been produced, distributed, and installed. Anomaly-based IDS can detect attacks that "look" suspicious with respect to the characteristics the IDS is monitoring / learning. Attacks that "look" normal can go unreported. And false alarms / false positives are a bane of all IDS systems. System administrators often need to "tune" IDS systems to eliminate false alarms. "Low and slow" attacks can defeat IDS as well – attacks that change the "normal" behavior of compromised assets over time so slowly that normal machine learning and false alarm elimination processes "tune out" the attack indicators. All IDS are also susceptible to alert flooding attacks, where the attacker creates a "noisy" distraction in another part of the business that creates many high-priority alerts while pursuing the attacker's real objective creating only a few low-priority alerts. And in the end, fast attacks risk bringing about unacceptable consequences despite IDS, because human or even automated incident response is too slow to prevent the consequence.

Network Intrusion Prevention Systems

What they are: Network IPS include network IDS. When the IDS function detects and reports a high-priority attack, the IPS function engages to interrupt the attack in progress. An external IPS may send TCP "reset" packets back into the tap or mirror port the IPS is using to access the packet stream. An in-line IPS built into a firewall can simply start dropping packets on the connection(s) involved in the attack so that further attack packets do not reach the target machine or network. Other attack interruption mechanisms are possible, such as contacting an agent installed on a host that is the endpoint of the attack and instructing that agent to drop the connection or take other protective actions.

Where to use: With all IPS products there is a risk of false alarms / false positives causing the IPS to interrupt benign communications, communications that may be essential to safe or reliable operations. Common wisdom is that IPS are deployed only at the very highest levels of control systems, such as on the IT/OT interface, where false alarms are likely to have only business consequences, not physical consequences. Network IPS that are designed for industrial environments though, generally have had their attack interruption actions tested and approved by vendors and engineering teams, so that even false alarms have only acceptable consequences.

Intrinsic Limitations: All network IPS are software, with vulnerabilities known and unknown that can be exploited. All network IPS include a network IDS, and so are subject to all the limitations of network IDS systems.

Secure Remote Access

What they are: Secure Remote Access (SRA) systems are collections of software and hardware that allow people to operate sensitive OT computers remotely. SRA systems almost always include VPNs, two-factor authentication, and remote access software such as the ubiquitous Windows Remote Desktop.

Where to use: Remote access into critical systems is strongly discouraged by most experts and in fact illegal in some jurisdictions. Remote access systems are used routinely inside industrial networks, all at the same level of criticality, to permit users on the one side of a large plant to manipulate automation equipment on the other side, or equipment that is in locations that are dangerous to physically walk into.

Intrinsic Limitations: All remote access systems are software, with vulnerabilities discovered and undiscovered. A phished password is often all an attacker needs to impersonate a legitimate user in the remote access system. Two-factor authentication systems for remote access are the subject of active exploitation by nation-state threat actors.

Security Updates / Patches

What they are: Security updates are new versions of software that are supposed to correct exploitable software defects (software vulnerabilities).

Where to use: Many experts recommend that security updates be applied universally, to all industrial systems as quickly as practical. This is practical on non-critical networks but can be extremely expensive on the most critical networks, because of the engineering effort involved in investigating and validating a new version of software on safety-critical or reliability-critical networks.

Intrinsic Limitations: Some security updates are defective, and either do not repair the vulnerability they are intended to or introduce new and sometimes even more serious vulnerabilities than the one they nominally fix. Security updates correct known defects in software – they do nothing to correct unknown "zero-day" defects, poorly chosen or leaked passwords, poorly configured security systems or firewalls, or insiders misusing their credentials.

Software-defined Networks

What they are: Software-defined networks (SDN) are network components such as firewalls, switches, routers plus management software. The software can reconfigure the network components to meet changing network and cybersecurity needs. For example, if a SOC declares a major compromise of the IT network, OT SDNs might reconfigure IT/OT firewalls to start blocking 100% of traffic, permitting nothing through until the emergency condition clears. Another example: a natural gas pipeline SCADA center might communicate with compressor stations across the pipeline's own fibre normally, but if the fibre is severed in a construction mistake, the SDN causes that communications to fail over transparently to satellite feeds, or VPNs through the Internet, or low-speed modems running through leased telephone lines.

Where to use: SDNs are used more commonly for high-availability communications than for security in industrial contexts. SDNs are occasionally connected to network IPS systems – when the IPS needs to interrupt a communications session carrying an attack in progress, the IPS interacts with the SDN software to block the session.

Intrinsic Limitations: All SDNs are software, with vulnerabilities already discovered and undiscovered. All SDNs control communications equipment and are blind to attacks carried on USB thumb drives or laptop computers.

Unidirectional Gateways

What they are: The US NIST glossary defines unidirectional gateways as a combination of hardware and software: the hardware is physically able to send information in only one direction, and the software makes copies of servers and emulates devices. Unidirectional Gateways are used routinely to send information from industrial networks out to business automation in IT networks, with no chance that cyber attacks can penetrate from the IT network into sensitive OT / industrial networks. Unidirectional gateways routinely replicate process historians, OPC servers and other industrial devices to IT networks, where IT users and applications access the replicas normally. Since unidirectional gateway vendors serve civilian rather than military markets, sales volumes are often higher than for data diode vendors, and thus gateway providers can often afford to invest in modern user interfaces, redundancy options and other features expected of industrial-grade equipment.

Where to use: The right place to use unidirectional gateways is at a consequence boundary – between an industrial network whose worst-case safety or reliability consequences of compromise are unacceptable, and a business network whose worst-case consequences include acceptable business losses and reputational damage. Unidirectional gateways can also be used to send information into classified military and government networks when the government in question recognizes the gateway supplier as sufficiently trustworthy to permit their equipment to connect to classified networks.

Intrinsic Limitations: Unidirectional gateways control the flow of network packets – they do nothing about potentially contaminated USB drives, or laptops, or cell phones being carried into OT networks. Unidirectional gateway software – like any software – has vulnerabilities that can be exploited. However, even if such vulnerabilities are exploited, the unidirectional hardware is still physically incapable of propagating any attack back into the protected OT network.

Virtual Local Area Networks

What they are: Virtual Local Area Networks (VLANs) are a feature of managed switches. These switches (LANs) can be configured to have groups of ports on the switch behave as if they were separate switches – "virtual" LANs. This might save a little money and can make the LAN configurations a little more flexible. When a machine needs to be moved from one LAN to another, only the switch needs to be reconfigured, no wires need to be moved.

Where to use: VLANs are recommended only when all virtual networks on the switch are at the same level of criticality. VLANs are not recommended to separate networks at different levels of criticality – for example, it is not recommended to host a gasoline pipeline's IT network and SCADA network in separate VLANs on the same switch.

Intrinsic Limitations: VLANs are software, with vulnerabilities discovered and undiscovered. Stolen switch passwords can reconfigure switches and VLANs very quickly, putting control system components at risk.

Virtual Private Networks

What they are: Virtual private networks (VPNs) encrypt and authenticate communications as they pass through an untrusted network, such as the Internet. VPNs provide the illusion of a direct connection between hosts, networks or a host and a network – a "virtual" direct connection, when hardware-based connections are not available. Modern VPN software often includes the ability to check the integrity of laptops and other endpoints when connecting to sensitive networks. Integrity checks often include: Is AV installed and up to date? Are all security updates installed? Is the laptop still otherwise configured in a way that is consistent with corporate security policy for the laptop? The VPN tends to permit a device to connect to a sensitive network only if all these checks pass. VPNs may also be built into firewalls as a feature.

Where to use: VPNs are used routinely to connect distant industrial stations, such as compressor stations, pumping stations, and electrical substations, into central SCADA systems. VPNs are used routinely as one of the security measures that is part of "secure remote access" systems.

Intrinsic Limitations: VPNs use encryption, and so all the limitations of cryptosystems apply here: VPNs have little value if keys have been stolen, VPNs are software that can be compromised, VPNs offer no protection against compromised endpoints, and so on.

Summary

The list above is not exhaustive – we could go on. If you do not find your favorite technology in the list above, take a few minutes and read related entries. A pattern emerges. All software has vulnerabilities, both known and unknown. Passwords can be stolen. Attacks can pivot throughout networks and through firewalls inside of encrypted connections. As much as we would like one, and as much as various vendors try to persuade us that they have one, there are no silver bullets.

Appendix B – Secure Operations Technology

This appendix is a copy of several chapters from *Secure Operations Technology,* describing the SEC-OT perspective, methodology and set of best practices for securing industrial control systems (ICS) from cyber threats.

Caution: The *Secure Operations Technology* book is very technical. Non-technical users may struggle with some of the material in this Appendix.

This section introduces SEC-OT and very broadly outlines how SEC-OT differs from Information Technology Security (IT-SEC). SEC-OT is focused on cybersecurity for physical operations. To this end, SEC-OT defines control system security as:

> ***Definition***
>
> ***Control system security*** *– protecting the safe and reliable control of physical operations from attacks embedded in information*

Important elements in this definition include:

- ***Safety:*** The first priority at all SEC-OT sites is safety. Safety is defined as preventing unacceptable risks of casualties at the site, threats to the public in nearby communities, and environmental disasters.
- ***Reliability:*** The second priority at SEC-OT sites is reliable operation of the physical process. Reliable operation includes correct, efficient, and continuous physical operations. Unscheduled downtime, production quality failures and equipment damage are all examples of reliability failures.
- ***Control:*** Industrial operations at SEC-OT sites are computer-controlled. Correct and authorized control of the computers that in turn control the physical process are essential to safe and reliable operations.
- ***Information:*** All attacks are information – the goal of SEC-OT is not to protect the information but to protect physical operations from attacks embedded in information. The key difference between SEC-OT and IT-SEC is therefore:

> ***Note***
>
> ***IT-SEC*** *– protects the information.*
>
> ***SEC-OT*** *– protects physical operations from information, or more specifically, from attacks that may be embedded in information.*

This difference in perspective has profound implications. For example:

- The classic "encrypt everything" IT-SEC response to protecting information has limited value in SEC-OT – all cyber attacks are information, and attack information can be encrypted just as easily as legitimate information.
- IT-SEC consequences of compromise are business consequences, such as damaged reputations, lawsuits and computers that need to be erased and restored from backups. SEC-OT consequences are physical consequences and generally cannot be "restored from backups."
- The IT-SEC philosophy of "let information flow where it will, so long as the information is protected" is directly at odds with the SEC-OT philosophy of controlling the flow of attacks by thoroughly limiting and controlling the flow of information.

Once physical operations are protected from cyber compromise though, preventing the theft of certain kinds of information is also important at many industrial sites. Production formulas, recipes, and other intellectual property, for example, may need protection from unauthorized disclosure. SEC-OT designs and best practices are always augmented with IT-SEC technologies and approaches, both to protect trade secrets and as a second line of software-based defences for safe and reliable operations.

SEC-OT Principles

The first three SEC-OT principles mirror the first three laws of control system security coined in this author's book *SCADA Security – What's broken and how to fix it.* The three laws are paraphrased:

First Three Laws of Control System Security

1. *Nothing is secure – security is a continuum, not a binary value.*
2. *All software can be hacked – all software has defects, and some defects are exploitable vulnerabilities.*
3. *All cyber attacks are information, and every piece of information can be an attack.*

The corresponding SEC-OT design principles are:

SEC-OT Principles

1. *To understand cyber risk, understand which attacks and consequences a security program does not defeat reliably.*
2. *To survive software compromise, physically protect control critical networks from cyber attacks.*
3. *To control attacks, inventory, and control information flows.*

Understanding Attacks

No security posture is perfect – given enough time, talent and money, any security posture can be breached. This means that every industrial control system, no matter how thoroughly protected, has residual risks due to cyber attacks. Businesses generally either:

- Mitigate these risks by changing the design of control systems or security programs to eliminate the risks,
- Transfer the risks for a fee to a willing insurer, or
- Accept the risks and if an attack occurs, suffer the consequences.

Understanding residual risks is therefore very important to business decision-making. Decision makers should understand the risks they accept on behalf of the business rather than accept risks blindly. *The Top 20 Cyber Attacks on Industrial Control Networks*[22], or Chapters 10-12 of the original *Secure Operations Technology* text provide an example of a SEC-OT-compatible, capabilities-based approach to risk assessment using a standard set of 20 ICS cyber attacks.

Physical Protection

All software can be compromised by cyber attacks, including security software, cryptosystems, and firewalls. Almost all software can be misconfigured as well, and modern attackers generally find it easier to exploit permissions than to exploit software vulnerabilities. For these reasons, SEC-OT requires physical rather than software-based protections.

For example, a security design that puts control-critical and IT computers both on the same physical switch and separates the two using VLAN software violates the physical-protection principle. If an attacker steals the password for the VLAN system, it is a simple matter to disable the VLAN and so eliminate the software separation between networks.

> **Note**
>
> *SEC-OT does not demand physical protection for all information flows, only for flows into control-critical networks from external networks, such as IT networks or the Internet that are not managed according to SEC-OT principles.*

The remainder of this Appendix explores physical protections from both offline and online attacks.

[22] *The Top 20 Cyber Attacks on Industrial Control Systems,* Waterfall Security Solutions, 2017, https://waterfall-security.com/ot-insights-center/ot-cybersecurity-insights-center/the-top-20-cyberattacks-on-industrial-control-systems-whitepaper/

Controlling Information and Attack Flows

All cyber attacks are information, and all information can encode attacks, therefore any comprehensive list of information flows into a control system is also a comprehensive list of attack vectors. The only way that a control system can change from an uncompromised to a compromised state is for attack information to cross a physical or network perimeter into the control system from outside the system.

> ***Note***
>
> *This Appendix routinely uses the term "information/attack flow" instead of "information flow" or "attack flow" to highlight the fact that all attacks are information, and every piece of information can encode an attack.*

Because any information can contain an attack, the SEC-OT ideal is the elimination of all information/attack flows from noncritical networks into control-critical networks. This ideal is generally impossible to achieve. SEC-OT principles and best practices dramatically reduce information/ attack flows from noncritical networks but generally cannot eliminate all such flows. SEC-OT, therefore, also demands strong procedures and technologies for inspecting, testing, and validating residual offline and online information/attack flows.

> ***Note***
>
> *The SEC-OT focus on controlling attack vectors is in sharp contrast with conventional IT-SEC practices whose focus is on reducing vulnerabilities, such as software defects and firewall misconfigurations.*

SEC-OT seeks primarily to eliminate or tightly control information flows and attack vectors and only secondarily to address remaining residual risks with software-based IT-SEC compensating measures. Chapter 9 explores such compensating measures.

Key Definitions

The first step in the SEC-OT methodology is to identify which cyber assets must be protected by SEC-OT measures. To this end SEC-OT defines:

> ***Definition***
>
> ***Cyber asset** – any electronic device containing a CPU*

Examples of cyber assets include:

- the obvious: cell phones, computers, laptops, PLCs and RTUs,

- less obvious: firewalls, routers, and network switches,
- the often ignored: some power tools and intelligent thermostats, and
- the sometimes surprising: USB drives, hard drives, keyboards, and mice, all of which contain embedded CPUs and firmware.

SEC-OT also defines:

> ***Definition***
>
> ***Industrial control system (ICS)*** *– a set of cyber assets that control, or influence the control of physical industrial operations*

A control system is therefore a set of cyber assets that have been grouped together for reasons that make sense to control systems engineers.

> ***Definition***
>
> ***Control-critical network*** *– a set of one or more ICS networks managed according to SEC-OT principles*

The distinction between ICS networks and control-critical networks is subtle. The ICS definition above is essentially the same as the IEC 62443-1-1 definition of "industrial automation and control system" (IACS)[23]. ICS engineers group assets into control systems for reasons of engineering capability or efficacy.

A control-critical network is a *set or group of ICS networks* where the entire set or group is managed according to SEC-OT principles. SEC-OT teams group ICS networks into control-critical groups to facilitate and optimize security. The focus of SEC-OT is preventing attack information from reaching into and compromising control-critical sets of ICS networks by eliminating, limiting and/or controlling both offline and online information flows through the physical and network perimeters of control-critical networks. Chapter 3 describes how to select which ICS networks belong in each control-critical network set.

> ***Note***
>
> *"Control-critical" networks are not the same as "critical-infrastructure" networks. For example, a home appliance manufacturer is not a critical infrastructure in any nation, but the ICS networks in such a manufacturing plant may still be control-critical to the manufacturer.*

---

[23] *IEC TS 62443-1-1:2009 Industrial communications networks – Network and system security – Part 1-1: Terminology, concepts and models,* International Electrotechnical Commission, 2009

While SEC-OT is designed to minimize information/attack flows into control-critical networks, large volumes of information typically flow much more freely between the ICS networks inside a control-critical set of networks. SEC-OT's stringent physical protections against information/attack flows apply to communications between the control-critical group and external systems, not between the control systems within the control-critical group.

In principle, a SEC-OT site may define many control-critical networks at an industrial site, each with many component ICS networks. In practice, most SEC-OT sites define a single site-wide control-critical network, containing a single ICS network, at least initially. Such designs help SEC-OT teams focus on their primary mandate: deploying a layer of physical protections to prevent attack information from external sources from reaching any control-critical components.

Many SEC-OT sites, therefore, use the terms “control-critical network,” “control network,” “critical network,” and “industrial control system” interchangeably, having defined a site-wide control-critical network as containing a single ICS. Such sites tend to refer to subsets of this single control network as “zones,” “network segments” or “ICS segments.”

This book uses terms as defined above, but often abbreviates “control-critical network” as “control network” or “critical network.”

When protecting control-critical networks from information/attack flows originating in external networks, SEC-OT observes that there are only two ways to transmit information between cyber assets:

Definitions

Offline communications *– any mechanism where information is encoded into a physical asset that is moved manually to enable the information to move*

Online communications *– any mechanism by which information is transmitted from one cyber asset to another without physically moving an information storage medium*

For example, USB keys, laptops and floppy disks that are carried from one cyber asset to another are examples of offline communications. Serial connections, Wi-Fi connections and twisted-pair Ethernet all facilitate online communications.

SEC-OT physical protections must address the threat of attacks embedded in both offline and online communications. A variety of physical protections for offline communications are described in the sections ahead. Air gaps and unidirectional gateway technology, which are the only two physical protection mechanisms supported by SEC-OT for online communications with critical networks, are described later in this Appendix.

Secure Operations Technology

The SEC-OT perspectives, principles and practices documented in this book are drawn from a decade of working with secure industrial sites, and with other experts who work with such sites.

The key difference between secure industrial sites and non-SEC-OT sites is not the sites' size or industry, but the degree of determination to reduce cyber risks to continuous operations.

> **Note**
>
> *The single most common reason industrial sites transition to the SEC-OT methodology is the sites' need to dramatically reduce cyber risks to continuous operations.*

Industrial enterprises generally adopt SEC-OT principles and practices because the business has decided that IT-SEC protections alone are not sufficient to address cyber threats to continuous, correct, and efficient operation of physical, industrial processes.

> **Note**
>
> *SEC-OT pioneers come from a wide range of site sizes and industries, including small electric substations, railway signalling systems, refineries, and power plants.*

The *Secure Operations Technology* methodology can be summarized in five steps:

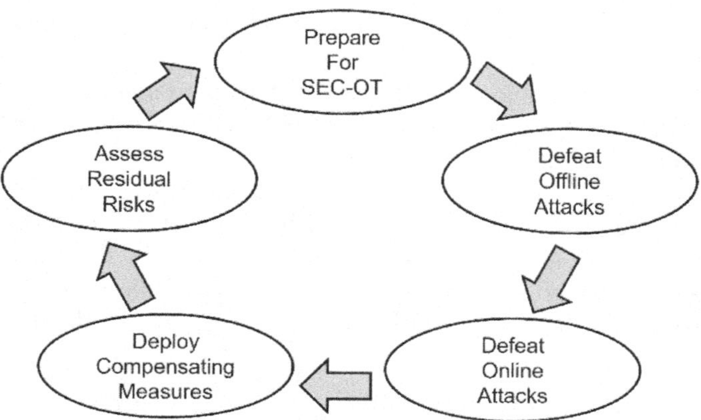

Figure (2) SEC-OT Methodology

1) **Prepare for SEC-OT** – Identify cyber assets whose compromise can cause unacceptable physical consequences, arrange them into ICS and control-

critical networks and then create inventories of information flows/attack vectors.

2) **Defeat Offline Attacks** – Deploy physical, technological, and procedural protections from removable media, removable devices, and other offline information/attack flows into control-critical networks.
3) **Defeat Online Attacks** – Deploy physical, technological, and procedural protections from online information/attacks flowing into control networks.
4) **Deploy Compensating Measures** – Deploy IT-SEC compensating measures and other software-based defences as a second line of defence.
5) **Assess Residual Risks** – Carry out a capabilities-based risk assessment of the resulting SEC-OT design to determine residual risks.

Some practitioners argue that the risk-assessment step should come first in the SEC-OT process to determine whether any change is needed to an existing IT-SEC design. In practice, capabilities-based assessments of IT-SEC designs have little value. Such assessments invariably conclude that IT-SEC designs reliably prevent few unacceptable physical consequences in the face of even unsophisticated attacks.

When transitioning to SEC-OT, few sites adopt all SEC-OT best practices at once. Most sites adopt essential principles and practices in a first phase of deployment and transition to a more comprehensive and mature SEC-OT posture over a course of years. Even after a site is mature in SEC-OT practices, SEC-OT security programs still evolve over time, as new best practices continue to be developed by SEC-OT pioneers.

This Appendix

This appendix is focused on the technical security controls and associated operating policies and principles essential to the SEC-OT methodology. This book does not describe a full security program. Readers who need full program guidance are encouraged to apply the SEC-OT methodology within the context of larger security program advice such as the NIST Framework[24] or the French ANSSI standards for industrial control systems[25,26].

This appendix is not an introduction to computer programming, operating systems, IP networking, industrial systems, cybersecurity, or industrial cybersecurity. Readers are assumed to be familiar with the basics of these disciplines – terms such as "drivers," "buffer overflow," "three-way handshake," "HMI," "PKI," and "IT/OT interface" are used throughout, without definition or introduction.

---

[24] *Framework for Improving Critical Infrastructure Security, Version 1.1,* National Institute of Standards and Technology, 2018

[25] *Cybersecurity for Industrial Control Systems – Classification Method and Key Measures,* Agence nationale de la sécurité des systèmes d'information, 2014

[26] *Cybersecurity for Industrial Control Systems – Detailed Measures,* Agence nationale de la sécurité des systèmes d'information, 2014

Summary

Secure Operations Technology is a perspective – a way of looking at and understanding security – as well as a methodology, a set of principles and a set of best practices. The key differences between SEC-OT and IT-SEC are:

- SEC-OT: protect physical operations from information/attack flows – do so physically rather than with only software and focus on attack capabilities, not vulnerabilities.
- IT-SEC: protect information wherever it flows – do so with encryption and security software and focus on reducing device and system vulnerabilities.

To this end, SEC-OT defines control system security as protecting the safe and reliable control of physical operations from attacks embedded in information. Fundamental SEC-OT principles include:

- Capabilities-based, not vulnerabilities-based risk assessments,
- Physical, rather than only software protections, and
- Inventories of and controls overflows of information/attacks into control systems.

The SEC-OT methodology includes five steps and associated sets of best practices: preparation, defeating offline attacks, defeating online attacks, deploying IT-SEC compensating measures and assessing residual risks.

Prepare for SEC-OT

This section describes preliminary steps and decisions essential to preparing for a SEC-OT deployment. These steps include carrying out an inventory of, and classifying cyber assets as, control critical or not critical, grouping assets into industrial control systems, grouping control systems into control-critical networks, physically separating control-critical assets from noncritical assets, and carrying out an inventory of information/attack flows.

Classify

Classifying cyber assets establishes a preliminary scope for the SEC-OT process. The goal of classification is to identify the cyber assets that are essential to safe and reliable physical operations. When a team applying SEC-OT has less than site-wide responsibility, the classification step is naturally constrained to only the assets for which the team has responsibility.

Even then, a SEC-OT team may further constrain the set of assets in scope for business reasons, such as seeking to gain experience with SEC-OT on a subset of the control assets at a site, before expanding the scope of the methodology to a larger set of assets. Asset classification identifies three classes of cyber assets:

- **Control-critical** assets – such as PLCs, RTUs, HMIs, safety systems, protective relays, communications front ends, and their associated switches and routers that are clearly involved in controlling physical processes,
- **IT-centric** assets – such as accounting workstations, sales laptops, customer-facing websites, and their associated switches and routers that should have nothing to do with physical control, and
- **Ambiguous** assets – such as some process historians, site-wide or enterprise-wide optimization systems, and/or control technician tablets, that are difficult to classify.

Ambiguous assets are labelled as such initially and are reclassified in subsequent steps of the methodology.

> ***Note***
>
> *All assets at a site that directly control physical operations must be classified as control critical.*

Asset classification is generally carried out in two phases. An initial assessment is typically based on an asset inventory based on high-level documentation and the recollection of experts in the room during the first-phase SEC-OT planning process. A later, more detailed assessment involves a comprehensive physical inventory of assets at a site and incremental classification of assets discovered by the detailed inventory that were missed in the initial assessment.

The most-thorough sites also consider physical consequences due to potentially unreliable, or improper operation of, external inputs that are essential to safe and reliable industrial operations. Many sites, for example, consider:

- Electric power to the site, which can be interrupted, or can be caused to exceed safe voltage and current levels,
- Natural gas pipelines for heating and other purposes, which can be interrupted, or can be over-pressurized leading to leaks, fires, and explosions,
- Air conditioning systems for control system server rooms and other rooms that must be climate-controlled, which can be interrupted,
- Heating, ventilation, and air conditioning (HVAC) for areas hosting 24x7 operations staff or other vital personnel, which can be interrupted,
- Uninterruptible power supplies for control-critical assets, which can be disabled, exhausted or over-charged, leading to fires, and
- Water supplies, which can be interrupted or contaminated.

In some cases, the cyber assets controlling these essential physical systems can be brought into scope for the SEC-OT methodology. Other cyber assets are more challenging to manage because they are owned or operated by some other department, enterprise, or government agency.

Group Assets

An industrial control system is defined as a *set* of cyber assets whose worst-case compromise results in unacceptable physical consequences, and a control-critical network is defined as a set of ICS networks. The next step to protecting an ICS is deciding how to group control-critical cyber assets into these sets.

> **Note**
>
> *All cyber assets identified as control-critical must become part of a control-critical network.*

When defining ICS sets, SEC-OT teams seek to group assets with similar functions, communications needs and security needs. When defining control-critical networks, these teams seek to minimize the volume and complexity of information flows into critical networks from noncritical networks. Initial definitions of ICS and control-critical network sets are typically revisited several times in the process of preparing for a SEC-OT design effort as information/attack flows are analyzed.

In practice, many SEC-OT sites initially define only one control-critical network per site and one ICS in that control-critical network. Such a design minimizes the number of ICS network perimeters that will require physical protection from offline and online information/attack flows.

> **Note**
>
> *SEC-OT demands physical segmentation and protection of control-critical networks from noncritical networks.*
>
> *Firewalls and other software segmentation may be used between the ICS members of a control-critical network, but not between a control-critical network and any other network.*

The most common exception to the "one control-critical network per site" rule of thumb is an exception for safety-instrumented systems (SIS). SEC-OT teams occasionally group SIS networks into one or more small control-critical networks separate from the main control-critical network at the site. Such networks are often referred to as "safety-critical" networks. All safety-critical networks are also control-critical networks.

A less common exception to the "one critical network" rule of thumb is for protective relays. Such relays are cyber assets that prevent damage to electrical equipment. When a control-critical network contains only protective relays and associated support assets, that network is often referred to as an "equipment-critical" network. All equipment-critical networks are also control-critical.

Physical Segmentation

With tentative groupings in place, SEC-OT practitioners design their networks to physically separate each control-critical network from all external networks. This physical separation is a prerequisite for physical protection. Physical separation means:

- Cyber assets in a control-critical network are not connected to the same physical switch, VLAN-enabled or not, as are IT assets, assets from a different control-critical network, or any noncritical assets, and
- Virtual cyber assets in one control network do not run as guests on the same physical server as IT assets, assets from a different control-critical network, or other noncritical assets.

When this physical segmentation results in significant re-cabling of control system networks, SEC-OT teams may revisit their initial asset classification or control system groupings. Reducing wiring changes for existing installations is one of the reasons that many sites define only a single control-critical network for the entire site. Such a definition permits the team to use VLANs and firewalls to separate ICS subnetworks of a control-critical network rather than physically separate the subnetworks.

SEC-OT teams also routinely reclassify small numbers of IT cyber assets as control-critical assets in order to leave those assets on the same physical switch as the control system.

> ***Note***
>
> *All cyber assets in a control-critical network must be managed as control-critical assets per the SEC-OT methodology.*

More specifically – an IT asset left in a control-critical network for convenience of wiring becomes a control-critical asset and must be managed as a critical asset in the SEC-OT methodology.

> ***Note***
>
> *When practical, SEC-OT sites locate IT and ICS assets in different server rooms.*

Additional physical separation, where practical, simplifies certain physical protection mechanisms. For example, separate control-critical and IT server rooms allow industrial sites to issue access badges for the IT room to IT personnel, for the control-critical room to ICS personnel, and not vice versa. Such separation also reduces opportunities for errors and omissions that might otherwise result in physical cross-connections between control-critical and noncritical network wiring and equipment.

Information/Attack Flows

With a tentative plan in place for the physical separation of control systems from other systems, a SEC-OT team can start considering all information flows – both offline and online – that bring information/attacks into control-critical networks.

An initial version of the survey is often carried out on a whiteboard, from the memory of experts in the room or from an examination of existing firewall rules. A more comprehensive survey is generally carried out later in the SEC-OT process to confirm this initial assessment. The comprehensive survey may inspect as-built documentation, physical devices and wiring, firewall rules, control system software configurations and other sources.

With initial segmentation and an inventory of control-critical perimeter-crossing information/attack flows in place, the team can start the process of revisiting assets whose classification was initially ambiguous.

> **Note**
>
> *The goal of critical-network definition is to minimize the volume and frequency of communicating information/attacks into control-critical networks.*

It is often possible for SEC-OT teams to reduce information flows into critical networks by carefully defining the criticality of cyber assets and occasionally moving an asset from one network to another.

For example, if a conventional operator HMI workstation was physically connected to an IT network, the SEC-OT team would observe that the HMI was sending commands into control-critical equipment every few seconds. Reclassifying the HMI workstation as a control-critical asset and moving the workstation from the IT to the control-critical network eliminates the HMI's cross-perimeter traffic into the control-critical network and introduces no new cross-perimeter flows.

In another example, an Enterprise Resource Planning (ERP) system located in the IT network of a chemicals business might send a small number of production orders to the main control-critical network every few hours or days. That ERP, however, exchanges large amounts of information with suppliers, banks, and other Internet-based systems. Reclassifying the ERP as an ICS asset would dramatically increase the amount of information/attacks flowing into the control-critical network, not reduce those flows.

> **Note**
>
> *Unidirectional reference architectures later in this Appendix can further reduce cross-perimeter information/attack flows into control-critical networks.*

While the goal of minimizing information/attack flows into ICS networks applies to both offline and online communications:

> **Note**
>
> *SEC-OT regards most online communications into control-critical networks as higher risk than offline communications – wherever practical, SEC-OT prefers offline communications.*

Online information flows allow attackers to attempt attacks whenever the attackers wish and for as long as they wish. Offline information moves only intermittently, at the whim of the person, truck or pigeon physically carrying the information, dramatically slowing the attack process. Once assets have been grouped into control-critical networks with an inventory of information/attack flows into ICS networks, SEC-OT practitioners can select whether given flows will be implemented via offline or online means. Such practitioners prefer offline flows wherever practical. Issues of online vs. offline practicality include:

- Required latency – online communications are almost always lower latency than offline communications, but not all communications require low latency.
- Capital versus operating costs – online communications incur technology and labour costs to establish, maintain and manage, while offline communications incur ongoing labour costs. The labour cost of offline communications depends directly on the frequency with which such communications are needed.
- Errors and omissions – offline communications are sometimes less accurate than high-frequency, automated communications, but the calculation is more ambiguous for low-frequency communications. For rare communications, automated online paths may fall into disuse and disrepair between transmissions, increasing their errors and omissions rate.

For example, at SEC-OT sites:

- Security updates are generally communicated manually into ICS test beds, and from test beds into control-critical networks. Most sites conclude that the small manual effort needed to write updates to a CD and carry the CD across a perimeter is not worth automating, given the extensive and time-consuming testing those updates must subsequently undergo before deployment.
- Second-by-second commands from a power grid control center to a power plant to produce more or less energy are communicated via online communications.
- Daily anti-virus (AV) updates are communicated manually via offline mechanisms at some sites, and online at others.

SEC-OT teams rearrange network boundaries to minimize all information/attack flows entering a network and minimize online information/attack flows in particular.

Summary

Preliminary steps in the SEC-OT methodology include:

- Carrying out a physical inventory of cyber assets at the industrial site and classification of each asset as control-critical, IT-centric or "ambiguous, where all equipment able to physically control industrial processes must be classified as control-critical,
- Grouping control-critical cyber assets into industrial control systems,
- Grouping industrial control systems into control-critical networks,
- Separating control-critical networks from other networks physically rather than with only software,
- Carrying out a comprehensive inventory of information/attack flows from external systems into control-critical networks,
- Reclassifying ambiguous cyber assets to minimize information/attack flows into ICS networks, and
- Rendering a decision for each information/attack flow as to whether to use offline or online mechanisms for the flow.

Physical separation sometimes extends to situating IT and ICS assets in separate server rooms.

Defeat Offline Attacks

To defeat offline attacks, the SEC-OT team carries out an inventory of all offline information/attack flows into ICS networks and then addresses the risks of such flows using a variety of techniques. We first look at offline information/attack flows and their remediation.

Offline Survey

All offline attacks are physically transported into industrial sites. Offline information/attack flows at most sites include:

- Removable media,
- Removable devices, such as vendor laptops, cell phones and USB drives,
- New permanent computers,
- People – who carry information in their heads and may have malicious intent, and
- Exotic attacks – shipments of physical products, such as structural steel, that might hide wireless scanners and attack tools, as well as automobiles, trucks, drones, remote-controlled robots, and other intrinsically mobile computing platforms.

Information and attacks arriving from "trusted suppliers" can be particularly deceiving.

> ***Note***
>
> *That a supplier is considered trustworthy does not mean that all the supplier's employees, contractors, and suppliers are trustworthy.*
>
> *That a person is considered trustworthy does not mean that all the data the person carries is trustworthy.*

Test Beds

A control-system test bed is an important tool for inspecting and testing offline information flows. Most industrial sites already have access to at a laboratory that contains at least "one of each" kind of ICS cyber asset, software, and version in use at the site sites. Ideally there is an accurate copy of each industrial control system available for testing – the more accurate the copy, the more useful the copy is for testing proposed changes. Most industrial sites already use their test beds to test new versions of software, security updates and other complex information artifacts for at least safety and reliability, before deploying these information artifacts on a live control system.

SEC-OT sites add security testing to the goal of the ICS test bed. An ideal test bed is:

- As accurate a representation of the industrial control system as possible,
- Thoroughly instrumented to enable testing for safety and reliability, and
- Thoroughly instrumented for security.

When new software versions, updates, complex configuration changes or other complex information/attack artifacts are candidates for deployment on an ICS network, those candidates are first tested on the test bed. The test bed is instrumented and operated to determine whether the new software correctly handles normal ICS operating conditions as well as a wide variety of upset conditions, including safety shutdowns and other emergency conditions.

The test bed is also instrumented for security, in much the same way as commercial anti-malware "sandbox" products are instrumented: allow the clock to move faster or slower into the future, test for the creation of unexpected files and network connections and look for other behaviours that differ from what is normal for the test bed. Security and performance monitoring sensors for the test bed are generally set to a very high level of sensitivity. This produces a high rate of false positive alarms, all of which must be investigated, but SEC-OT sites would rather use the test bed to thoroughly understand the behaviour of new information artifacts than see those artifacts deployed on a live control system without such understanding.

Test beds must not be connected to live control-critical networks by firewalls or other software artifacts. If an attack compromises a test bed because of some inbound information flow, that attack must have no physical means of propagating to the live control system.

Most often ICS test beds are part of IT networks. IT and Internet connectivity can simplify the detection of malware that connects to Internet-based command and control centers. A risk with such connectivity though, is that targeted malware can be programmed to shut down and betray no symptoms on the test bed when the malware detects Internet connectivity. The malware uses the fact that the test bed is Internet-connected, and the knowledge that no control-critical network is even Internet-connected, to hide from the test bed's security sensors.

A less common but more thorough design connects the ICS test bed unidirectionally to the IT network, in the same way as a production ICS network is connected. Unidirectional gateways may also be used to emulate live ICS data sources to the test bed to make the test bed a more realistic emulation of the live ICS, for testing the safety, reliability, and security characteristics of new information artifacts. Unidirectional gateways and unidirectional network reference architectures are discussed later in this Appendix.

Removable Media

Removable media are the source of many compromises of non-SEC-OT networks by common, high-volume malware and ransomware. SEC-OT defines removable media as:

> ***Definition***
>
> ***Removable media*** *– any mechanism for information storage that does not contain a CPU*

> ***Note***
>
> *By this definition, USB devices are not removable media, because all such devices contain a CPU.*

For example, CDs, DVDs, magnetic tapes, and floppy disks are removable media, but USB hard drives, solid state drives and flash drives are not. All USB devices contain CPUs and so must be treated as removable devices. By this definition, pieces of paper are removable media as well, particularly when the contents of such papers are electronically scanned into control system equipment.

To deal with removable media, SEC-OT sites generally implement security controls that include:

- Operating system and application software policy changes that forbid mounting removable media on control-critical cyber assets and raise alerts when mount attempts are detected,

- Anti-malware scanning computers or kiosks,
- Physical protection, disabling or removal of removable media hardware and connectivity mechanisms from critical assets, and
- A security near-miss protocol analogous to the U.S. Occupational Safety and Health Administration (OSHA) safety near-miss protocol.

Each control is discussed in detail below.

Automated Policies

Microsoft Windows Active Directory servers can be configured to apply a security policy to all managed Windows computers, instructing those computers to refuse to mount removable media, or refuse such mounts to all but privileged users on special machines. Denying all removable media mounting is preferred at SEC-OT sites – that a site trusts certain users does not mean the site should trust the contents of those users' CDs.

Individual Linux computers can be similarly configured but forbidding the "root" administrative account from mounting removable media is very difficult. Preventing such mounts on industrial devices can be equally difficult or impossible, depending on which operating system the dedicated devices use. Even on Windows machines, sophisticated attackers with physical access to the machines can often find ways to defeat Active Directory permissions. Nonetheless, SEC-OT sites use software policies and derive what protection is possible from software.

Software policies are also configured to report all attempts to mount removable media, whether successful or not. These alerts are generally transmitted in real time to a central SOC. When security analysts at the SOC sees these alerts, the analysts correlate the alerts with open work orders. Any alerts outside the scope of approved work orders trigger at least a phone call to the affected site and result in either an incident response escalation or a near-miss report as described below.

Anti-Malware Scanning Stations

SEC-OT sites routinely deploy anti-malware scanning workstations or kiosks at the security desks or badged doors that are the physical security boundary of control-critical networks. A scanner/kiosk is one or more physical computers running one or more anti-malware scanning engines. Roll-your-own installations may use multiple computers with as many scanning engines running simultaneously on each computer as can coexist – multiple anti-malware engines frequently do not coexist well on a single computer. Commercial multi-scanning solutions generally require only a single scanning computer or "kiosk" and are typically configured with between four and eight anti-malware scanning engines.

Multi-scanning solutions generally have a user interface that shows users the files on their media, allows users to select the files to scan, and then writes the scanned files to brand new physical media taken from a dispenser beside the kiosk. The new media are then carried to a nearby file server, which is the only device on the control-critical network with removable media mounting hardware and software enabled. The files are read into the file server and then transferred electronically to the critical network from the file server.

Physical Protection

SEC-OT sites physically disable or eliminate removable media readers on as much control-critical equipment as is practical, excepting only the file servers adjacent to scanning workstations and kiosks. At many sites however, some low-level PLCs, RTUs and other equipment require the use of removable media or USB drives to update firmware or carry out other routine maintenance. Such sites deploy physical locks on any remaining media readers with manual procedures to authorize, prepare for and follow up on operations that involve unlocking the devices.

These sites colour-code or otherwise label very prominently all physical media that is produced by the scanning stations. Workers at the site are trained that such control-critical media must never leave the control-critical area at the industrial site and must never be inserted into a noncritical computer or laptop. Any such insertion risks writing new attack information to the media. Leaving the site with such media and bringing it back to the site later poses the risk that someone may have inserted the media into a distant, unmonitored computer and deliberately or inadvertently written malicious information to the media.

The goal of these procedures is to provide a reasonably strong assurance that any media inserted into ICS equipment is free of common malware.

Near Miss Protocol

The US Occupational Safety and Health Administration (OSHA) defines a near miss as:

> ***Definition***
>
> ***Near miss** – an incident in which no property was damaged, and no personal injury was sustained but where, given a slight shift in time or position, damage or injury easily could have occurred*

When potentially compromised media or cyber assets are connected to control-critical components in violation of procedures that minimize the risk of compromise, such connections are a threat to safe and reliable operations. SEC-OT sites define incidents that could have compromised control-critical networks, but did not, as "cyber near misses."

Establishing a cyber near-miss program analogous to widely used OSHA programs increases the visibility of removable media and device mistakes. An OSHA-inspired system of reviewing, prioritizing, and remediating near misses involves both individual contributors and managers and, over time, nearly eliminates the erroneous use of unauthorized removable media on control-critical networks.

Inspecting Contents

Anti-malware scanning is only one form of inspection for removable media contents. In addition to such scanning, manual inspection of files entering control-critical networks is preferred at SEC-OT sites. Such inspection is practical for short, high-level, abstract instructions such as "Schedule pumps A, B and C to start at 2 AM every morning, to help minimize electric power costs."

Manual inspection is generally not practical for software updates, new anti-virus signatures or new control recipes that contain a schedule of hundreds or thousands of digital and analog values paired with cryptically named devices and device registers. SEC-OT sites generally require that these complex information/attack artifacts be deployed first into test beds, not directly from IT networks into live ICS networks. These complex files are first tested in the heavily instrumented test bed before they are moved into the live ICS.

Removable Devices

Removable devices are a threat as serious as removable media:

> ***Definition***
>
> ***Removable device*** *– any cyber asset with temporary online access to a control-critical cyber asset*

By this definition, all laptops, cell phones and USB devices are removable devices. Even modern hard drives, keyboards and mice frequently contain CPUs and firmware. Removable device CPUs communicate with connected ICS cyber assets, however temporarily. The risk with such connections is that a removable device running attack software, however inadvertently, can launch active attacks against software in all connected cyber assets.

> ***Note***
>
> *SEC-OT sites generally forbid connecting external removable devices to any ICS asset.*

When SEC-OT sites need portable computers and other removable devices on the ICS network, the sites address this need in standard ways:

- **Vendor laptops:** When vendors require access to certain software tools on a laptop at a SEC-OT site, the vendor requests such a laptop from the site before the visit. The site provisions a control-critical laptop with known-good media and makes the laptop available to the vendor during the visit. This laptop is never connected to noncritical networks, and no vendor laptop or other external laptop is ever permitted to connect to critical networks.

- **Network Access Control (NAC):** To help enforce the "no external laptops" rule, many SEC-OT sites enable Network Access Control on their ICS networks. NAC is software protection and so is not proof against sophisticated attacks but is sufficient to block, and alarm on, accidental connections by vendor laptops.
- **Alerts:** All SEC-OT sites enable alerts for connections to unauthorized removable devices to the greatest extent practical, including unauthorized USB drives, keyboards, and mice. Such alerts are generally routed to a central SOC. SOC analysts investigate the alerts and trigger either incident investigations or near-miss reports.
- **Contracts:** Whenever practical, vendor contracts include penalties for unauthorized connections of any kind of removable device to any kind of control-critical cyber asset.
- **Labelling:** Control-critical assets and network connections are clearly labelled, and unused network and other removable device connectors are physically blocked to prevent mistaken connections.
- **USB chargers:** Some SEC-OT sites have programs to easily request, provision and maintain USB charging stations throughout the site, to reduce the temptation to subvert physical blocks and charge cell phones or other portable noncritical equipment from control-critical equipment USB ports.

Again, these provisions are applied to all removable devices, including USB mice and keyboards. Such devices are not permitted temporary connections to control-critical equipment. When USB mice, keyboards or other devices are required on critical networks, the devices are first tested on the relevant ICS test bed, labelled as control-critical equipment, and permanently assigned to the critical network, as described in the section "New Cyber Assets" below.

> ***Note***
>
> *Unauthorized wireless access points are singularly dangerous removable devices.*

Rogue access points, if permitted to operate, provide a path for attack information to bypass some of the physical protections on which SEC-OT sites rely. Well-meaning technicians and vendors may expect that they can routinely attach such equipment to critical networks, at least temporarily. Preventing such attachments is a high priority for SEC-OT personnel, vendor training and awareness programs, as well as NAC and near-miss programs.

Encrypted USB Drives

SEC-OT sites generally avoid USB drive encryption systems. Vendors of such systems maintain that encryption makes the control-critical drives unrecognizable on IT networks and vice versa, so that cross-contamination is impossible. SEC-OT sites distrust such claims because:

- Encrypting drive contents does not address the risk of malware compromising USB drive firmware, and every removable drive contains a CPU and firmware,
- All cryptosystems are software and can be hacked, and
- Relying on software to protect control-critical computers rather than strict alerting and near-miss protocols makes users complacent in the use of USB drives. This increases the opportunity for sophisticated, firmware-based attacks at the affected sites.

New Cyber Assets

New and replacement cyber assets are introduced into all control-critical networks from time to time, with occasional bulk additions of new assets when control systems are upgraded or expanded. When new cyber assets are being prepared for use on a critical network, whether those assets be USB mice, laptops, displays or servers, the assets must be inspected and tested to ensure that they do not contain embedded attack information.

The problem with inspection is that modern devices are complex and often packaged to defeat inspection. Dismantling most hard drives, flash drives or monitors to thoroughly inspect their circuit boards, for example, generally destroys the device being inspected. Even for equipment where inspection is possible, circuit boards in laptops and servers can be very complex and beyond the means of most sites to inspect.

SEC-OT sites currently take all the following measures to assure the integrity of new cyber assets entering a control-critical network.

- **Test bed:** All new cyber assets destined for control-critical networks are first deployed on the safety, reliability, and security test bed and monitored closely throughout functional and security tests.
- **Consumables:** Commodity “consumable” types of equipment that are difficult to inspect physically, such as keyboards and mice, are purchased from unpredictable vendors. This way, the new equipment may still contain common, high-volume attacks, but is much less likely to contain the most sophisticated attacks that are targeted at a specific SEC-OT site.
- **Inspection:** When inspection is possible, the contents of new cyber assets are compared to vendor schematics, photographs of similar equipment, and purchasing information, to determine whether delivered circuit boards and chipsets match vendor specifications and whether unwanted hardware components, especially wireless communications components, have been delivered as part of the new equipment.
- **Contracts:** Whenever practical, hardware and systems integration contracts include penalties for delivering equipment that contains unauthorized hardware, especially additional CPUs, firmware, or wireless communications hardware. Such penalty clauses increase the motivation for

product and service providers to include supply chain integrity measures in their own purchasing and handling procedures.
- **Labelling:** Control-critical cyber assets are clearly labelled as such, and site personnel are trained never to connect noncritical assets to control-critical networks and vice versa.

Most SEC-OT sites maintain an inventory of pretested control-critical cyber assets that can be deployed to address emergency hardware failures. When ICS assets are decommissioned, their labelling is removed, and the assets are erased and reprovisioned for use outside the critical network, or physically destroyed, or first erased and then destroyed.

The greater question of cyber risks due to new cyber assets is the subject of ongoing "supply chain integrity" research in the ICS security community.

Insider Attacks

Insiders with physical access to critical cyber assets are a perennial concern at SEC-OT sites as well as non-SEC-OT sites. SEC-OT sites apply as many of the usual personnel precautions as are permitted by local privacy and other laws, including:

- **Auditing:** Enable detailed auditing of local and remote user actions on all control-system assets as a deterrent to deliberate misoperation.
- **Forensics:** Write these audit records and other records through a unidirectional gateway into a physically tamper-proof forensic repository.
- **Video monitoring:** Deploy video monitoring and recording, to help associate malicious insiders to forensic records.
- **Investigations:** Use forensic records and video recordings routinely and visibly in routine safety and security near-miss investigations – monitoring is a deterrent only when potential perpetrators know that they are being monitored.
- **Personnel surety program:** Deploy a comprehensive program for evaluating insider risks, for example including periodic background checks for criminal convictions and other indicators of risk, psychological profiling, and periodic employee interviews.

The above is only a summary. SEC-OT sites routinely draw from subdisciplines of personnel security in conventional physical security and IT-SEC domains.

Deceived Insiders

Even well-meaning insiders carry information into control-critical sites, networks, and cyber assets. Sometimes this information is a physical object such as a cell phone or USB drive – the risks posed by these physical objects are addressed by the measures described earlier in this Appendix. Sometimes though, the attack information flows through the minds of insiders – if an attacker can persuade an insider to act on false information, there can be physical consequences.

SEC-OT sites train their insiders to be suspicious of all information received from outside of control-critical networks, including information that may appear to have originated in the critical network, but which has travelled through a noncritical network and is therefore no longer as trustworthy as information that has never left the critical network.

> ***Note***
>
> *SEC-OT sites must take care to avoid creating animosity between ICS, IT, and vendor personnel. That ICS personnel must be suspicious of externally sourced information and advice does not mean that the people providing such advice or maintaining external systems are incompetent or malicious.*

It is external networks, cyber assets, and any information potentially contaminated by contact with noncritical assets that are suspect – not capable and well-intentioned IT or vendor colleagues.

The most difficult part of training ICS personnel to suspect external devices and information is not the principles, but the practice of identifying data sources that are more open to tampering than SEC-OT-protected sources.

For example, a site may replicate an ICS historian unidirectionally to an IT network. This replica could then supply data to a web application whose output is available on the cell phones of ICS personnel. The cell phone app may have the same look and feel as other critical-network ICS applications from the same vendor. This familiarity does not mean that the information provided by the cell phone app is safe – information received by the app has traversed both an IT network and the Internet and may have been compromised in transit.

ICS personnel must be trained to verify externally acquired information, before transferring that information to ICS assets or physically acting on the information. This includes:

- **Important instructions in email** – including instructions that appear to be from their supervisor or another credible authority – such instructions should be verified verbally with the source authority, and
- **Optimization advice or settings** – provided by external applications or that traverse an external network before reaching the ICS personnel. This includes any advice received wirelessly. Such settings, instructions and advice should always be verified against internal ICS status and measurements before acting on the advice, to ensure that the advice will not cause unacceptable physical consequences when applied to physical equipment.

It is often easier to train site personnel with a "whitelist" of acceptable sources of information than try to explain data flows in enough detail for people to determine for themselves which data is trustworthy, and which requires verification from control-critical sources.

Nonessential Equipment

Some equipment on control-critical networks does not need to run continuously. All such equipment should be configured to shut down automatically when idle.

For example, shutting down the engineering workstations used to program, test and manage ICS networks and especially SIS networks is very important. The same is true of laptops the site keeps in stock for visiting vendors. Such workstations and laptops are often populated with copies of powerful tools that can manipulate, reconfigure, and reprogram live control equipment. Even with SEC-OT-recommended physical protections against cyber compromise, best practice dictates keeping these powerful tools password-protected and turned off until needed.

Exotic Attacks

Attack information that is physically shipped into industrial sites becomes a threat only if that information becomes available to a control-critical cyber asset. For example, a hexadecimal rendering of a ransomware executable printed on the side of a steel girder entering a site is a threat only if that code is somehow scanned and converted into a form that can be executed.

A more credible threat is when cyber assets enter a site surreptitiously, especially those with wireless communications capabilities. For example, a battery-operated Wi-Fi scanner taped to the side of a steel girder that reports discovered Wi-Fi networks at the site through a cellular connection to an attacker is a credible threat. Threats like these are one of many reasons SEC-OT sites generally disable all Wi-Fi connections to control-critical networks. Note that a compromised cell phone in the pocket of an employee at the site poses the same threat as the scanner taped to the girder – both can discover and remotely attack control-critical Wi-Fi networks.

A comparatively new threat vector is intrinsically mobile cyber assets that enter a site. Drones can carry physical assaults into a site, as well as Wi-Fi sniffers and attack tools. Modern automobiles contain over 100 CPUs each, many of which are accessible via Wi-Fi, Bluetooth, cellular or other wireless connections. The compromise of a cyber asset in an automobile or truck at a site can result in significant casualties and physical damage to the site.

Some of these threats can be mitigated by limiting wireless networks at the site to unidirectionally-protected, monitor-only functions as described in the Wireless Networks reference architecture later in this Appendix. Others are the subject of active debate, research, and SEC-OT best-practice development.

Summary

The only way for a control-critical network to change from an uncompromised to a compromised state is if attack information passes into the network via offline or online means. A survey of offline information flows reveals all possible offline cyber attack vectors.

An ICS test bed is an essential SEC-OT tool for testing complex incoming information such as anti-virus signatures, security updates and new software versions. Such a test bed should be as accurate a copy of the live ICS systems at a site as is practical. These test beds should be thoroughly instrumented and monitored for safety, reliability, and security issues.

At most sites, offline attack vectors and protections include:

- **Removable Media:** Deploy anti-malware scanning kiosks and workstations to test media entering a site. Physically disable removable media ports. Configure control-critical components to report alerts when media are used anywhere else and manage these alerts using a near-miss process.
- **Removable Devices:** Ban vendor laptops, USB drives and other external computers from connecting to control-critical hosts and networks. Physically disable removable device ports, such as unused network and USB ports. Configure control-critical networks and cyber assets to raise alerts when unauthorized connections are attempted and manage these alerts using a near-miss process. Deploy known-clean control-critical laptops provisioned with required software for visiting vendors and other personnel who need the equipment.
- **New Cyber Assets:** Deploy all new equipment first on the test bed and test the equipment for safety, reliability, and security.
- **Insider Attacks:** Deploy detailed auditing and surveillance. Use these tools routinely in security and safety near-miss remediation.
- **Deceived Insiders:** Teach ICS personnel to trust only control-critical equipment. All instructions, setpoints and monitoring information received via other means – such as cell phone apps and electronic mail – should be verified against trustworthy sources before acting on the information in a way that might have unacceptable physical consequences.
- **Nonessential Equipment:** Turn off nonessential equipment when not in use, especially ICS laptops and engineering workstations.
- **Exotic Attacks:** Some exotic attacks can be mitigated by the Wireless Networks reference architecture. Others are the subject of active research, debate, and best-practice development.

Defeat Online Attacks

To defeat online attacks, the SEC-OT team carries out an inventory of all online information/attack flows into ICS networks and then addresses the risks of such flows using unidirectional gateways primarily, and air gaps more rarely.

Air gaps and unidirectional gateway technology are the only two physical boundary protection mechanisms supported by SEC-OT as protection against information/attack flows into control-critical networks from external networks. Firewalls may be used in series with unidirectional gateways and for internal segmentation within control-critical networks, but not as primary perimeter protection – firewalls are software protection, not physical protection from information/attack flows.

This section introduces and gives examples of both unidirectional gateways and air gaps. Later on, we provide a more comprehensive catalogue of unidirectional network reference architectures, including architectures that may seem counter-intuitive, such as those providing vendor remote access, central engineering teams and continuous high-level control of industrial sites from external authorities.

Online Survey

At industrial sites with ICS firewalls already deployed, a preliminary inventory of information flows can be as simple as reviewing existing firewall rules. Online information flows often include:

- IT client connections to ICS databases, historians and even monitoring and control devices to acquire operations data that supports business decision making,
- OT equipment connecting to IT infrastructure servers such as Active Directory, DNS, AV and WSUS servers,
- Control-critical equipment connected to vendor monitoring and update sites via modems and the Internet,
- IP and serial connections to wireless LAN and WAN infrastructure, including leased-frequency microwave communications, and
- Interactive remote access connections to permit systems integrators, product vendors, IT personnel, management, and others unrestricted access to control-critical equipment.

A more comprehensive inventory often includes a physical inspection of the ICS site to detect undocumented firewalls, wireless routers, modems, and other online connections to control-critical equipment.

Air Gaps

> ***Definition***
>
> ***Air-gapped network*** *– any set of cyber assets with no means of online communications with any external assets*

For at least thirty years, industrial control systems have seen steadily increased connectivity. Air gaps have become increasingly rare. Examples of air gaps at modern SEC-OT sites include Safety Instrumented Systems (SIS) and LED displays on portable tools. Air gaps are frequently criticized though:

- Air gaps impede the movement of valuable status monitoring information out of control systems and into enterprise applications, and
- Air gaps impede the movement of security monitoring information that is increasingly seen as essential to assessing equipment status and assessing the strength of security postures.

In the cases where air gaps are still practical, however, such gaps represent the most thorough possible physical protection from online cyber attacks.

> ***Note***
>
> *The term "air gap" is frequently used in a cavalier fashion by stakeholders not familiar with their control systems' as-built designs.*

Security assessors routinely report finding many "unexpected" connections to control systems that were described as air gapped. When converting a site to SEC-OT methodology, any claims that existing equipment is air-gapped should be verified by a physical inspection of the affected equipment, its associated cabling, and any possible wireless interfaces. Where practical, an inspection of network communications within air-gapped networks can be valuable as well – packets that are received from or sent to cyber assets outside of the air-gapped network can indicate online connections outside of the network.

Unidirectional Gateways

> ***Definition***
>
> ***Unidirectional gateway*** *– a combination of hardware and software. The hardware is physically able to send information in only one direction and the software replicates servers and emulates devices.*

Unidirectional gateways are essential to SEC-OT in any environment where impaired industrial production is an unacceptable consequence. The most common deployment of such gateways is at the IT/OT interface, where the gateway can transmit monitoring data out of a control-critical network without the ability to send any information or attacks back into the system from the IT network.

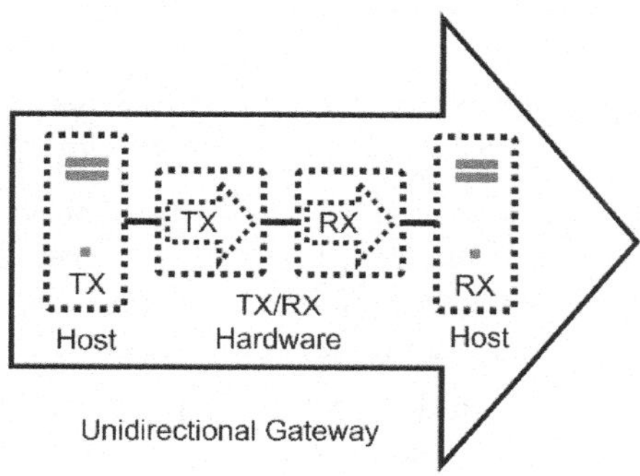

Figure (3) Unidirectional Gateway Internals

The most robust unidirectional hardware design consists of a fibre-optic transmitter connected to a fibre-optic receiver with a short piece of fibre-optic cabling. The receiver in such designs has no laser, and so is physically unable to send any information or attack back to the transmitter. The transmitter has no photocell or fibre-optic receiver able to receive a signal, even if one were sent.

With this type of physical protection in place, it does not matter if the software components of a unidirectional gateway are compromised – no software compromise can impair the ability of the gateway to physically prevent online attacks from reaching the transmitting network.

> **Note**
>
> *Unidirectional gateways of varying quality are available from a variety of vendors. The best equipment uses unidirectional optical signalling described above and is certified as unidirectional by an accredited Common Criteria laboratory or its equivalent.*

Unidirectional gateway software replicates servers and emulates devices. For example, a gateway may be deployed to replicate a historian server or other database from a control system to an IT network. The replica database is a normal part of the IT network. IT users and applications requiring real-time data interact normally with the IT replica database, sending the replica queries and receiving as responses the same data that the ICS database would have provided.

In another example, a unidirectional gateway may be deployed to emulate an OPC-UA server from a control system to an IT network. The gateway polls the control-system OPC-UA server periodically and sends snapshots of control-system state information unidirectionally to the IT network. In the IT network, the unidirectional gateway implements a second OPC-UA server. This replica OPC server is a normal part of the IT network. IT users and applications requiring real-time data interact normally with the emulated OPC-UA server on the IT network, sending poll requests to the replica and receiving as responses the same data as the ICS server would have provided.

> ***Note***
>
> *Common questions about unidirectional gateways include "how can they negotiate a TCP 3-way handshake?" and "why replicate servers?"*
>
> *Unidirectional gateways are not routers – they never forward network traffic from one network to another. Instead, the gateways are endpoints of TCP connections on source and destination networks.*

Unidirectional gateways forward device state information from one or more devices on a source network to one or more replicas on a destination network. Queries from the destination network are sent to the replicas. Unidirectional gateways, by design, cannot forward polls and queries into protected networks.

The TCP connections from unidirectional gateways to networks on either side of the gateways are independent connections and often exchange very different kinds of packets. For example, a gateway configured for database replication would send queries to the source database on the ICS network and would send "insert" and "update" commands to the replica database on the external network.

> ***Note***
>
> *Another common question is "What happens if the IT replica is attacked, corrupted, and the corrupted information is used to make decisions – can this process misoperate the ICS?"*
>
> *Incorrect decisions can be made from business network replicas, but to control the physical process, such decisions must be communicated somehow back into the ICS.*

The offline protections discussed earlier in this Appendix address such potentially compromised information/attack flows, especially the section "Deceived Insiders."

Network Layers

IT-SEC defence in depth advice recommends many layers of software protection for ICS sites as protection from online attacks originating on IT networks and the Internet. Layers of firewalls and networks are one kind of layered defence that defence-in-depth recommends – usually a minimum of the following, depending on the source of guidance:

- An Internet firewall between the Internet and an IT DMZ network
- A DMZ firewall between the DMZ and the IT network
- An IT/OT firewall between the IT network and an ICS DMZ,
- An ICS DMZ firewall between the ICS DMZ and the ICS plant-wide network,

- Production unit firewalls between the plant-wide network and individual DCS, SCADA, or production cell controllers,
- Device network firewalls between production units and their networks of connected PLCs, and
- A SCADA WAN firewall between a SCADA system and the WAN that connects the system to remote sites and equipment.

IT-SEC best practice recommends that no two layers of firewalls be sourced from the same vendor, in hopes that no single vendor's firewall vulnerability can be used to traverse multiple layers in this defensive structure.

This design has many intrinsic limitations, which is why SEC-OT practitioners prefer physical protections, such as air gaps and unidirectional gateways, to firewalls and other software protections. The IT-SEC design is not fundamentally flawed however – SEC-OT sites still tend to arrange their networks this way, with one key difference:

> ***Note***
>
> *SEC-OT sites generally deploy unidirectional gateways to replace or augment at least one complete layer of firewalls in an IT-SEC defence-in-depth architecture.*

One complete layer of unidirectional protection between the Internet and the control devices that directly control physical operations is sufficient to prevent online attacks from pivoting through firewalls and intervening networks to misoperate the physical process.

More generally, SEC-OT sites use unidirectional gateways to separate control-critical networks from noncritical networks. Noncritical networks always include:

- The Internet,
- IT networks, through which Internet-based attacks often pivot into ICS targets, and
- Any wireless network, since wireless communications are intrinsically broadcast, and it is impossible to which nearby wireless devices have access to the wireless communications.

Wide-area networks, such as SCADA WANs, are most often modelled as non-control-critical networks, since, by definition, WAN communications extend outside of any physical security perimeter controlled by the industrial site. There are exceptions to this rule though, discussed later in this Appendix.

Test bed networks are most often considered non-control critical as well. The most thorough testbeds though, are provided with most of the same physical protections against information/attack flows as control-critical networks, to make the test-beds faithful emulations of such networks.

Summary

Air gaps and unidirectional gateways are the only physical protections that SEC-OT endorses to defeat online attacks from noncritical networks reliably.

- Air gaps permit no online information/attack flows at all, and
- Unidirectional gateways are a combination of hardware and software – the hardware is physically able to transmit information in only one direction, and the software replicates servers and emulates devices.

Unidirectionally-replicated databases and emulated devices are normal participants in IT networks. Users query the replicas and receive the same answers from the replicas those queries would have produced from the original ICS databases and servers.

Unidirectional gateways are most commonly oriented to send information from a control-critical network to external networks and physically permit no information/attack flows back into the critical network. Unidirectional gateways are most commonly deployed to completely replace one layer of firewalls in a defence in depth, layered network architecture.

SEC-OT sites use firewalls extensively within control-critical networks and between ICS networks in the same control-critical groups but not between critical and noncritical networks.

Unidirectional Architectures

This section documents unidirectional network reference architectures that are used routinely in SEC-OT network designs.

> ***Note***
>
> *SEC-OT practitioners are cautioned that most unidirectional gateway vendors support only a subset of these patterns without costly custom engineering.*

SEC-OT pioneers continue to invent new patterns for new ICS applications and needs.

#1 Database Replication

Database replication is one of the most common reference architectures. Most ICS networks are designed to simplify application integration by concentrating operations information in a small number of data repositories such as Microsoft SQL Server databases or process historians.

In the database replication architecture, a replica database is established on the enterprise IT network and a unidirectional gateway copies the contents of an industrial database in a control-critical network to the enterprise replica. Enterprise users and applications access the replica normally.

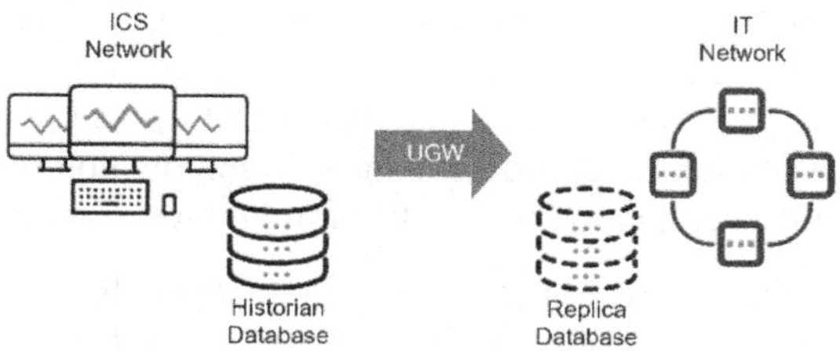

Figure (4) Unidirectional Database Replication

The replica may be local, in an IT network at the industrial site, or may be remote, typically at a head-office data center or other central site. A local replica at the industrial site reduces latency and other communications costs for applications on the site's IT network that make intensive use of industrial data. A central enterprise database aggregating data from many industrial sites provides an industrial enterprise with an information resource that can be used to compare performance and other details between industrial sites. SEC-OT businesses may use local replicas, central enterprise databases, or both.

> **Note**
>
> *When replica databases develop gaps, for example due to scheduled downtime to apply security updates to unidirectional gateway components, those gaps can be repaired by manually triggering the retransmission of data from the source database.*

Retransmitting data to fill historical gaps is called "back-filling" the replica database. The back-fill process retransmits data from the industrial database and populates missing records into the replica database, without duplicating any records that already exist there. The process is generally triggered manually from the industrial network. Less commonly, the process is carried out regularly and automatically, for example a daily retransmission of all the previous day's data. Such regular, programmed retransmissions though, increase network and other resource utilization.

> **Note**
>
> *Practitioners not familiar with unidirectional gateways sometimes ask how they can send queries from an IT application, through a gateway, into an industrial database.*
>
> *Database replication means no such queries ever need to be sent – queries from IT users are sent to the IT replica database, which answers such queries normally.*

This is the essence of database replication. Source databases are normal parts of control system networks and respond normally to queries and commands from ICS equipment and users. Replica databases are normal parts of IT networks and respond normally to queries and commands from IT applications and users.

Database replication is one of the most common unidirectional network architectures and is used in a wide variety of industries. For example:

- Historian databases are replicated routinely from ICS to IT networks in many industries, including electric power generation and transmission, offshore platforms, oil and gas pipelines, refining, chemical and pharmaceuticals, and water and wastewater treatment.
- Relational databases are replicated routinely to IT networks in railway signalling and Industrial Internet of Things (IIoT) applications.
- Proprietary, real-time databases are replicated routinely to IT networks and vendor cloud systems in vendor monitoring and predictive maintenance applications.

An extra feature of some database replications is meta-data replication. When new tables, points or tags are added to source databases on industrial networks, some unidirectional gateways can automatically propagate those new data sources to the replica databases. This feature, when available and enabled, reduces database maintenance costs by reducing data entry costs for the replica database.

#2 Device Emulation

When no industrial database is deployed on a control-critical network, or when software licensing costs or other considerations make replication of such a database undesirable, SEC-OT sites may elect to emulate industrial devices to the IT network. A unidirectional gateway typically polls communications servers or devices directly, using device protocols such as OPC-UA, Modbus, or Siemens S7. The gateway transmits device state snapshots to the IT network where the gateway emulates the industrial devices to the IT network. IT applications, such as IT databases and historians, access the emulated replicas as if those replicas were the original industrial devices.

> ***Note***
>
> *Practitioners not familiar with unidirectional gateways sometimes ask how they can send poll requests through the gateways from an IT application into an industrial device.*
>
> *Device emulation means no such polls need be sent through a gateway – poll requests are sent to the IT replicas, which answer those requests as the original devices would have.*

For example, an enterprise may decide to deploy a single enterprise historian at a head office rather than a plant historian at every site. SEC-OT teams then deploy unidirectional gateways to emulate ICS devices or OPC servers to the IT network to provide data to the enterprise historian.

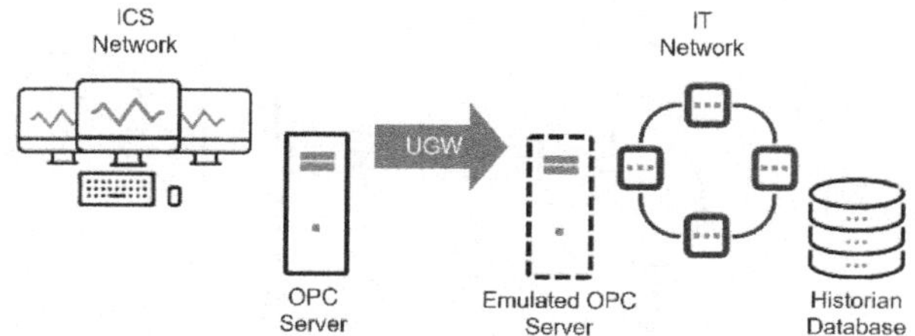

Figure (5) OPC Server Emulation

With device emulation however, there is often no "back-fill" function possible. This is because most industrial protocols have no way to ask a device for data that the device observed in the past. When a complete record of device readings is essential in central database, SEC-OT sites generally either:

- Deploy a high-availability unidirectional gateway, one that is tolerant of single points of failure, thus preventing gaps from appearing in enterprise databases,
- Deploy a short-term historian at the industrial site, recording all the data in all the devices at the site, so that if a gap develops in the enterprise historian, that gap can be back-filled manually from the short-term historian, or
- Replicate a database instead of emulating a device.

Device emulation is sometimes referred to as "protocol emulation." The term is not entirely accurate but does provide insight into how the reference architecture can be applied. Device emulation can be used to emulate many kinds of servers that use "protocols," including:

- Publish/subscribe messaging endpoints,
- Video surveillance cameras,
- Network printers, and
- Network time servers.

These emulations are in addition to a wide variety of PLCs, RTUs and other industrial devices and OPC servers.

#3 Application Replication

Many control systems include HMIs, web servers and other sophisticated applications that are difficult to replicate or emulate. Instead, unidirectional gateways are deployed routinely to replicate the relational databases, historians, OPC servers and other data sources that serve data to ICS applications. A second instance of the sophisticated application is then deployed on the IT network. The ICS instance serves critical-network users, and the IT instance serves IT and sometimes Internet-based users.

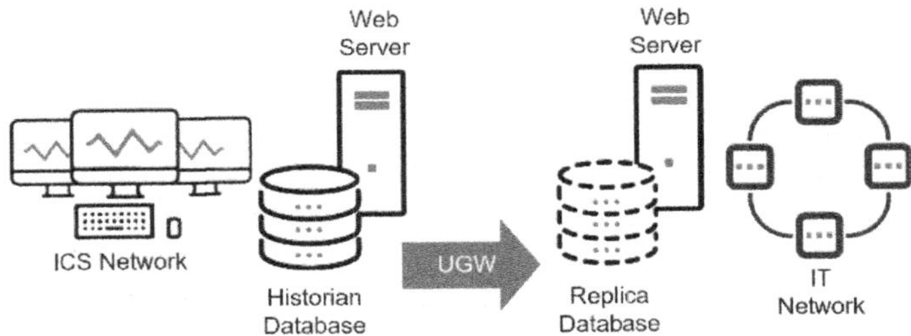

Figure (6) ICS Web Server Access via Database Replication

In many cases, these applications also store configurations, images, or other supporting information in files. SEC-OT sites often deploy file server replication for the folders containing these files so that when configuration changes are made to the ICS application, such as adding new web pages or editing HMI screens, those changes propagate automatically to the IT instance of the application. Such replication reduces management costs for the replica application.

#4 Remote Diagnostics and Maintenance

ICS product vendors are experts as to the operation, troubleshooting and maintenance of their physical and/or software products. Increasingly, such vendors offer remote diagnostic and maintenance services for their products. Such offerings may be very attractive to industrial sites, especially to those sites and organizations too small to maintain their own expert-level personnel for every important technology used at their sites.

The Remote Diagnostics and Maintenance reference architecture enables remote diagnostic and maintenance services for unidirectionally-protected control-critical networks. In this architecture, a unidirectional gateway replicates industrial databases or devices to an IT network or DMZ. Vendors connect to the replicas using VPN connections, as if the replicas were the original industrial systems. Vendors and their expert/analysis software systems use the unidirectional replicas to draw conclusions about when the vendors' products at an industrial site need service or adjustment.

When a vendor sees an opportunity to improve a product through remote adjustment, they contact the customer site and schedule a remote screen view session. At the scheduled time, an engineer with access to the control -critical network at the site calls the vendor over the phone and activates remote screen view. Remote screen view sends real-time images of the screen of a cyber asset through a unidirectional gateway to a web server on the IT network or a DMZ. The remote vendor connects a browser to the web server to see the screens but cannot send any command, mouse movement or attack back through the gateway into the control network.

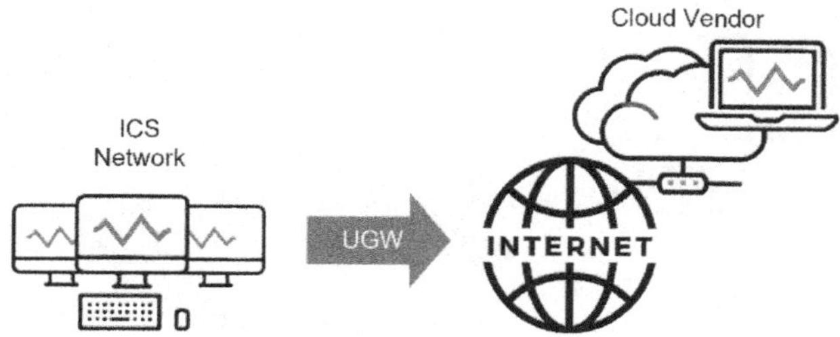

Figure (7) Unidirectional Remote Screen View

The vendor provides instructions over the phone to the engineer at the site. The engineer works with the vendor to understand the problem and the proposed solution. Only when the engineer understands both, does she apply the vendor's recommended corrective actions.

The vendor interprets this process as supervising site personnel in the application of a complex correction to the vendor's products at the site. The engineer at the site interprets the process as supervising the vendor. Both perspectives are legitimate, and both sets of needs are met by this approach to remote support, without the risks that come from firewalled remote access.

An additional advantage of this approach to remote support is that vendor personnel do not need to be screened and trained for every site they service, as would be the case if these vendors had been given unescorted remote access to the site.

This Remote Diagnostics and Maintenance reference architecture is applied routinely to electric power turbines and less commonly to a wide variety of other hardware and software systems.

#5 Emergency Maintenance

In an emergency, a qualified engineer may not be available with access to control-critical networks to operate a remote screen view session. To support emergency maintenance requests, SEC-OT sites may deploy emergency access hardware. This hardware is typically a network appliance with two twisted-pair Ethernet interfaces and a physical key or keypad on the front panel. In an emergency, personnel at the site contact their support providers. Those providers advise site personnel to go to their key closet, sign out the key for the emergency access hardware, insert the key in the access hardware and activate the hardware.

This physical process engages the access hardware function and physically connects two copper or optical cables inside the device, temporarily enabling bidirectional communications with a control-critical network. The emergency access device has a built-in timer. When the timer expires, or when electric power to the device is lost, the device automatically and physically disconnects the cables again.

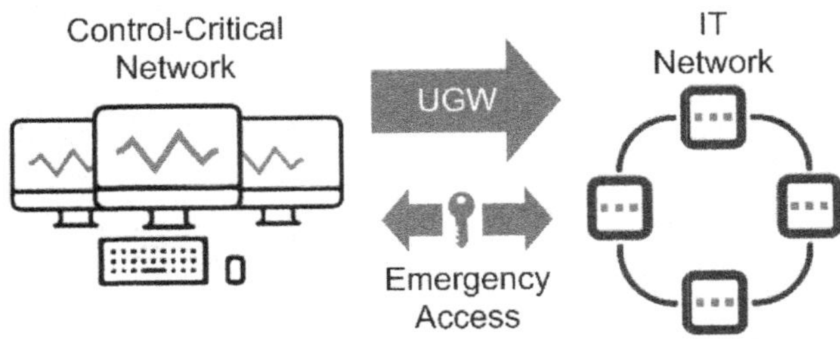

Figure (8) Emergency Maintenance

The access unit is typically deployed in parallel with a unidirectional gateway and in serial with a conventional firewall/VPN server, jump host and/or other IT-SEC remote access mechanisms. In normal usage, the control-critical network is physically, unidirectionally protected. For the duration of a declared emergency at the site, the emergency access unit temporarily enables a software-protected remote access path into the control-critical network.

> ***Note***
>
> *Most SEC-OT sites prefer remote screen view to emergency access hardware, because unidirectional hardware protection for the control-critical network is preserved during remote screen view sessions but not during emergency access sessions.*

Most hardware and software vendors, though, prefer the Emergency Maintenance reference architecture to the Remote Diagnostics and Maintenance architecture. With the Emergency Maintenance architecture, vendors can do what they wish to systems at a remote site without explaining anything to site personnel. Some SEC-OT sites acquiesce to vendor demands and provide remote access via the Emergency Maintenance architecture. Other sites explain to their vendors that if the vendors are not prepared to provide their remote support services securely, the site will need to cancel the support agreement and pay some other service provider for remote diagnostics and maintenance. Vendors frequently accommodate sites who phrase the choice this way.

#6 Continuous Remote Operation

Some industrial sites require continuous or nearly continuous remote control from another site. For example, a tank farm storing oil for an oil pipeline might have an operator 8x5 but shift off-hours control to a 24x7 pipeline operator at a central site. In another example, some industrial sites do not have engineers on site and rely on a central engineering or IT team. These central teams generally have one or more people connected remotely, continuously to every industrial site in the enterprise. Neither the Remote Maintenance and Diagnostics nor the Emergency Maintenance architecture is appropriate to these continuous, long-term connectivity needs.

At such sites, SEC-OT practitioners define a control-critical WAN that contains all the equipment, local and remote, that can control a given industrial process. In the tank farm example, the tank farm control systems and pipeline control systems form a single control-critical network. In the central engineering example, all the managed plants as well as the central engineering office are modelled as a single control-critical network. Private telecommunications capacity is used to connect the distributed sites, not public switched networks. Firewalls and site-to-site VPNs are deployed at every site's interface to the private WAN.

SEC-OT permits firewalls in the connection to the private WAN because the entire WAN is modelled as a single control-critical network. In this instance, the firewalls represent internal network segmentation, not an interface to an external, noncritical network.

This means though, that all the component sites in this critical WAN must be protected as thoroughly as the most sensitive of the connected sites is protected. For example, if any of the connected industrial sites has "guards, gates and guns," so must every site, including the central engineering office. This also means that physical, unidirectional protections against information/attack flows from external networks must be deployed at the interface between any part of this extended control-critical WAN and any noncritical network such as an IT network or the Internet.

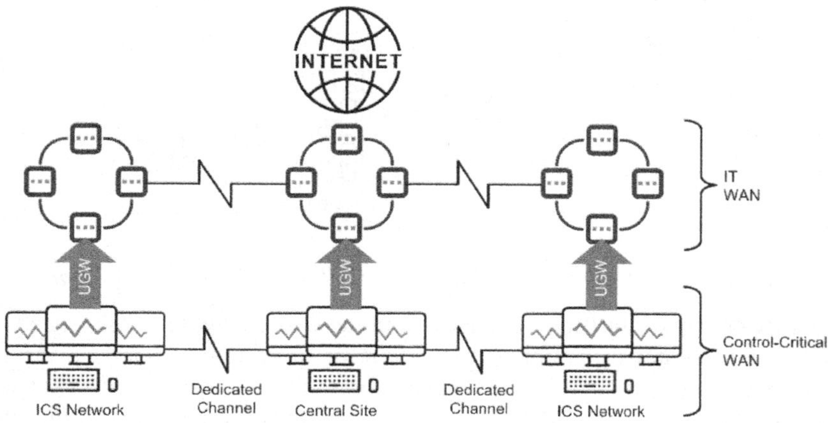

Figure (9) Continuous Remote Operation via Control-Critical WAN

In this architecture, unidirectional gateways may be deployed centrally, at a large site or an engineering office, or may be deployed at each industrial site that is part of the critical WAN. Most businesses prefer to deploy the gateways at a central site with 24x7 engineering staff, but this may increase telecommunications costs when all communications must be routed through the central site.

The decision whether to deploy gateways at each site vs. centrally is a business decision, not a security decision, provided that the entire control-critical WAN is managed as a SEC-OT network, not an IT network.

#7 Device Data Sniffing

Test and training systems can benefit from access to live data feeds rather than simulated sources. Normally, the Database Replication and Device Emulation architectures are sufficient to provide such data unidirectionally into test beds, without risk to control-critical networks. In some cases, though, ICS systems or devices cannot tolerate the unidirectional gateway sending additional queries in order to replicate the systems.

For example, some control and monitoring devices support only one TCP connection at a time to a central control system, and so cannot be queried by both the control system and a unidirectional gateway serving the test bed. In another example, some WAN connections to monitoring and control devices are low-bandwidth and cannot tolerate doubling network traffic – one set of traffic to send live values to the control system and another to send values to the gateway serving the test system.

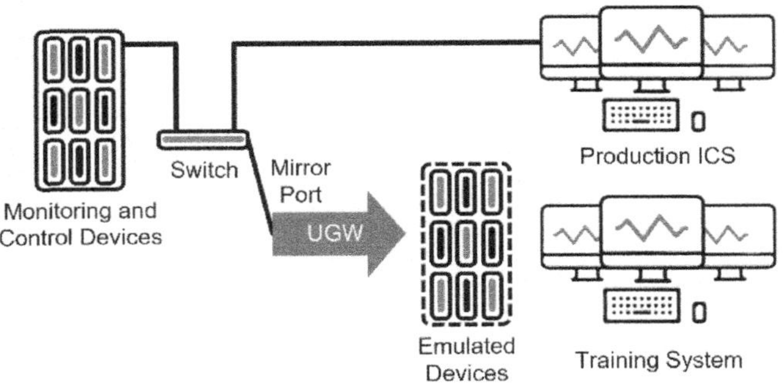

Figure (10) Device Data Sniffing for a Test and Training System

The Device Data Sniffing reference architecture addresses these needs. A unidirectional gateway is connected to one or more mirror ports on the ICS switches through which device communications pass. Special gateway software examines the replicated traffic captures and extracts device values from those captures so that the ICS devices can be emulated to the test network. The unidirectional gateways then respond to queries from the test bed using the values observed in device-to-control-system communications. This architecture enables emulating devices to a test bed without new connections to those devices and without increasing network traffic to the devices.

The Device Data Sniffing reference architecture is used most commonly in electric power transmission and distribution networks, where hundreds of limited-functionalities remote RTUs may be accessible only via costly, low-speed, leased telecommunications capacity.

#8 Central or Cloud SOC

Most enterprises have a central security operations center (SOC) rather than a SOC at each industrial site. Increasingly, central SOCs are hosted by a third-party cloud provider, and may be staffed by that provider's experts. Central SOCs have many benefits, not least that they can gather and correlate information from many industrial and IT sites to determine whether and what kind of attacks might be in progress.

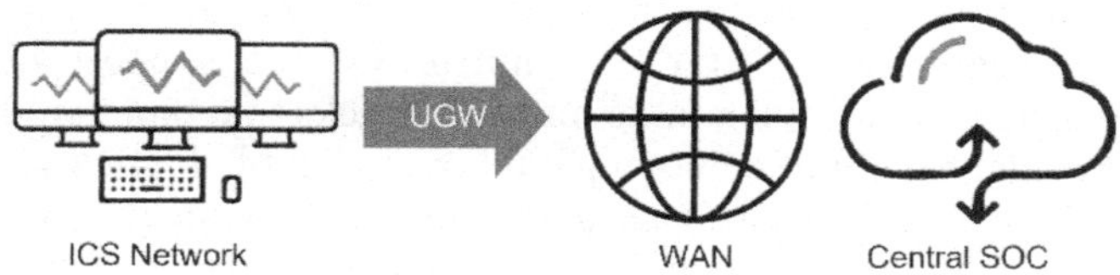

Figure (11) Central or Cloud SOC

Unidirectional gateways are deployed routinely to enable central monitoring by emulating Syslog devices, SNMP clients, log file servers and other security-relevant devices into central monitoring sites. This architecture enables central monitoring of security conditions in control-critical networks without introducing the attack paths back into the monitored equipment that firewalled SOC connectivity would introduce.

#9 Network Intrusion Detection Systems

Unidirectional protections are deployed routinely to enable both signature-based and anomaly-based network intrusion detection systems (NIDS). The gateways replicate traffic captures from SPAN and mirror ports on ICS switches to intrusion detection sensors. Using a unidirectional gateway for this function allows the IDS sensor to be deployed safely on an IT network.

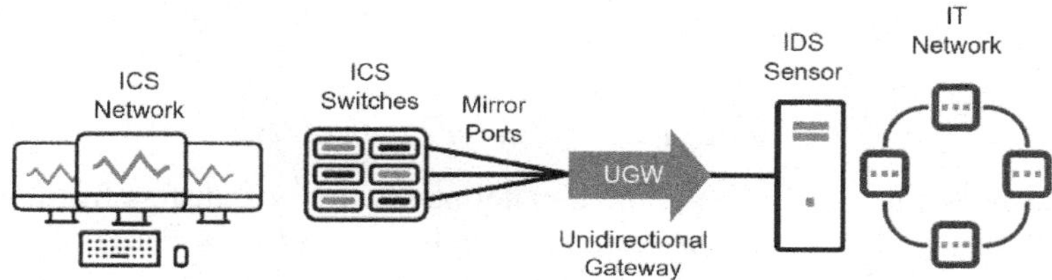

Figure (12) ICS IDS Sensor Deployed on IT Network

Connecting the IDS sensor to the IT network is an advantage because most IDS sensors need frequent adjustment, which is typically carried out remotely by security analysts in a central SOC. Deploying a unidirectionally-fed IDS on the IT network makes such remote adjustment straightforward for IT-based SOCs, without introducing the risk of an attack pivoting from the IT network, through a NIDS sensor, into the monitored control-critical network.

> **Note**
>
> *Many switch vendors document their SPAN and mirror ports as unidirectional. Such documentation is often inaccurate.*

Worse, any unidirectional assurances on the part of network switch vendors are software assurances – a stolen password or other compromise of switch software can quickly reconfigure a SPAN or mirror port to support bidirectional communications with the potential to transmit attacks into monitored networks.

An additional benefit of deploying unidirectionally fed NIDS sensors on IT networks is that, in the event of an upset condition on an ICS network, IDS sensors can sometimes generate large volumes of alert traffic. Some ICS networks are very sensitive to changes in traffic volumes and these bursts of alerts destined for a central SOC can pose a threat to correct operations of the ICS. Deploying the NIDS sensor on the IT network ensures that alert traffic traverses the IT network exclusively, with no impact to operations.

#10 Convenient File Transfer

SEC-OT sites frequently replicate file servers from control-critical networks to IT networks to facilitate ad-hoc file transfers. Replicating an ICS file server allows ICS technicians to drag and drop files to a folder on the ICS network and have those files appear automatically on a replica IT file server a few moments later.

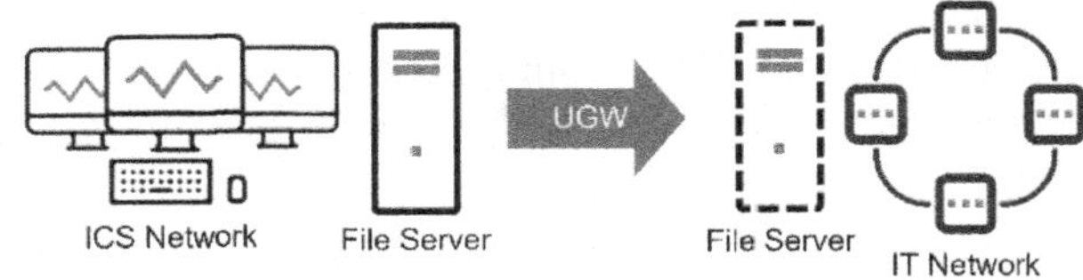

Figure (13) File Server Replication

At most sites, almost all ad-hoc file transfer needs are for transfers from the ICS network to the IT network. At such sites, replicating a file server from the ICS network to the IT network dramatically reduces any need to use removable media or transient devices. Earlier in this Appendix we discussed more comprehensive physical protections for offline threats due to removable media and removable devices.

#11 IIoT and Cloud Communications

The Industrial Internet of Things (IIoT) is a catchphrase for dramatically increased connectivity for control-critical cyber assets or "edge devices." Such connectivity generally enables:

- The flow of information from edge devices at an industrial site into Internet-based cloud services for "big data analysis,"
- Automatic updates of firmware in edge devices, and occasionally
- Information/attack flows returning to edge devices to control the devices and/or physical infrastructure.

SEC-OT sites have two ways to respond to these requirements:

- Edge devices that monitor physical operations but are physically incapable of controlling those operations can be deployed on their own networks. These networks may be connected directly or wirelessly to IT network segments at the plant or connected directly or indirectly to cellular and Internet networks. Sites with such mixed networks must take care to label IT and ICS cabling and other communications components carefully and prominently to prevent accidental cross-connections at the site.
- Edge devices that control physical operations are control-critical assets and must be deployed and managed using SEC-OT best practices. These assets may be deployed on a main ICS network, on their own ICS network that is part of a control-critical group of ICS networks, or as a separate control-critical network.

A unidirectional gateway is generally deployed to gather information from these edge devices and possibly other systems in a control-critical network, translate the information to Internet/cloud friendly formats, and send the information across the Internet to a cloud service.

When edge devices are part of a control-critical network, software updates must be applied by an IIoT update server that is part of the control-critical network, not applied directly from the cloud. SEC-OT permits no automatic mechanism to send information as complex and potentially dangerous as a firmware update into a control-critical network automatically, without first testing that artifact and verifying its safety, reliability, and security characteristics on an ICS test bed.

When information/attack flows must return from the cloud to act on physical equipment, SEC-OT sites inspect and control those flows thoroughly. Most commonly, such inbound information is very abstract, such as a message saying, "equipment X will fail shortly – schedule downtime and send a work crew as soon as possible." Such information is sent to the people responsible for a work process, who inspect the information to make sure it is safe, and then manually apply the new knowledge to the industrial process – for example: by manually scheduling process downtime.

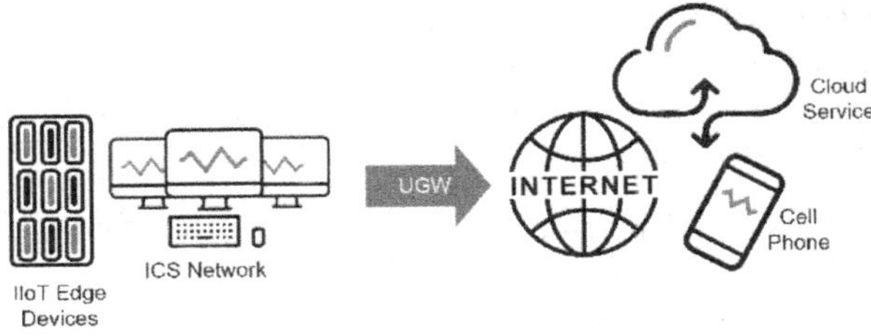

Figure (14) Cloud Communications

Continuous, detailed control from an Internet-based cloud is not permitted for control-critical networks. For example, some vendors sell cloud-based HMI services, where remote operators connect through the Internet and send detailed, second-by-second instructions to complex, powerful, and dangerous industrial sites all over the world. Such connectivity is forbidden by SEC-OT.

#12 Electronic Mail and Web Browsing

Plant operators and other control system personnel at SEC-OT sites frequently need access to corporate electronic mail systems and sometimes Internet web browsing. Such activities are never permitted on control-critical networks. Instead, SEC-OT sites deploy one or more IT-managed computers and screens at 24x7 operator workstations.

Operators can see the IT equipment as part of their array of displays and can use the IT equipment and services as needed. The IT equipment, however, is connected to an IT network and managed as an IT resource, not a control-critical resource.

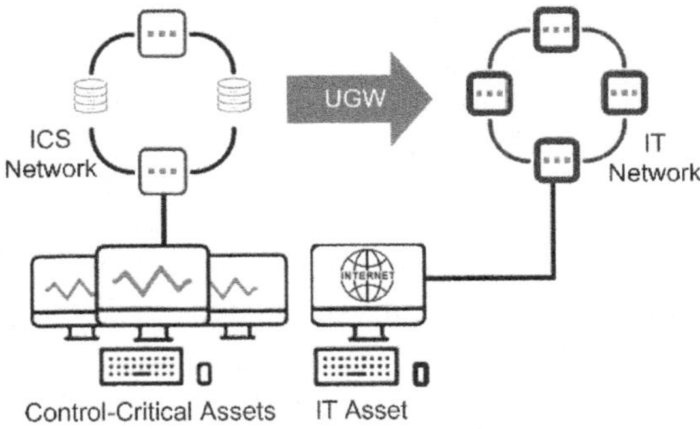

Figure (15) Email and Web Browsing

#13 Partial Replication Protecting Trade Secrets

Some industrial sites may have trade secrets embedded in their industrial systems. A pharmaceutical plant for example, may have batch recipe information embedded in a process historian database, preferring to store this sensitive information exclusively in their physically protected control-critical network rather than in IT networks.

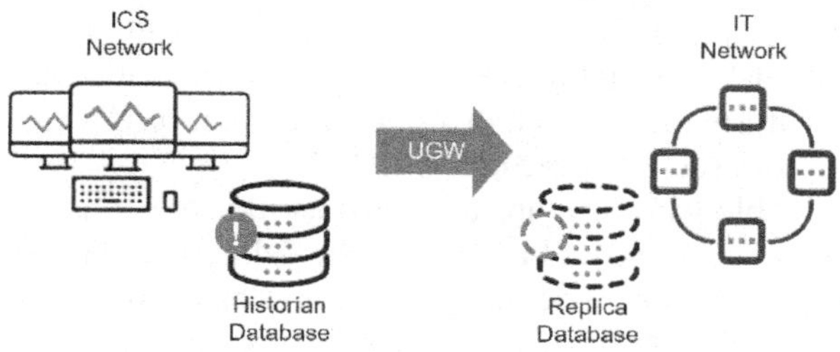

Figure (16) Partial Replication

At such sites it is important to configure unidirectional gateways that replicate information out of control-critical networks in a manner that avoids replicating trade secrets. The most common way to do this is to replicate only a subset of information from each ICS server and device to the site's IT network.

The partial replication may select data to replicate by specifying a list of data source names to replicate exclusively, by replicating an entire data source except for a list of names to exclude from replication, or to segregate trade secret information into separate servers and data sources entirely. Complete separation is practical in only some cases. Selecting between a list of names to replicate versus a list of names to exclude from global replication depends on the length of each kind of list of data names and each site's tolerance for errors and omissions in the maintenance of these lists.

#14 Scheduled Updates

Many industrial sites require scheduled updates of some types of information, such as batch production orders and anti-virus updates. Some sites adopt a daily, manual process for such updates – burning the updates to a CD, carrying the CD through the offline protections documented earlier in this Appendix and deploying the updates on a test bed. On the test bed, the updates are tested for safety, reliability and security impacts and are ultimately carried into the control system.

Other sites deploy a reversible unidirectional gateway[27] to automate these processes.

Reversible Unidirectional Gateways

A reversible gateway is a unidirectional gateway that replicates servers across one-way hardware, but the hardware can reverse orientation. The hardware can send data one way into a control network, or one way out of such a network, but

[27] At this writing the only reversible unidirectional gateway on the market is Waterfall Security Solutions' FLIP

never both at the same time. The gateway-reversing function can be triggered by a manual input such as a physical button, a key, or a touchpad on the front panel of the device or can be triggered automatically on a schedule. When the schedule is controlled by a CPU in the reversible gateway, that CPU must be air-gapped and blind to any data traversing the device. If this orientation-scheduling CPU can receive no information from either control-critical or IT networks, the CPU cannot be compromised by either network.

When reversible gateways are deployed as the sole connection between a control-critical network and an IT network, the delivery of data from the control network to the IT network is delayed while the gateway is oriented into the control network, and vice versa. When such delays are unacceptable to business users, the reversible gateway may be deployed in parallel with a conventional "always-on" unidirectional gateway as illustrated in Figure (19).

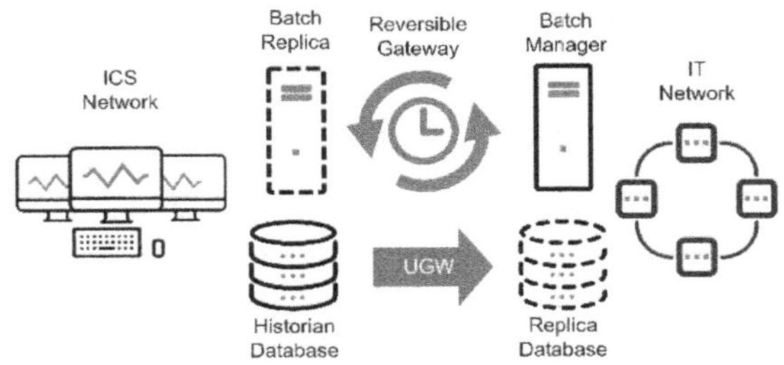

Figure (17) Reversible Gateway and Conventional Gateway in Parallel

Reversible Gateway Security

The degree of security provided by reversible unidirectional gateways is comparable to the security provided by the offline removable media controls described earlier. Like offline information/attack flows, information through a reversible gateway does not move when the attacker needs the attack information to move but moves when the gateway reverses orientation on a schedule, or because of physical intervention at the site.

A half-duplex communications medium that reverses orientation only a small number of times per day dramatically impairs the command-response capabilities of online, remote-control attacks. Prompt command-response capabilities are essential to the Remote Access Trojan (RAT) malware that attackers prefer to use for high-consequence attacks.

Reversible gateways are most often configured as clients of both control-critical and IT networks, not servers to those networks, and not as routers that forward network traffic. When the time comes to reverse orientation, the gateway software actively fetches batch orders, AV signatures or other content from an authoritative source on an IT network. The gateway verifies the authenticity of this content as well, both in the external IT network and again on the internal network. Configuration as a client rather than a server or router further reduces remote-control attack communications opportunities.

> ***Note***
>
> *Unlike firewalls and routers, reversible unidirectional gateways do not forward application protocol requests in one direction and replies in the other.*
>
> *Instead, they replicate one type of server into a control-critical network, and a different type back out to IT networks. Applications on either side of the gateway interact normally with their respective servers or replicas.*

The most cautious SEC-OT sites using reversible gateways also use firewalls to separate the network segment hosting servers that are replicated *from* the IT network from the network segment hosting servers that are replicated *to* the IT network. This makes it even more difficult for attackers to find any round-trip mechanism that might permit command/response round-trip communications of any sort.

#15 Safety Systems

Some SEC-OT sites unidirectionally segment safety systems from their control networks. When SEC-OT sites do this, it is generally because they:

- Conclude that safety systems are very important control systems and so warrant a second level of unidirectional protection, or
- Conclude that safety systems are comparatively simpler than larger control systems to protect unidirectionally, and so deploy SEC-OT physical protections for safety networks first in a series of progressive deployments of SEC-OT designs and best practices.

Syslog and SNMP clients are routinely replicated unidirectionally from safety networks to SOCs and network operations centers (NOCs), while the safety devices are emulated to ICS networks. ICS network integration permits detailed safety system status information to be represented in general-purpose ICS HMI displays. Plant operators often prefer to integrate safety system alarms and indicators into their primary HMI rather than monitor a second HMI containing only safety information.

In some cases, operators must occasionally send a small number of online commands into safety systems, such as "reset" commands to restore normal operations when safety issues are resolved. The most common way to meet this need is to deploy a small safety-critical HMI console as part of the 24x7 operator workstation, with that console physically wired into the safety-critical network. Operators can see the status of safety systems on their main HMI but can issue control commands to the safety system only via the dedicated safety HMI keyboard and mouse.

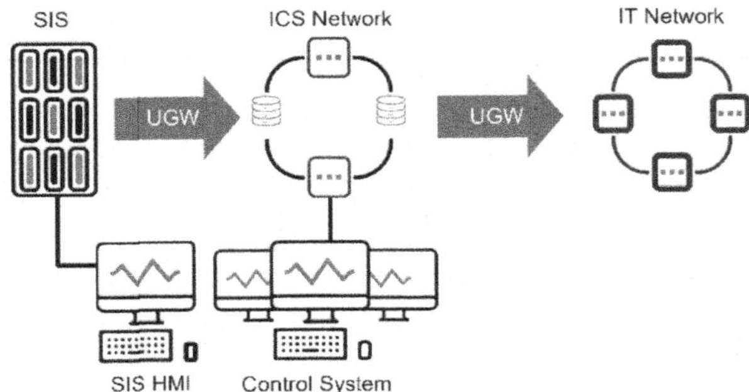

Figure (18) Integrated SIS Display with Separate SIS Control Computer

#16 Continuous High-Level Control

Some sites require very limited continuous remote control from an external source, such as a customer or regulatory authority. For example, electric power plants often require second-by-second instructions from a generating dispatch center that dictates how much power the plant should produce, reflecting the constantly changing power demands of an electric grid.

In such cases, two unidirectional gateways are deployed. An "outbound" gateway replicates control-critical servers unidirectionally to an external IT or other communications network, while an "inbound" gateway replicates the external control system back into the critical network.

> **Note**
>
> *An inbound/outbound gateway that sends arbitrary queries through one unidirectional path and forwards responses to those queries back through the other path is not a gateway but a forbidden firewall or router.*
>
> *Unidirectional gateways do not forward packets. Gateways replicate servers and emulate devices.*

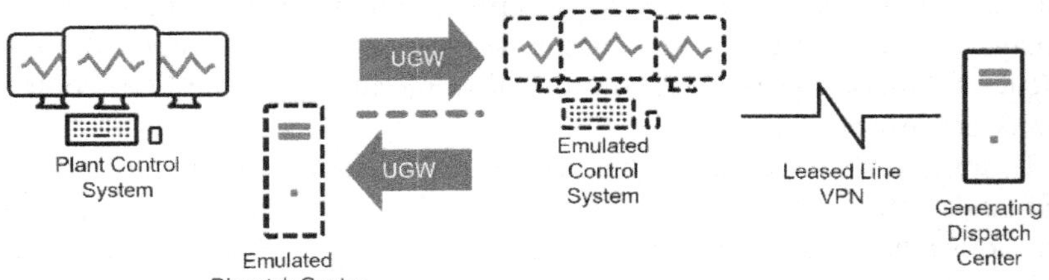

Figure (19) Power Plant with Continuous Control from Dispatch Center

Like the reversible unidirectional gateway, inbound/outbound gateway designs are stronger than firewalls:

- Unidirectional gateways do not forward network traffic from one network to another, and so cannot forward the content of attack packets from an external network into a control-critical network.
- Compromising a software component that communicates through a firewall is a one-step process – the attacker finds and exploits a software vulnerability in that software component by sending attack packets through the firewall. Compromising ICS software through a unidirectional gateway that is oriented into a control-critical network is at least a three-step process: first compromise the external host running the server replication software using one vulnerability or exploit, then compromise the internal gateway host with a different vulnerability and exploit, and then do the same again to an ICS component inside the ICS network.

This last step of compromising an ICS component must be carried out "blind" – without feedback of any sort to the attacker. This is because neither the inbound nor outbound unidirectional gateways forward network traffic. There is, therefore, no kind of network traffic that RAT attack code can generate that will result in feedback returning to the external attacker.

Compromising the control-critical network by attacking through an inward-oriented unidirectional gateway is a realistic threat only when there are ICS insiders deliberately cooperating with the remote attackers. The insiders must provide the attackers with detailed information about the progress of the attack, the design of the control-critical network and the configuration of ICS components. The attack is more credible when ICS insiders actively assist the attackers. In-person assistance is essential to this type of online attack, because the attackers are otherwise blind to the progress of their attack and the nature of the ICS network they are attacking.

Sites deploying the Continuous High-Level Control reference architecture tend to prioritize the deployment of insider threat management systems documented earlier as well.

#17 SCADA WAN

WANs are intrinsic parts of SCADA systems – SCADA systems must communicate across a WAN to distant and often unstaffed locations such as pumping stations, compressor stations, electric substations, and wind turbines. The most robust design for SCADA systems observes that elements of the SCADA WAN reside outside of any site's physical security perimeter and so cannot be modelled as part of a control-critical network. Instead, each remote site and the central site are modelled as their own critical network, with unidirectional gateways at interfaces to the SCADA WAN.

Most often, the central site must be able to both monitor remote sites and control them – for example: turn pumps and compressors on and off, open and close switches or valves and activate, deactivate, or tune wind turbines. This means that unidirectionally-protected remote sites use the Continuous High-Level Control reference architecture at their interfaces to the SCADA WAN. In that architecture, unidirectional gateways emulate the central SCADA system to each remote site so that equipment at the site can interact with the local replica as if the replica were the original SCADA system, and vice versa – emulate site equipment to the central SCADA system.

Figure (20) Remote Site with Continuous Control from SCADA System

When remote sites are distant from support staff, the ability to carry out some kinds of remote maintenance is advantageous. In practice, only a fraction of maintenance issues can be resolved remotely – for example, when physical equipment malfunctions there is generally no alternative to dispatching a repair crew to replace the failed component. Still, reducing the number of times that crews must be dispatched reduces costs.

To facilitate remote cyber maintenance, one or more maintenance workstations are generally deployed at the central SCADA site, and unidirectional gateways replicate maintenance information and requests from these workstations into remote sites. Maintenance commands from these workstations though, are generally not arbitrary commands with unknown consequences.

Instead, remote maintenance is typically managed by a workflow mechanism. Permitted remote maintenance actions for each station are enumerated and only short identifiers, such as small integers, are communicated to each remote station to activate maintenance actions. When these commands arrive at a remote station, the unidirectional gateway checks to ensure that the numbered actions exist and then triggers predefined actions, such as the execution of numbered scripts or batch files.

In many SCADA installations, some remote sites are more valuable or more consequential than others. Enterprises may initially deploy the full SEC-OT methodology at their most important remote sites and only a subset of SEC-OT practices at lesser sites. Such enterprises lease dedicated, private network capacity to their remote sites and protect the most valuable sites unidirectionally with the "Continuous High-Level Control" architecture and maintenance systems described above. Less-valuable and less-consequential sites use software protection – most commonly including encrypting firewalls.

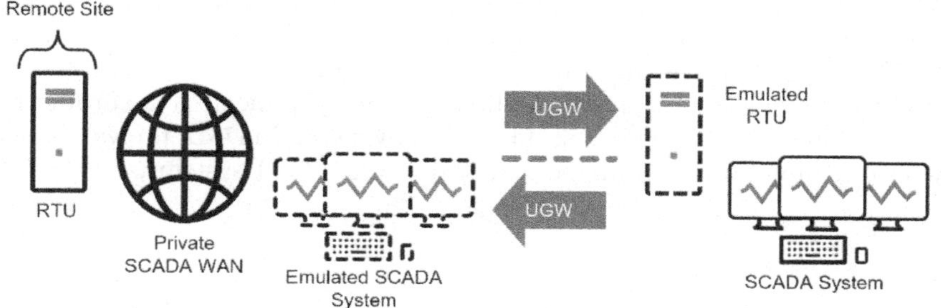

Figure (21) Software-Protected Remote Site with Continuous Control

#18 Protective Relays

Protective relays are deployed to protect electrical equipment from damaging conditions such as lightning strikes, ground faults, overheating and overloading. Most commonly such relays are deployed in high-voltage substations distributed throughout a large geography. Because of their role in preventing damage to costly equipment, protective relays are generally regarded as very important to the reliability of industrial sites.

Some SEC-OT sites therefore choose to deploy SEC-OT best practices for their protective relays, even if the utility is not yet ready to deploy physical protections for other equipment. For example, electric transmission utilities sometimes deploy two Ethernet switches in each of their high-voltage substations: one switch hosting the equipment-critical protective relay network and the other hosting monitoring and control equipment for non-protective functions such as high-voltage power switches and capacitor banks. A unidirectional gateway is deployed to monitor the equipment-critical network while preventing any online attacks on the protective relays.

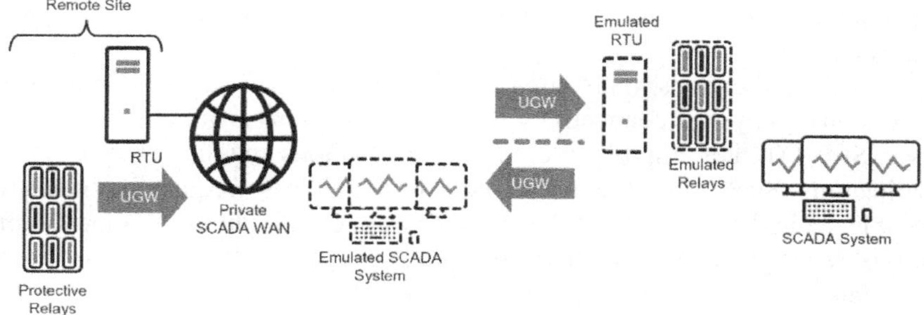

Figure (22) Unidirectionally-Protected Relays and Central SCADA Site

#19 Replicas DMZ

Information transmitted from control-critical to IT networks is frequently very valuable – this value is generally the motive for integrating ICS with IT networks. The IT teams responsible for protecting the information in replica servers and emulated industrial devices often deploy these replicas in a DMZ network, separated from the main IT network with an IT-managed firewall, as part of an IT-SEC system of protecting replicated information.

In this architecture, a unidirectional gateway protects a control-critical network from information/attacks in an IT network, and a DMZ firewall protects the information flowing from the critical network into IT systems.

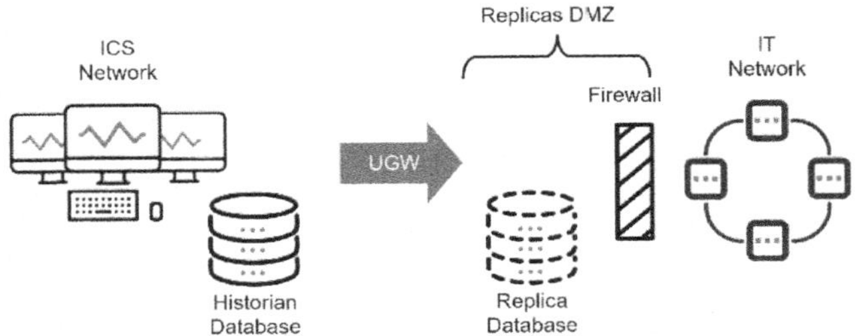

Figure (23) Database Replication to a Replicas DMZ

#20 Wireless Networks

Wireless networks have intrinsic security limitations – the wireless communications medium is inherently broadcast, which permits attackers to both listen to and interfere with wireless communications, without gaining physical access to the industrial site.

Worse, cell phones and a wide variety of other inexpensive, commonplace cyber assets increasingly use wireless communications and sometimes use multiple kinds of wireless communications simultaneously. The ability to use multiple wireless communications mechanisms simultaneously allows cyber attacks to pivot between wireless networks through compromised wireless devices. These characteristics make commonplace devices increasingly convenient as pivot points for wireless attacks on industrial sites for distant attackers.

There are situations when wireless communications are unavoidable, though, such as when physical connectivity with remote stations is not possible. In such cases, SEC-OT sites employ wireless communications and the "SCADA WAN" architecture. Such sites use dedicated/leased wireless frequencies whenever possible, and whenever practical avoid the use of commodity signalling systems such as Wi-Fi and SMS, which are available to even unskilled attackers.

There are also circumstances when wireless communications are very desirable, to reduce capital and operating costs at industrial sites. One reference architecture with minimal risk uses wireless communications to send monitoring data to IT networks or portable devices through a unidirectional gateway.

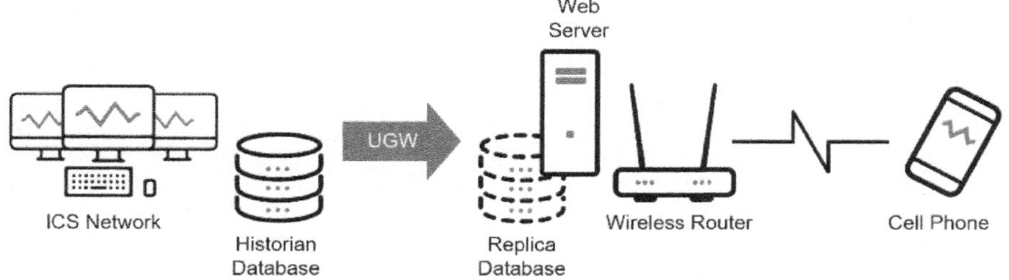

Figure (24) Unidirectional Database Replication to a Wireless Network

With this design, no compromise of the wireless equipment or portable devices can reach back into the critical network to affect operations. There is, however, still a risk that a sophisticated attack can tamper with the monitoring data that reaches portable devices.

For such attacks to have physical consequences, information from the devices, or in wirelessly reachable external networks, must return into the control-critical network to mis-control physical equipment. SEC-OT best practices address this threat. Sites using unidirectionally-protected wireless monitoring are advised to review the "Deceived Insiders" section earlier in this Appendix.

Summary

Unidirectional database replication and device emulation are the most commonly used unidirectional reference architectures. The complete list of reference architectures is:

Database Replication	Device Emulation	Application Replication	Remote Diagnostics & Maintenance
Emergency Maintenance	Continuous Remote Operation	Device Data Sniffing	Central or Cloud SOC
Network IDS	Convenient File Transfer	IIoT and Cloud Communications	Electronic Mail and Browsing
Partial Replication	Scheduled Updates	Safety Systems	Continuous High-Level Control
SCADA WAN	Protective Relays	Replicas DMZ	Wireless Networks

SEC-OT pioneers continue inventing new reference architectures as they encounter new kinds of industrial networking needs.

Appendix C – Acronyms

2FA - Two Factor Authentication
AD - Active Directory
AI - Artificial Intelligence
ANSSI - Agence nationale de la sécurité des systèmes d'information
API - American Petroleum Institute
ASCII - American Standard Code for Information Interchange
ASIC - Application-Specific Integrated Circuit
AV - Anti-Virus
BES - Bulk Electric System
BSI - Bundesamt für Sicherheit in der Informationstechnik
CCE - Consequence-Driven Cyber-Informed Engineering
CD - Compact Disc
cDBT - Cyber Design-Basis Threat
CEO - Chief Executive Officer
CIE - Cyber-Informed Engineering
CIP - Critical Infrastructure Protection
CISO - Chief Information Security Officer
CNC - Computer Numerical Controllers
COM - Component Object Model
CPU - Central Processing Unit
CRT - Cathode Ray Tube
CSF - Cybersecurity Framework
CSO - Chief Security Officer
CSV - Comma-Separated Value
DBT - Design-Basis Threat
DCOM - Distributed Component Object Model
DCS - Distributed Control System
DHS - Department of Homeland Security
DMZ - Demilitarized Zone
DNP3 - Distributed Network Protocol 3
DNS - Domain Name System
DOE - Department of Energy
DVD - Digital Versatile Disc
ECC - Engineering Change Control
EKANS - Snake Ransomware
EPRI - Electric Power Research Institute
ERM - Enterprise Risk Management

ERP - Enterprise Resource Planning
FERC - Federal Energy Regulatory Commission
HART - Highway Addressable Remote Transducer
HFLI - High-Frequency, Low-Impact
HILF - High-Impact, Low-Frequency
HMI - Human-Machine Interface
HTTP - Hypertext Transfer Protocol
HTTPS - Hypertext Transfer Protocol Secure
HVAC - Heating, Ventilation and Air Conditioning
IACS - Industrial Automation and Control System
IAM - Identity and Access Management
ICS - Industrial Control System
IDS - Intrusion Detection System
IEC - International Electrotechnical Commission
IED - Intelligent Electronic Device
IIoT - Industrial Internet of Things
IP - Internet Protocol
IPS - Intrusion Detection System
ISA - International Society of Automation
ISAC - Information Sharing and Analysis Center
IT - Information Technology
JSON - Javascript Object Notation
LAN - Local-Area Network
LED - Light Emitting Diode
MES - Manufacturing Execution System
MPLS - Multiprotocol Label Switching
MQTT - Message Queuing Telemetry Transport
NAC - Network Access Control
NAT - Network Address Translation
NERC - North American Electric Reliability Corporation
NERC-CIP - NERC Critical Infrastructure Protection
NIDS - Network Intrusion Detection System
NIST - National Institute of Standards and Technology
NISTIR - National Institute of Standards and Technology Inter-Agency Report
NOC - Network Operations Center
OPC - Open Platform Communications
OPC-DA - OPC Data Access
OPC-UA - OPC Unified architecture
OPC-HDA - OPC Historical Data Access
OSHA - Occupational Safety and Health Administration
OT - Operational Technology
PCN - Process Control Network
PHA - Process Hazard Analysis
PID - Proportional-Integral-Derivative

PII - Personally-Identifiable Information
PKI - Public Key Infrastructure
PLC - Programmable Logic Controller
PPE - Personal Protective Equipment
QR code - Quick Response code
RAT - Remote Access Trojan
ROI - Return on Investment
RSV - Remote Screen View
RTUs - Remote Terminal Unit
SBOM - Software Bill of Materials
SCADA - Supervisory Control and Data Acquisition
SDN - Software-Defined Network
SEC-OT - Secure Operations Technology
SIM card - Subscriber Identity Module card
SIS - Safety-Instrumented System
SMS - Short Message Service
SNMP - Simple Network Management Protocol
SOAP - Simple Object Access Protocol
SOC - Security Operations Center
SPAN - Switched Port Analyzer
SPR - Security PHA Review
SQL - Structured Query Language
SRA - Secure Remote Access
T1 - T-carrier 1
TCP - Transmission Control Protocol
TLS - Transport Layer Security
TSA - Transportation Security Administration
TTP - Tactics, techniques, and procedures
TV - Television
UK - United Kingdom
US - United States
USA - United States of America
USB - Universal Serial Bus
USD - United States Dollar
VLAN - Virtual Local-Area Network
VM - Virtual Machine
VP - Vice-President
VPN - Virtual Private Network
WAN - Wide-Area Network
WSUS - Windows Server Update Service
XML - Extensible Markup Language

About the Author

Andrew Ginter lives in Calgary, Alberta, Canada. He holds a BSc. in Applied Mathematics and an MSc. in Computer Science, both from the University of Calgary. He is the author of *SCADA Security – What's broken and how to fix it*, *Secure Operations Technology*, and now *Engineering-Grade OT Security – A manager's guide.*

Andrew spent a decade developing control system software products for Hewlett Packard, Agilent Technologies and other vendors. He spent half a decade developing IT/OT middleware products for Agilent Technologies and Verano. These products connected control and manufacturing networks to IT networks, thereby contributing to the industrial security problems that now plague many industries. This last 18 years Andrew spent as CTO and CSO at Industrial Defender and then VP Industrial Security at Waterfall Security Solutions, working to design, develop and deploy industrial security products and technologies.

Andrew is the eldest of seven children born to refugees who made a new life in a strange land and worked hard to live their faith and raise their children. He is married 35 years to a woman he adores, has two grown daughters of whom he is enormously proud, and writes in his spare time.

A request to my readers: *If you liked this book, please consider leaving a short review on Amazon. Thank you!*